The Moral Argument

The Moral Argument

A History

DAVID BAGGETT AND JERRY L. WALLS

OXFORD
UNIVERSITY PRESS

Oxford University Press is a department of the University of Oxford. It furthers
the University's objective of excellence in research, scholarship, and education
by publishing worldwide. Oxford is a registered trade mark of Oxford University
Press in the UK and certain other countries.

Published in the United States of America by Oxford University Press
198 Madison Avenue, New York, NY 10016, United States of America.

© Oxford University Press 2019

All rights reserved. No part of this publication may be reproduced, stored in
a retrieval system, or transmitted, in any form or by any means, without the
prior permission in writing of Oxford University Press, or as expressly permitted
by law, by license, or under terms agreed with the appropriate reproduction
rights organization. Inquiries concerning reproduction outside the scope of the
above should be sent to the Rights Department, Oxford University Press, at the
address above.

You must not circulate this work in any other form
and you must impose this same condition on any acquirer.

Library of Congress Cataloging-in-Publication Data
Names: Baggett, David, author.
Title: The moral argument : a history / David Baggett and Jerry L. Walls.
Description: New York : Oxford University Press, 2019. | Includes bibliographical references.
Identifiers: LCCN 2019009506 | ISBN 9780190246365 (hardback) | ISBN 9780190246372 (pbk.) |
ISBN 9780190246389 (updf) | ISBN 9780190246396 (online) |
ISBN 9780190068646 (epub)
Subjects: LCSH: God—Proof—History.
Classification: LCC BL473 .B25 2019 | DDC 212/.1—dc23
LC record available at https://lccn.loc.gov/2019009506

1 3 5 7 9 8 6 4 2

Paperback printed by Marquis, Canada
Hardback printed by Bridgeport National Bindery, Inc., United States of America

For J. P. Moreland

To Madelyn Rose, Mackenzie Grace, and Abigail Joy: I hope you will always love and respect the beauty and goodness of moral truth, and even more the awesome reality that lies behind it.

Contents

Acknowledgments ix

Introduction 1

1. Precursors to Kant 8
2. The Sage of Königsberg: Immanuel Kant 19
3. A Contentious, Contemplative Cardinal: John Henry Newman 34
4. An Agnostic Moralist: Henry Sidgwick 49
5. That Adorable Genius and a Prime Minister: William James and Arthur Balfour 62
6. A Knightbridge Professor: William Sorley 72
7. An Edinburgher: Andrew Seth Pringle-Pattison 88
8. The Theo-Philosopher of Carlisle: Hastings Rashdall 97
9. An Oxford Nolloth Professor: Clement Webb 114
10. The Gregarious Aristocrat: W. G. de Burgh 130
11. An Eminent and Erudite Platonist: A. E. Taylor 139
12. Dean of St. Paul's: W. R. Matthews 155
13. A Dinosaur: C. S. Lewis 162
14. A Reverend Don: H. P. Owen 181
15. Contemporary Moral Apologists 198

Conclusion 210

Notes 219
Index 253

Acknowledgments

It is our delight to thank some of the many people whose assistance proved invaluable as we worked on this book. Cynthia Read and the team at Oxford University Press were, as always, eminently supportive, patient, and encouraging. Many thanks to Assistant Editor Drew Anderla, and warm thanks to the production team at Newgen; copyeditor Gretchen Gordon, indexer Cynthia Landeen, Vani Vidhya, and project manager Richa Jobin. We greatly appreciate you all.

Thanks to the administrations of our schools, Houston Baptist and Liberty Universities, for steps they took to enable us to have the time to complete this project.

Dave taught three doctoral level courses (and a few masters level courses) on this material in the Rawlings School of Divinity while work on the book was underway. All the students in each class made important contributions to the discussion, but for now we especially want to mention Brett Seybold, T. J. Gentry, Peter Van Kleeck, John Fraser, James Morris, Dale Kratt, Isaac Seo, Michael Obanla, Zach Breitenbach, Steve Jordan, Peter Morgan, Lori Peters, Daphne Edmondston, Heather Bradley, Will Honeycutt, Chris Berg, Nehemiah Hanson, Shane O'Neill, Roy Mattson, John McCard, Delia Ursulescu, Doug Geivett, and Elton Higgs.

Thanks to friends and colleagues with whom we've discussed these issues for many years, a few of whom include Mike Jones, Mark Foreman, Kegan Shaw, Sloan Lee, Tyler McNabb, and Ronnie Campbell. Jonathan Pruitt, managing editor extraordinaire at MoralApologetics.com, deserves special mention. Thanks to Dave Beck, whose forthcoming book came into our hands too late to make its presence felt in this volume. It's called *The Reality of God: A Narrated History of the Case* (IVP Academic, 2019). He includes in his sketch of the history of the moral argument a few thinkers we don't cover, including ancient figures like Zeno, Chrysippus, Cleanthes, Epictetus, Marcus Aurelius, and Marcus Minucius Felix.

We each have some individual thanks to offer as well. *From Dave*: I am thankful for my talented and endlessly patient wife, Marybeth Baggett, who read and edited the whole manuscript, which was a wonderful gift.

I am thankful for her, as well as for our son, Nathaniel, who's given us ample opportunities to grow in sanctification.

I remain deeply grateful to my mentor Tom Morris for his profound impact on my thinking and career. Everything I write bears his influence. As always, . . . *From Jerry*: I am thankful for the love and support of my children: Timothy and Angela Amos; Madelyn Rose, Mackenzie Grace, and Abigail Joy; Jonathan and Emily Walls. They inspire and make more meaningful every worthwhile thing I do, and I hope that includes making discernible moral progress.

And a final word from Dave: As work on the book drew to a close, my sweet, brave cat Francesca Josephine breathed her last. Before she died, when the end was in sight, I promised her I'd put her in the book, so here she is. She was always a kitten in my eyes, even though she died at nearly sixteen. I'm convinced that she may have seen her inner lion every time she looked in a mirror. The prospect of ever seeing her again brings to mind this passage from C. S. Lewis's *Problem of Pain*: "I think the lion, when [she] has ceased to be dangerous, will still be awful: indeed, that we shall then first see that of which the present fangs and claws are a clumsy . . . imitation. There will still be something like the shaking of a golden mane: and often the good Duke will say, 'Let [her] roar again.'"[1] (Nathaniel, she always loved you; it was just hard for her to tell you.)

Introduction

> Like so many Americans, she was trying to construct a life that made sense from things she found in gift shops.
> Kurt Vonnegut, *Slaughterhouse-Five*

As I (Dave) sit here in the anterior alcove of the Forest Public Library in central Virginia, through the decorative recessed windows before me I take in a beautiful scene. Foregrounded by a thoroughfare that extends in a few miles to the cemetery where my mother is buried, in the distance is a sprawling mountain range that dominates my whole vision. Punctuating the panoramic range are distant peaks and valleys that have inspired painters and poets alike for centuries. Just a half hour away, in Appomattox, Virginia, the Civil War officially drew to a close. Mere minutes from here can be found Thomas Jefferson's Poplar Forest home, a smaller replica of Monticello. Off to my far left I can see Sharp Top, a particular peak that is famous, among other reasons, for bequeathing some of its sacred stones to the Washington Monument. As I reflected on all this enchanting history on a crisp autumn day, I was reminded afresh that these mountains have stood tall throughout the centuries and represented an excellent vantage point to witness all these events with their many vagaries and vicissitudes. And they will persist long after our own stories, and those of our contemporaries, have come to an end.

Ours is but a brief chapter in the history of the world. The point is not meant as morbid, but rather a sober but telling reminder that quite a lot has come before us. It behooves us all to take that seriously and to cultivate a teachable spirit, a measure of humility, and a rapacious curiosity. We have much to learn from cultivating an ear to hear echoes from the past. None of us need start from scratch in figuring out life's mysteries. We can and should enter into animated conversation with the greatest minds and most generous hearts from the past, and stand on their shoulders as we strive to see farther and further.

This book intends to do just that with the so-called moral arguments for God (primarily) and the afterlife (secondarily). The moral argument for the existence of God presents us with a curious and somewhat puzzling irony.

On the one hand, the moral argument has had enormous appeal in popular literature. It was the starting point and a pivotal argument in the most widely read and influential work of Christian apologetics in the twentieth century, C. S. Lewis's *Mere Christianity*, a book that continues to enjoy remarkable sales and staying power as we move well into the twenty-first century. In the same vein, the prominent Christian philosopher and apologist William Lane Craig reports that the moral argument has been the most effective one for reaching his audiences when he lectures on college and university campuses.

On the other hand, however, in recent times it has suffered neglect in academic philosophical circles compared to the other classic theistic arguments. For a salient example of this, consider how the argument has fared in the seminal work of two of the leading philosophers of religion of the twentieth century—namely, Alvin Plantinga and Richard Swinburne. In his groundbreaking work *God and Other Minds: A Study in the Rational Justification of Belief in God*, published in 1967, Alvin Plantinga did not even discuss the moral argument, limiting his attention to the cosmological, the ontological, and the teleological arguments. Richard Swinburne advanced a larger set of arguments for God in his landmark volume *The Existence of God*, published in 1979, but still the moral argument received scant attention and support compared to most of the other arguments. Adding to the irony is the fact that the first major proponent of the argument—namely, Immanuel Kant—famously declared that there were only three possible arguments for the existence of God, the very three that Plantinga considered in his 1967 volume, and that all three were fallacious. Despite his famous argument that the existence of God is a necessary postulate of practical reason that we require to make full rational sense out of morality, Kant insistently maintained that his argument was in no way a speculative argument in support of a theoretical claim.

We believe there are good reasons why the moral argument has enjoyed acclaim in popular apologetics, but also that it deserves as much respect and attention in academic discussion as the other theistic arguments. Indeed, we believe the moral argument possesses a unique appeal that may well make it the most powerful of all theistic arguments—at least for many. To fully appreciate this argument, however, we need to have a grasp of its historical development and elaboration, which often goes neglected. The moral argument, to be sure, does not enjoy the same sort of heritage that can be traced back to the medieval period with towering progenitors such as Thomas Aquinas and Anselm of Canterbury. However, it has its own rich history, one that can illumine its own illustrious pedigree that may be missed in the deceptive simplicity of Lewis's famous formulation. Appreciating this story, moreover, is vital for contemporary philosophers who want to advance the argument and articulate it as forcefully as possible. To that end, this is an extended essay in historical recovery, an archaeological dig for ideas that can shed some badly needed light on a number of the most important questions human beings can ask. These perennially pressing questions are arguably more critical than ever in our morally ambivalent times.

The history of the moral argument in the English-speaking world after Kant is a fascinating tale to tell.[1] Like any good story, it's full of twists and unexpected turns, compelling conflicts, rich and idiosyncratic characters, both central and ancillary players. The narrative is as labyrinthine and circuitous as it is linear, its point remains to be fully seen, and its ending has yet to be written. What remains certain, however, is the importance of telling it. Why this is so, and why readers will find it worth their while, requires a bit of explanation, including an elaboration of a central and recurring conflict at the heart of the story—another nonnegotiable requirement for any good yarn.

After accepting his new post at Cambridge, Lewis—on his fifty-sixth birthday, in 1954—gave his inaugural address, titled "De Descriptione Temporum," a description of the times, in which he aimed to identify the central turning point in Western civilization: "Somewhere between us and the Waverley Novels, somewhere between us and *Persuasion*, the chasm runs." To make the case for his proposal, Lewis adduced germane examples from the realms of politics, the arts, religion, and technology. With respect to religion, what Lewis primarily had in mind was the un-christening of culture. Exceptions abound, but the "presumption has changed."

A critical aspect of his strategy here was simply to face head-on the reality that the tide had turned against many of his deepest convictions. Since he believed that the new direction was mistaken, he would often point backward. To the charge that this was retrograde, he famously said, "We all want progress, but if you're on the wrong road, progress means doing an about-turn and walking back to the right road; in that case, the man who turns back soonest is the most progressive."[2]

One of the telltale indicators of modernity (that Lewis subverted) is the relegation of morality to a second-class status—among not just philosophers but many writers of fiction and poetry as well. A prominent American poet of the twentieth century, Wallace Stevens, once said that ethics are no more a part of poetry than they are of painting. In philosophy, too, business as usual in metaphysics is to construct an interpretation of reality that draws exclusively on nonmoral considerations, such as the deliverances of the sciences. Only then does one go on to draw out various ethical consequences of the resultant view, even if that means domesticating morality or even emaciating it to fit an otherwise morally indifferent system.

In 1935 the Cambridge philosopher William Sorley, another luminary in moral apologetics, expressed misgivings about this demotion of morality, which is bound to result in an artificially truncated worldview in which moral ideas are paid short shrift. "If we take experience as a whole," Sorley wrote, "and do not arbitrarily restrict ourselves to that portion of it with which the physical and natural sciences have to do, then our interpretation of it must have ethical data at its basis and ethical laws in its structure."[3]

At the heart of moral arguments, as this book will chronicle, is the abiding conviction that morality provides an indispensable and vitally hopeful window of insight into ultimate reality. Hermann Lotze, a nineteenth-century German philosopher, went as far as to say that the true beginning of metaphysics lies in ethics, a sentiment with which both Sorley and Lewis, among others, resonated. Indeed, those who intend to sideline ethics may actually end up inadvertently displaying their moral commitments, and we should be alert to their presence as Friedrich Nietzsche suggested: "Whenever explaining how a philosopher's most far-fetched metaphysical propositions have come about, in fact, one always does well (and wisely) to ask first: 'What morality is it (is *he*) aiming at?'"[4]

Those best able to speak to a cultural moment aren't always the ones simply swept up in it, but rather may be those who recognize it as only the latest chapter in an ongoing story. Ideas don't arise in a vacuum, ex nihilo, out of whole cloth, but have their antecedents, precursors, and influences. History is a vital reminder to neither fall prey to the tyranny of the urgent and forget what's truly important, nor yield to the dogmatism of the present. As C. S. Lewis reminded us, "Every age has its own outlook. It is specially good at seeing certain truths and specially liable to make certain mistakes. We all, therefore, need the books that will correct the characteristic mistakes of our own period. And that means the old books."[5] The resources of history offer a refresher course, a teachable moment, a cautionary tale about the need to avoid making sacrosanct the trends of the times, and an often sobering lesson in why reigning plausibility structures may need to be rejected. It takes us out of the present, not for good, but for a season, so that we can return to contemporary discussions and pressing matters of the day with a new lens and fresh perspective.

The persuasive power of the moral argument rises or falls on this central question of the role morality is to play in shaping our understanding of reality. Feeling the force of the moral argument requires permitting the deliverances of morality to inform metaphysics. In an age of reductionism, skepticism, and deconstruction, however, morality is often less explained than explained away, relegated to the distinct periphery when it comes to the serious business of figuring out life's meaning and purpose (or lack of it).

In such a context, preoccupation with the minutiae of technical details can supplant the traditional concern of philosophy to pursue wisdom and virtue. Mindful of this recurring trend, Roger Scruton, while discussing the present state of British philosophy, laments the narrowness of much of the analytic tradition. As an illustration, he makes the following point: "That Derek Parfit is referred to as the greatest moral philosopher of our time is a sign of how isolated analytic philosophy has become. His utilitarian arguments are clever, but there are no human beings in them! In answer to the question, 'how should I live?' he has nothing to say, or nothing that a grown person would not laugh at." Scruton thinks there's plenty of smart philosophy generated nowadays, but he admits he finds depressing how, too often, the "analytical narrowness has driven away the human questions."[6]

Some readers, of course, might be convinced that the moral argument is hardly worth their time. Even if they're right, though, there seems little harm in hearing what its historical representatives have had to say. If their assumptions were so mistaken, if the challenges they would pose to contemporary understandings are in fact ineffectual, it is worthwhile to see why this is so. But if their insights prove penetrating, their challenges formidable, and their case powerful, then an intentional effort to recapture the richness and fertility of the history of the moral argument will likely prove to be profoundly illuminating. In this book we propose to let the argument's advocates, many long dead, come alive again and speak for themselves. Perhaps the exercise, rather than proving to be an adventure in archaeology, will be just what's needed to imbue an old argument with new vitality, and provide invaluable insight for contemporary culture.

In short then, a historical study of the moral argument is important for several reasons. It's a reminder of how classical philosophers were unafraid to ask and explore the big questions of faith, hope, and love; of truth, goodness, and beauty; of God, freedom, and immortality. It gives students and scholars alike the chance to drill down into their ideas and arguments, rather than settling for cursory summaries of their rich analysis. It invites us all to learn to live with the moral argument, rather than reducing it to a tactical weapon in one's apologetic arsenal, or something merely to acknowledge before quickly dismissing its contemporary relevance. Only by a careful analysis and assessment of the history can we come to see its richness and the fertile range of resources it offers.

As we embark on this journey, we encourage readers to keep an eye out for certain recurring themes that add richness and coherence to the unfolding story and that can serve as hooks on which to hang important ideas. First, guiding epistemological assumptions are important to notice, since many of the central understandings are at variance with what's assumed today. Second, consider the relative expansiveness of the germane theories of rationality among those whose work we examine. Is it a narrow empiricism, for example, or something much wider? Are aesthetic or relational or affective elements allowed in such theories, or excluded? How do such operative assumptions compare to what goes on today?

Third, take note as we go along of the various forms of argument that make an appearance. Are they all deductive? Or are some inductive or abductive? How often are cumulative cases to be found, either within the moral argument or in the larger natural theological case to be made of which the moral argument is just a part? Fourth, assess our claim that an exposure to these historical thinkers sheds light on contemporary discussions. If that's where the evidence leads, what is its significance? If not, why were we wrong to suggest as much?

Fifth, pay special heed to an argument's interlocutors at the time. Was it Nietzsche, or G. W. F. Hegel, or David Hume? Idealists, rationalists, or empiricists? By turns, be forewarned, it's each of these and more. Milieu matters; context counts. Scholars, like words, are best understood in their native habitat. Sixth, and finally, be inspired by the sheer range of learning and meticulous, patient rigor of so many of these eminent thinkers, leading scholars, and brilliant philosophers. Oxford dons, Cambridge philosophers, Gifford lecturers, and leading churchmen grace these pages, and even a British prime minister. Readers may not finally be persuaded by their collective case, but so impressive a group cannot be responsibly ignored.

The modern moment may not be quite as bleak as the picture Vonnegut paints in the epigraph at the beginning of this chapter, with Billy Pilgrim's mother cobbling together meaning from vestiges of kitsch gathered from gift shops. Still there's something distinctly recognizable in Vonnegut's insight: the misguided nature of asking the wrong questions and not asking the right ones; looking for meaning in the wrong places; ignoring the rich resources we have at our ready disposal to find meaningful and substantive answers to life's most important and existentially central questions.

We hope that telling the story of the moral argument can serve as a partial corrective to this lamentable trend. More positively, we trust it will serve as inspiration for a new generation to recapture some of the vision and passion shared by these luminaries in the field who had learned to live long and well with these arguments, making them part of the air they breathed, and in so doing breathing new life back into them.[7]

At the end of each chapter is a concise, aerial synopsis of the chapter's content. It's intentionally broad in scope for the sake of not losing the proverbial forest for the trees.

1

Precursors to Kant

One of the best current shows on television, as delightful as it is idiosyncratic, is *The Good Place*, starring, among others, Ted Danson (of *Cheers* fame) and Kristen Bell (former star of *Veronica Mars*). Created by the prodigiously talented Michael Shur (who also created such comedic powerhouses as *The Office* and *Parks and Recreation*), *The Good Place* doesn't just make viewers laugh; it makes philosophy cool. It's a winsome example of creatively transforming the ideas of moral philosophy, otherwise recondite, into a form both accessible and engaging.

Three of the main characters are the ethics professor Chidi Anagonye (played by William Jackson Harper), the morally incorrigible Eleanor Shellstrop (Bell), and Michael (a demon played by Danson). Yes, a demon, as Eleanor and Chidi have died and are now in the afterlife. Long story short, Chidi tries to teach Eleanor to be a better person—by studying ethics, which is a funny enough premise in itself. Along the way all sorts of frivolity unfolds, and in the process a wide array of fascinating philosophical questions arise: What constitutes the right moral motivation? Is altruism possible? Is there such a thing as meaningful moral agency? And a question that will recur in numerous forms over the course of this chapter and book, a query central to the moral apologetic enterprise: Does hope for an afterlife help or hurt moral maturation?

The brilliant humor of the show gives the heady topics a light touch, and the moral philosophy is legitimate. The Clemson professor Todd May serves as philosophical advisor to the show, as does the UCLA philosophy professor Pamela Hieronymi; but the content is tempered and rendered palatable, even delectable, by writing that is consistently sharp and hilarious. Consider Chidi's *Hamilton*-style rap musical: "My name is Kierkegaard and my writing is impeccable! / Check out my teleological suspension of the ethical!" Or, directly relevant to this chapter, one day in "class" Eleanor dismissively asks, "Who died and left Aristotle in charge of ethics?" to which an exasperated Chidi replies, "Plato!"

Socrates, Plato, and Aristotle

Alfred North Whitehead once said that all of Western philosophy is a footnote to Plato (420s–348/347 BC), so we might as well start there. William Lane Craig writes that the reasoning at the heart of the moral argument goes all the way back to Plato.[1] Most especially in the early dialogues, Plato recorded the words of Socrates, who saw himself as under a divine mandate. Socrates was also a firm believer in objective moral obligations. C. Stephen Evans points out that Socrates seemed to have thought of obligations much as we do: their four salient features are that moral obligations (1) provide a verdict on our actions, (2) bring reflection to closure, (3) involve accountability or responsibility, and (4) hold for persons *as* persons.[2]

Apart from that issue, we find in Plato the notion that things have goodness insofar as they stand in some relation to the Good. The Good, Plato believed, subsists in itself. The Good, for Plato, is the "Form" that has primacy over all the other Forms, the ultimate standard used in all evaluations of goodness. It was likened to the sun and was said to be the source of all that exists. With the advent of Christian theism, the Good became naturally identified with God himself.

George Mavrodes argues that Plato's worldview, though not Christian, has very often been taken as congenial to a religious understanding of the world. He writes that the idea of the Good seems to play a metaphysical role in Plato's thought. In other words, it is somehow fundamental to what *is* as well as to what *ought to be*, much more fundamental than atoms. "A Platonic man, therefore, who sets himself to live in accordance with the Good aligns himself with what is deepest and most basic in existence."[3] Evans elaborates by suggesting it is no accident that there is a long tradition of theistic (and even Christian) Platonism, running from Augustine to Robert Adams. He suggests that it seems almost irresistible for a Platonist to ask what it says about the nature of ultimate reality that moral truths are deep truths about the universe.[4]

Plato was Socrates's student, and Plato's famous student was Aristotle (384–322 BC). At seventeen Aristotle went to Athens, the richest city and most famous cultural center of the age, and he lived there for the better part of his life. There he became a student of Plato at the famous Academy and soon became Plato's favorite student. Later Aristotle would found his own school: the Lyceum. Eventually returning to Macedonia for ten years, he became tutor to Alexander the Great; he was also the teacher of Cassander and Ptolemy, who would eventually be crowned kings of the kingdoms of Macedon and Egypt, respectively.

The first polymath in history, Aristotle was a pioneer in meteorology, biology, zoology, astronomy, and botany as well as philosophy. Indeed, he is considered by many historians and scholars to be the most intelligent individual who ever lived. According to Pantheon, a project from the Macro Connections Group at the MIT Media Lab, Aristotle's theories have influenced human history more than any other personality. Another great philosopher of antiquity, the Roman politician, lawyer, orator, political theorist, and constitutionalist Cicero, used to refer to Aristotle's literary style as "a river of gold."

Although Plato's protégé, Aristotle took a different approach to ethics from that of his mentor. Aristotle was more inclined to speak of a thing's flourishing. A knife's goodness depends on the effectiveness with which it serves its purpose, for example. Likewise with human beings: how effectively do they serve their purpose? And this question raises another—namely, *what is* the purpose, goal, or end of human beings?

Much of the Judeo-Christian tradition would share with Aristotle a strong sense of human and moral teleology. A life of virtue, for example, is thought to *fit our nature* somehow, Aristotelian and Christian ethicists would agree. For Aristotle, the highest activity in which we can be engaged is contemplation of the divine. This is the apex of the life of rational contemplation. Aristotle conceived of God as a magnet drawing people to himself.[5] The ease with which one like Aquinas could incorporate Aristotle's philosophy into a framework of divine law reveals quite a bit of consistency between aspects of Aristotelian and Christian thought.

Augustine and Aquinas

Plato and Aristotle exerted a huge influence on medieval Christian thinkers, including the two we are about to discuss who framed this important era: Augustine (354–430 AD) and Thomas Aquinas (1225–1274). The goodness of God was a central, if not *the* central feature of Augustine's thought. Augustine endorsed the classical moral psychology, according to which we do all that we do in relation to what we take to be our *summum bonum* (highest good).[6]

Augustine referred to the supreme good as something we seek, the good that somehow serves at the foundation of all we do. He thought we desire it not for the sake of something else, but for its own sake. We require nothing further in order to be happy than obtaining *it*. It is truly called the "end," because we want everything else for its sake, but we want *it* only for itself. What is the highest good that everyone is ultimately seeking? God himself, Augustine thought. In book 8 of *The Trinity*, Augustine's aim was to show that God is the good and that humans find happiness when they love God. Loving what is good Augustine took to be a natural and obvious thing to do. This is the human telos. Augustine noted that there are different goods found in different finite things. There is the good of friendship and of the beauty in nature, for example. Humans prefer some of these goods more than others.

In light of this, Augustine thought two points are in need of explanation: the human ability to distinguish among the goods and a way to make sense of the ranking of different goods. Augustine suggested that God as *the* good explains both of these. God impressed upon the human mind "some notion of good itself."[7] And God is the standard by which all finite goods are ordered so that God is properly thought of as *the* good. Since the human telos is loving the good, and God is identical to the good, human happiness—or eudaimonia—is found in loving God.[8]

Born almost a millennium after Augustine, Aquinas is often cast as the original "natural law" theorist, paving the way for the long and distinguished history of natural law in Christian thought ever since. Natural law is especially effective at explicating aspects of general revelation. Theistic natural law theorists believe that God has manifested his moral law by writing it into human nature and into other aspects of his ordered creation.[9]

Aquinas's famous "fourth way" has been interpreted by some as a type, or at least a potential type, of moral argument. He began this argument based on an observation that we find in the world a gradation of values. Some things are better, truer, and nobler than other things. Such comparative terms describe the varying degrees to which things approach a superlative standard: the most good, truest, noblest. There must therefore exist something that is the best and truest and noblest of all. Aquinas believed that whatever possesses a property more fully than anything else is the cause of that property in all other things. Hence, there is some being that is the cause of the existence, goodness, and any other perfection of finite entities, and this being we call *God*. Such an argument is one way to infer that moral values exist per se in a spiritual realm inaccessible to sense-experience. The basis of this proof is that relative degrees of perfection imply the existence of perfection in an absolute degree.[10]

In Aquinas, the classical understanding of good as desirable is at the heart of both his moral psychology and teleology.[11] For Aquinas, the "perfect good" toward which all human desires ultimately point is God himself, even beyond the full realization of the specific potentialities of human nature. God is the ground or "supreme fount" of goodness and its true fulfillment, as the vision of the Divine Essence fills the soul with all good things, since it unites it to the source of all goodness.[12]

Like Augustine, Aquinas saw the universal human hunger for goodness as an expression, most fundamentally, of the longing to know God. There is but one Sovereign Good, namely, God, by enjoying Whom, men are made happy. The deep connection between goodness and God also shaped Aquinas's natural theology. Near the beginning of his initial metaphysical reflections on the nature of God, prior to his arguing for God's infinity or even unpacking the nature of God's existence, Aquinas devoted two full questions of his *Summa Theologica* to the nature of goodness and God's goodness. He developed a rich account of goodness that underwrites the teleology and moral psychology noted previously in this chapter. At the heart of Aquinas's thought was seeing God as good, indeed as the supreme good.[13]

Descartes and Pascal

In his *Closing of the American Mind*, Allan Bloom wrote that most everyone in France self-identifies as either a Cartesian or Pascalian. It's thought that René Descartes (1596–1650) and Blaise Pascal (1623–1662), two national authors, offered contrasting casts of mind for the French. They represent a "choice between reason and revelation, science and piety, the choice from which everything else follows," and a chasm there's no crossing.[14]

Descartes and Pascal were both brilliant philosophers and mathematicians, and their lives actually overlapped. Indeed, they even met in person once, resulting—according to a piece of reigning lore—in a later dispute over who had the idea for a particular experiment in barometric pressure. Ironically enough, though, especially in light of Bloom's observation, both Descartes and Pascal were religious believers. They both offered reasons and evidence in favor of God's existence, and, most relevantly for present purposes, both said things relevant to later developments of the moral argument in particular. It's instructive and sufficient for present purposes to identify a few suggestive kernels in their writings that arguably gestured in a direction that certain future moral apologists would travel. What matters here is less their differences—such as their radically different views about Jesuits—and more their similarities, Bloom's characterization notwithstanding.

In his "Dedicatory Letter to the Sorbonne," introducing the work of his famous *Meditations*, Descartes wrote in baldly bold and ambitious terms about the vital role that belief in God and the soul play in providing a robust incentive for morality. Indeed, he thought there could practically be no morality for unbelievers until the reality of God and the soul could be proven to them by natural reason. "And since in this life the rewards offered to vice are often greater than the rewards of virtue, few people would prefer what is right to what is expedient if they did not fear God or have the expectation of an afterlife."[15] Admittedly, this is perhaps less a moral apologetic than something else: not an inference from morality to God as much as, at first approximation, a claim that we generally need belief in God and an afterlife to motivate virtue. It's their vital connection his insight discerns, and for now this is all we wish to point out.

Descartes was an example of a philosopher and theist who believed that moral, mathematical, and logical truths are contingent (or at least not necessarily necessary) because of God's ability to alter their content. This is why Descartes is often described as a "universal possibilist," someone who believes that anything at all is possible if only God wills it. Descartes wrote that God laid down the mathematical truths that we call eternal, just as a king lays down laws in his kingdom, and that they depend on him completely.[16] He added that it is

> useless to inquire how God could from all eternity bring it about that it should be untrue that twice four is eight . . . for I admit that that cannot be understood by us. Yet since on the other hand I correctly understand that nothing in any category of causation can exist which does not depend on God, and that it would have been easy for him so to appoint that we human beings should not understand how these very things could be otherwise than they are, it would be irrational to doubt concerning that which we correctly understand, because of that which we do not understand and perceive no need to understand.[17]

Three features stand out about Descartes for present purposes. First, Descartes saw the practical connections between morality and its authoritative stature with the issue of the afterlife, an issue that will recur numerous times in the history of the moral argument. Second, Descartes saw the vital importance not just of an afterlife, and not just of God's existence, but also of God's character. He thought nothing less than the classical or "Anselmian" conception of theism was philosophically powerful enough to merit our allegiance. Interestingly enough, Descartes offered two or perhaps three arguments for God's existence in his *Meditations*, depending on how one reads *Meditation III*, but for our purposes, the most interesting is his variant of the ontological argument in *Meditation V*. Anselm, of course, was the originator of the latter, and the first best to articulate the need for God, in order to be maximally great, to instantiate the omni-qualities. An adequate theology is vital for solving problems associated with theistic ethics emanating from the "Euthyphro dilemma" and the like, which is a crucial part of an overall moral apologetic. Third, Descartes apprehended the need to acknowledge God, in virtue of who he is, as the ground of all reality in one sense or another. The extreme voluntarism he adopted, not unlike the extreme idealism of George Berkeley, however misguided or unnecessary in certain ways, had the wisdom of seeing the need for God to function as the ontological foundational of all of reality.[18]

Descartes's contemporary, the junior French fellow philosopher Blaise Pascal, was another mathematical prodigy. He contributed to the study of fluids and clarified the concepts of pressure and vacuum. While still a teenager, he started some pioneering work on calculating machines, establishing himself as one of the first two inventors of the mechanical calculator. As a mathematician he created two major new areas of research: he wrote a significant treatise on the subject of projective geometry at the age of sixteen, and later he corresponded with Pierre de Fermat on probability theory.

Before dying at age thirty-nine, he was reputed by many to be the leading thinker in Europe. In his book *Men of Mathematics*, a generally excellent book, E. T. Bell makes the provocative case that, whereas Pascal's work in mathematics was an accurate measure of his brilliance, his later morbid religiosity and work in the philosophy of religion marked a precipitous decline in his intellectual prowess and achievement. In Bell's words, Pascal was a highly gifted mathematician who "let his masochistic proclivities for self-torturing and profitless speculations on the sectarian controversies of his day degrade him to what would now be called a religious neurotic."[19] Of course another possibility about Pascal is that his mathematical talents and piercing insight into matters metaphysical were deeply related to each other, both products of his keen intellect (instances of tendentious and partisan polemicism notwithstanding).

After Pascal's dramatic conversion, which he referred to cryptically as his "night of fire," he made it known that he thought none of us can rationally ignore the existentially urgent question of whether or not there's an afterlife. For him this question makes a huge difference not only in how we should understand morality but indeed in how we should approach our entire lives. In his *Pensées*—the posthumously organized notes he was compiling in his preparation to write his Christian apologetic—he wrote,

> The immortality of the soul is something of such vital importance to us, affecting us so deeply, that one must have lost all feeling not to care about knowing the facts of the matter. All our actions and thoughts must follow such different paths, according to whether there is hope of eternal blessings or not, that the only possible way of acting with sense and judgment is to decide our course of action in the light of this point, which ought to be our ultimate objective.[20]

Like Descartes (and others) before him, and Kant (and others) after him, Pascal saw morality, God, and the afterlife as intimately related. In philosophical circles "Pascal's wager" is his best-known contribution, and readers may naturally associate an intentional connection of morality and the afterlife with the merely prudential desire to avoid getting flames on one's cosmic rear end (as J. P. Moreland once put it). But there's much more to Pascal than the wager; much more to his recognition of the importance of immortality than prudential concerns; and much more to the wager than is commonly assumed.

Again, Pascal was in the process of constructing an elaborate book-length apologetic for the truth not just of theism generally but of Christianity in particular, of which notes on the wager filled only a few pages. What's at stake when it comes to the ultimate coherence of happiness and holiness is nothing less than the full rationality of morality. So when Pascal used his mathematical acumen, in this context, to quantify the irrationality of indifference to an eternal good for which there's excellent evidence, it was anything but something merely mercenary or prudential.

Locke and Reid

Continuing on the same general theme, the great English philosopher John Locke (1632–1704) was well known for emphasizing the importance of divine rewards and punishments in moral motivation. The forthrightness with which he occasionally emphasized their centrality, in fact, has elicited from some quarters accusations that he fell prey to the misguided notion that the matter of moral motivation can be reduced to aiming for a beneficial outcome—again, something more prudential than intrinsically moral.

We don't generally look to Locke for anything like a full-fledged moral argument for God's existence; he's better known for his work in epistemology and political philosophy than in ethics.[21] Nevertheless, it's worth at least brief mention that his writings articulated, however imperfectly, the insight or intuition that morality and a system of divine punishments and rewards are inextricably connected.[22] However bluntly or crassly drawn some of these connections may be, Locke does put his finger on a sound insight close to the heart of the moral enterprise when he insists upon an ultimate reckoning and balancing of the scales. Unless ultimate reality is itself committed to justice, many of our cherished hopes for the rectification of wrongs and redemption of sufferings are in vain. Of course this line of thought requires quite a bit of fleshing out before it can become a discursive apologetic, for otherwise it might be seen as wishful thinking and a hope that is bound to disappoint.

In fairness to Locke, his discussion of moral motivation was more nuanced and textured than is often acknowledged. In addition to fear of punishment or hope for reward, he also wrote about the legitimacy of acting according to conscience. Whereas some argue that Locke underwent a shift in his view, and others see the rational and prudential dimensions usefully dividing up the relevant labor, yet others see as deeply compatible both sorts of motivations. Although we're inclined toward that third alternative, we have no intention of entering that debate here, but simply instead to make mention of the essential role Locke felt that a providential and authoritative God plays in morality.

In his more mature work, *The Reasonableness of Christianity*, Locke reiterated that moral law functions as a way of ensuring obedience. Humans can appreciate the intrinsic goodness of virtue, and even its appeal, but this is not nearly enough to motivate virtuous behavior: "The philosophers indeed showed the beauty of virtue: they set her off so as drew men's eyes and approbation to her. The generality could not refuse her their esteem and commendation; but still turned their backs on her, and forsook her, as a match not for their turn."[23]

To remedy this problem, on Locke's view, God attaches clear and explicit sanctions to ensure that the virtuous course of action will always be the more attractive option:

> [Virtue] has another relish and efficacy to persuade men, that if they live well here, they shall be happy hereafter. Open their eyes upon the endless, unspeakable joys of another life, and their hearts will find something solid and powerful to move them. The view of heaven and hell will cast a slight upon the short pleasures and pains of this present state, and give attractions and encouragements to virtue which reason and interest, and the care of ourselves, cannot but allow and prefer. Upon this foundation, and upon this only, morality stands firm, and may defy all competition. This makes it more than a name; a substantial good, worth all our aims and endeavours; and thus the gospel of Jesus Christ has delivered it to us.[24]

One more figure of note to mention prior to Kant is the Scottish philosopher Thomas Reid (1710–1796). Reid offered a few arguments in support of the "coincidence thesis," according to which well-being and virtue go together. His first argument wasn't that they are necessarily coextensive, but rather that they are bound together in various important ways. In the process he made it clear that he saw virtue and well-being as distinct. The way to secure their coincidence, despite their distinctness ontologically and conceptually, Reid thought, is by positing the existence of a benevolent deity. As Reid put it, "While the world is under a wise and benevolent administration, it is impossible, that any man should, in the issue, be a loser by doing his duty. Every man, therefore, who believes in God, while he is careful to do his duty, may safely leave the care of his happiness to Him who made him."[25]

The scholar Terence Cuneo points out that Reid held that the coincidence thesis lies deep in the moral life. Reid thought it a virtuous coincidence that the moral life is, or is at least likely to be, good on the whole for the virtuous agent. At the same time, Reid recognized that certain experiences of evil can shake this conviction. Cuneo adds that "Reid sees no way to defend the coincidence of virtue and well-being apart from supposing that the world is under benevolent administration. There is an important sense, then, in which Reid's ethical views are ineliminably theistic."[26]

As it happens, Reid would agree after all with the writers of *The Good Place*, convinced that genuine virtue requires being committed to the moral life for its own sake, not for some reward. Importantly, though—and this is a crucial insight—he saw no way to make sense of that commitment apart from holding "that there is a God who is just and benevolent in the administration of the world, ensuring that an agent's virtue and good on the whole coincide if not in this life, then in the next."[27] As Reid put it, "Virtue is his [i.e., God's] care. Its votaries are under his protection & guardianship."[28] Unlike Joseph Butler, who engaged skeptics of the coincidence thesis in an effort to change their minds, Reid thought a commitment to that thesis, though virtuous, natural, and intuitive, goes beyond the evidence in some sense. Another step was needed before it could become fully evidentially significant. It was for Immanuel Kant, born just fourteen years after Reid, that these considerations would provide the material for an argument for God's existence. To Kant—perhaps the best-known moral apologist of all—we now turn.[29]

> Synopsis: Although Kant is often thought of as the first significant moral apologist, hints and intimations of the moral argument can be found before him. Plato's conception of the Good has been thought congenial to a theistic conception, and Aristotle's robust teleological conception of reality and sturdy commitment to final causes resounded with much of the later Judeo-Christian tradition. Augustine and Aquinas, in particular, were committed religious believers and thinkers who forged clear connections between their theism and key moral ideas found among such Greek thinkers as Plato and Aristotle. The contemporary Frenchmen Descartes and Pascal both saw the relevance of the afterlife to fundamental questions of the moral quest. Locke and Reid were both drawn to an early version of the "coincidence thesis," according to which well-being and virtue go together. In all of these ways the stage was set for Kant's landmark work.

2

The Sage of Königsberg

Immanuel Kant

After his retirement, with his canon complete, Immanuel Kant (1724–1804) endured a short bout with senility—a historical twist as cruelly ironic as Beethoven's deafness. After the death of the eccentric genius, inscribed on his tombstone near the cathedral of Kaliningrad were his bold words in German about what never ceased to touch and move him: "Zwei Dinge erfüllen das Gemüt mit immer neuer und zunehmender Bewunderung und Erhfurcht, je öfter und anhaltender sich das Nadenken damit beschäftigt: der bestirnte Himmel über mir, und das moralische Gesetzt in mir."

Translated to English, the immortal words read: "Two things fill the mind with ever-increasing wonder and awe, the more often and the more intensely the mind of thought is drawn to them: the starry heavens above me and the moral law within me."[1] Kant is widely regarded as the first significant proponent of the moral argument. Most everyone after Kant who talked about the argument did so in at least implicit conversation with him.

Since Kant was not without his precursors, we wanted to share in chapter 1 at least a few intriguing tidbits from earlier thinkers who, though they didn't offer robust moral arguments for God's existence, seemed to apprehend at least a hint of the intuitions and insights at the foundation of such arguments. Other names could no doubt have been included, and we make no claims to be exhaustive there, only suggestive. With Kant, however, the story really began to take identifiable form.

Kant gave two main moral arguments for rational faith, or rational postulation of belief in God's existence, and these are our main concern in this chapter. The first argument is an "argument from grace," and the second is an "argument from providence."[2] Before delving into the arguments, let's first briefly consider the diminutive philosophical giant himself and take an all-too-cursory look at his deeply influential work on ethical theory.

Kant's Life and Ethical Works

The great German philosopher was born in Königsberg, Prussia, the fourth of nine children. Both parents were simple and devout pietists. Religious devotion, humility, and a literal interpretation of the Bible along with the sacredness of work, duty, and prayer all played an important role in the reformist movement within the Lutheran church of which Kant was part. Pietism assigned primacy to the sovereignty of conscience, a teaching that would exert a lasting influence on his thinking, particularly when it came to what he said about consciousness of the moral law.

Because of a wise and benevolent pastor, the young Immanuel—he changed his name to "Immanuel" after learning Hebrew, having been baptized "Emanuel"—attended a pietist school there in Königsberg. Kant lost his parents as a young man and suffered from ill health, but before long he became a popular citizen of his city for his grace, wit, and ready conversation. He entered the University of Königsberg at the age of sixteen and graduated six years later. He then took work as a private tutor until, at age thirty-one, he obtained a post at the university as private docent. This marked the "precritical" period of his written work, much of it focused on mathematics and physics.[3]

David Appelbaum and others suggest that, between 1766 when Kant published "Dreams of a Visionary" and 1770, Kant became more antimetaphysical, in part from his deeper commitment to scientific knowledge and in part from the influence of the French philosopher Jean-Jacques Rousseau, who had written with deep insight on the subject of freedom.[4] Rousseau made a large impact on Kant; a framed picture of Rousseau was the one picture adorning Kant's home. Legend also has it that Kant deviated from his scrupulous schedule the day Rousseau's *Émile* arrived in the mail.

Speaking of *Émile; or, Treatise on Education*, Lewis White Beck argues that one of Rousseau's influences on Kant is actually a moral argument for God's existence that is imbedded in *Émile*:

> First among [views Kant shared with Rousseau] is the moral argument for the existence of God anticipated in *Émile*. In order to voice his protest against contemporary naturalism, Rousseau, lacking speculative power, had to fall back on personal faith. Kant, by formulating and defending a metaphysics that was both a priori and practical, developed Rousseau's insight into an indispensable part of his own more critical philosophy.[5]

As a teacher, Kant was not, as often portrayed and pictured, distant, unemotional, or coldly stoic. His approach was anything but that of a detached speculative philosopher. He developed an infectious and animated lecture style that drew huge crowds. His pupil Jachmann noted his spirited oratory that swept the heart and emotions along with the intelligence. In a letter to a friend, Jachmann wrote, "How often he moved us to tears, how often he stirred our hearts to their depths, how often he lifted our minds and emotions from the shackles of self-seeking egoism to the exalted self-awareness of pure free-will, to absolute obedience to the laws of reason and to the exalted sense of our duty to others!"[6]

In 1770 Kant was appointed Ordinary Professor of Logic and Metaphysics in the University of Königsberg. Living during the European Enlightenment of the seventeenth and eighteenth centuries, he himself was one of its most important luminaries, deeply imbibing the Enlightenment spirit. Kant published landmark contributions to metaphysics and epistemology, but here we will confine our focus to his work in ethics.[7]

His first major treatise on ethics came in 1785: the *Groundwork for the Metaphysics of Morals*. In 1788 came *The Critique of Practical Reason*, which extended his analysis of ethics. It both built on and added to the work of his famous first *Critique*.[8] In 1791 came an interesting article on the Old Testament book of Job in which Kant, while expressing reservations about theodicy and likening Job's false comforters to theodicists, affirmed the propriety of rational faith in the face of the otherwise seemingly intractable problem of evil.[9] His 1793 *Religion within the Bounds of Reason Alone* landed him in trouble with religious authorities.[10] After discontinuing his university lectures in 1796, he published *Metaphysic of Morals* in 1797, one part of which deals with justice, the other with virtue. *Lectures on Ethics* was posthumously published by some of his students.

As an ethicist, Kant is often cast as one who embraced a moral law without a lawgiver, which explains why so many secular ethicists try to enlist him to their cause. But such efforts tend to overlook the many and profound ways in which Kant connected God and ethics. Admittedly he didn't connect them with as straight a line as some might prefer, but he nevertheless did see them as integrally related.

For Kant, when it comes to ethics, the nonempirical, purely a priori aspect of the investigation is what constitutes the heart of the matter: the "metaphysics of morals." Since the moral law, if it exists, is universal and necessary, the only appropriate means to investigate it is through a priori rational reflection, by which one can find the guide and supreme norm for morals. Rather than turning his attention to "practical ethics," then, Kant doubled down on the centrality of "pure ethics," a priori investigation into the parts of ethics that are universal and necessary.

Morality isn't about what makes us happy, he thought, but about what is needed for us to deserve happiness. A good will is what makes one *worthy of happiness*, a will guided by reason rather than inclination. Kant thought that all of our actions, whether motivated by inclination or morality, must follow some law; but the moral law must bind universally and necessarily regardless of ends and circumstances. But what sort of law can that be? He was convinced that the only alternative is a law that reflects the form of law itself—namely, that of universality. Kant thus arrived at his well-known categorical imperative, one version of which says only to act on those maxims we can consistently will to become universal laws. Whereas hypothetical imperatives provide the rules an agent must follow when she adopts a contingent end, categorical imperatives apply to everyone and are universal and necessary; they are independent of anyone's particular contingent aims. Kant went on to provide three different formulations of the categorical imperative: the universal law of nature, the formula of humanity, and the formula of autonomy.

As we turn to his moral argument(s), note his recurring willingness, even insistence, to use morality and its deliverances, implications, and prior requirements as evidentially significant to warrant conclusions about what it is rational to believe or postulate about reality, a methodology on which the whole endeavor of moral apologetics is centrally predicated.

The Argument from Grace

The two main moral arguments that Kant provided are the "argument from grace" and the "argument from providence." To illustrate the connections between them, let's start with Kantian moral faith, which features two parts: (1) that the moral life is possible, and (2) that a life of true happiness must be a moral life, that morality and happiness must converge (which we saw in chapter 1). The argument from grace will pertain to the first aspect of moral faith: that the moral life is possible, that radical transformation is possible. The argument from providence will pertain to the second aspect of moral faith: that morality and happiness ultimately converge perfectly.

The argument from grace, in light of the biblical principle of "by grace through faith," might be expected to do primarily with the issue of forgiveness. After laying out various versions of the moral argument (including Kantian variants), Robert Adams once wrote,

> I have focused, as most philosophical discussion of the moral arguments has, on the connections of theism with the nature of right and wrong and with the idea of a moral order of the universe. I am keenly aware that they form only part of the total moral case for theistic belief. Theistic conceptions of guilt and forgiveness, for example, or of God as a friend who witnesses, judges, appreciates, and can remember all of our actions, choices, and emotions, may well have theoretical and practical moral advantages at least as compelling as any that we have discussed.[11]

Writers from Newman to Taylor to Lewis did indeed focus heavily on the role of grace and forgiveness in their variants of moral apologetics.

Forgiveness for wrongdoing, theologically speaking, pertains to issues of (theological) *justification*. The variant of the argument from grace that Kant advanced, however, is more closely associated with the process of moral transformation, often referred to theologically as *sanctification*, at least when it comes to the radical transformation possible after justification. Kant would make the Methodist founder John Wesley proud, however, by emphasizing (at least at times) that such transformation, every bit as much as justification, essentially requires the operation of God's grace (an important motif in Wesley's preaching).

The argument stems from recognizing both a very high moral demand and the human inability to meet that demand without some sort of outside assistance. Kant believed that consciousness of the moral law reveals an exacting moral standard. Ultimately morality insists on nothing less than the effort of seeking perfection. The moral requirement is neither indulgent nor compromised. Since perfection obviously can't be attained in this life, and because of the Kantian deontic principle *ought implies can*, death must not be the end.[12] We must be able to continue the quest subsequent to death. This posthumous dimension is Kant's argument for immortality. The quest for moral perfection is never completed; rather, the "holy will" that is the possession of God alone is only forever approached and approximated asymptotically.[13] It is also an argument for God, though, or at least rational postulation of God.

Here is a discursive formulation of Kant's argument from grace.

1. Morality requires us to achieve a standard too exacting and demanding to meet on our own without some sort of outside assistance.
2. Exaggerating human capacities, lowering the moral demand, or finding a secular form of assistance aren't likely to be adequate for the purpose of closing the moral gap.
3. Divine assistance is sufficient to close the gap.
4. Therefore, rationality dictates that we must postulate God's existence.[14]

What leads us to think the moral demand is beyond our reach? The inability on the part of human beings to meet such a demand. Human beings have a profound moral problem, a deeply flawed moral disposition in need of a revolution of the will.[15] No mere tweaking of the paradigm will do. Radical change is needed. We are all, Kant thought, born under the evil maxim. Out of all the plethora of subjective maxims, they all boil down either to the good maxim, which subordinates desire to duty, or the evil maxim, which subordinates duty to desire. It's not that we are as evil as we could be, but the human race is surely tainted; our "dear self" tends to reign supreme. Commentators on Kant sometimes attribute Kant's recognition of human moral frailty and self-consumption to Kant's Lutheran upbringing that depicts the essence of our sinful condition as being curved in on oneself.[16]

The most important consequence of Kant's recurring insistence that moral judgments must be universalizable is that a moral agent is not allowed to make special exemptions or exceptions for himself. This would require individual reference to himself, of course, which would be problematic for Kant in its own right. Kant's aversion to such a maneuver went beyond that issue, however; it's at least partially a function of his recognition that the root moral malady is the human tendency to privilege our own interests above our moral duties.

Kant saw clearly that the moral demand is very high, while also recognizing that we have a natural propensity to depart from it, privileging instead what John Duns Scotus (and Anselm before him) called the "affection for advantage" over the "affection for justice." We have a natural tendency, when forced to rank these, to privilege evil over good, self over others, desires over duty. This needs to change, but how can we do it on our own? We can't. As A. E. Taylor would later put it, we can't pull ourselves up by our own hair. Kant likewise saw that we find ourselves in a dilemma: we need to privilege the good maxim, but our natural tendencies are too strong in the other direction of privileging the self and our own desires. Born under the evil maxim, we can't reverse the ranking by our own devices. John Hare sees Kant in the tradition of Augustine here, who said that God bids us to do what we can't, in order that we might learn our dependence on God.[17]

It is telling that implications from the three variants of the categorical imperative concern our duties to others and the communities of which we are a part. We've already been discussing the first variant and the challenge egoism poses to universal legislation. An implication of the second variant drives home the point that preoccupation with oneself is at odds with the moral demand. The formula of the end in itself—treat others as ends in themselves and not merely as means—requires more than paying heed to others as centers of agency. We are, as far as we legitimately can, to assume the ends of others as our own. And on Kant's conception of the "kingdom of ends," we are tied together by our needs and abilities into a single unit or kingdom (of which God is the head), which we must be prepared to will into existence as a whole. We are to act as though we are, through our maxims, lawmaking members of a kingdom of ends—a systematic union of rational beings under common objective laws.

What results from the combination of a high moral standard and our own inabilities is a recurring emergence of a dissonance and disconnect between how we behave and how we ought to behave, between indicatives and imperatives, between is and ought. On a Kantian picture, we all ought to behave in a certain way, in accord with the moral law, but at the same time we encounter intractable obstacles. Our natural capacities are not up to the task. Yet the moral demand remains pressing on us—a demand whose deliverances we lack the sensitivity and sympathy to figure out and abide by, but whose content *can* be both figured out and actualized by the perfect moral thinker and paradigm. The moral gap then generates its consequent sense of moral failure and the conceptual difficulty that we labor under a demand too prohibitive, well beyond our capacities.

If morality is beyond our capacities, but ought implies can, how can morality be authoritative for us? The problem can be resolved if there are additional resources outside ourselves we can tap into. Then the operative deontic principle becomes "ought implies can with the help available." But this means we *ought* to seek that help, and we are culpable if we don't. To close the gap without appealing to divine assistance, there are three possibilities: (1) to exaggerate our capacities to be moral; (2) to lower the moral demand; or (3) to identify some set of secular substitutes for divine assistance in meeting the demand.

Kant anticipated the first strategy, but rejected it when he referred to man's self-conceit and the exaggeration of his powers. Kant also anticipated the second effort when he said that we may imagine that the moral law is indulgent as far as we are concerned, but it's not an approach he condoned. The last effort to answer the challenge of the moral gap tries neither to exaggerate human capacities nor to lower the moral demand; rather, it aims to recognize the gap but then locate some nontheological substitute for God's assistance to close it. Kant was skeptical such secular help would suffice.

At least at crucial junctures Kant was clear that divine assistance was needed to effect radical moral transformation. His argument to this effect offered resources for a performative version of the moral argument. Interestingly, on a specifically Christian understanding, hope for moral transformation is at the center of its soteriology. Indeed, contra Kant, a holy will, something like impeccability, is a living hope. Total transformation, complete conformity to the image of Christ, is within our grasp. The yearning for perfection isn't a pipe dream or wishful thinking—it is a veridical intimation of reality. If such a thing is possible, isn't it worth pursuing? Isn't it something all of us should care about, particularly if the realization of such a possibility depends on our doing so?

Moreover, not only does the argument from grace have implications for individuals, it also bears on larger social structures and dynamics, which themselves can harden systemic injustices, promote dysfunctions, and perpetrate evils of various sorts, on the one hand, or, more positively, advance social justice, lift up the downtrodden, and give hope to the marginalized. Although Rousseauian readings of Kant may go too far, Kant did seem to recognize the potentially corrupting nature of certain social interactions. It's not surprising, therefore, that his ethics have important applications on more communal levels beyond the merely individual one. Kant's language of an ethical commonwealth, for example, invoked the image of what a society would look like when virtue is widespread, when it becomes common practice not to privilege self over others and over duty. Recall the various ways that versions of the categorical imperative demanded a rejection of self-focus together, instead, with an abiding concern and preoccupation for the larger communities of which we're a part.[18]

An important truth test of a worldview is its fruit. Here it's relevant to adduce what Paul Copan has dubbed an historical aspect of moral apologetics: the historical role played by Jesus Christ and his devoted followers. Morality has implications for more than individuals; it demands deep cultural transformation as well. On this score Christianity can point to a laudable track record. Even the outspoken atheist Jürgen Habermas, in his later work, acknowledged the inescapable and profound debt human rights discourse today owes to the biblical worldview.

"Christianity has functioned," Habermas wrote,

> for the normative self-understanding of modernity as more than just a precursor or a catalyst. Egalitarian universalism, from which sprang the ideas of freedom and a social solidarity, of an autonomous conduct of life and emancipation, the individual morality of conscience, human rights, and democracy, is the direct heir to the Judaic ethic of justice and the Christian ethic of love. This legacy, substantially unchanged, has been the object of continual critical appropriation and reinterpretation. To this day, there is no alternative to it. And in light of current challenges of a postnational constellation, we continue to draw on the substance of this heritage. Everything else is just idle postmodern talk.[19]

Argument from Providence

The other aspect of Kantian moral faith was that a life of true happiness must be a moral life. Morality and happiness must ultimately perfectly converge. Something of an airtight relationship between them is needed, if morality is to be a fully rational undertaking. More specificity is needed, however, for the Stoics and the Epicureans both assumed, in their own way, such an airtight connection. Kant disagreed with both of their formulations, insisting that happiness can't be reduced to virtue or vice versa. Rather, they remain distinct.

In addition, our experience gives us no particular reason or realistic hope to think that morality and happiness will perfectly correspond in this life; nature is indifferent to our moral purposes, as far as we can tell from our sense experience. Unless such a perfect correspondence ultimately obtains, however, morality becomes rationally unstable. We must seek to find a rational way to assure ourselves that morality and happiness are ultimately consistent.

Kant concluded that we need belief in God to give us this assurance. Kant gave this argument in the Dialectic of the *Critique of Practical Reason* but also at the beginning of *Religion within the Bounds of Reason Alone*, and at the end of the first and third *Critique* (*Pure Reason* and *Judgment*). The fundamental issue here pertains to a lack of rational fit if we lack the assurance of a correspondence between happiness and virtue. Since rationality dictates our obligation to pursue this congruence—which is the highest good as it applies to us as inhabitants of both the phenomenal and noumenal realm—the rationality of the moral enterprise demands that such a goal be obtainable. Ensuring such a correspondence is not within our powers.[20] Since morality and rationality give us this end (union of virtue and happiness), we must, if we are to pursue the morally good life in a way that is rationally stable, believe that this highest good is really (and not merely logically) possible.

In order to sustain our belief in the real possibility of the highest good, we therefore have to postulate the existence of a supersensible author of nature who can bring about the conjunction of happiness and virtue. In this way morality inevitably leads to religion. In this context Kant suggested we have to recognize our duties as God's commands. Why? Because by so doing we can rationally believe in the real possibility of the highest good, the end that morality itself gives us. When Kant defined religion as recognizing our duties as God's commands, the notion of religion is of a moral faith that how things ought to be is ultimately how they will in fact be, thanks to the providential governance of the universe.

Here is a more discursive formulation of the argument.

1. Full rational commitment to morality requires that morality is a rationally stable enterprise.
2. In order for morality to be a rationally stable enterprise, it must feature ultimate correspondence between happiness and virtue.
3. There is no reason to think that such correspondence obtains unless God exists.
4. Therefore, rationality dictates the postulation of God's existence.

To get a better grasp on the argument, let's get more specific on this issue of rational stability. Why do we need to believe in the possibility of the highest good in the conjunctive sense? We have been speaking in terms of rational stability, which is a legitimate category of its own, but it could also be cashed out or augmented in several other ways. We wish to make mention of two such ways, and then offer our own take on how best to identify what's at stake here, which strikes us as vitally important.

The issue of *rational stability* primarily raises the question of whether morality is a fully rational endeavor. If morality is less than fully rational, it's unclear we should remain committed to it when doing so is painful or costly. An intuition that many share is that morality is nonnegotiably important and ineliminable, overriding and authoritative. If this is right, then such a view seems to be assuming its fully rational nature, but the fully rational nature of morality requires explanation.

What is it about morality that ensures its rationality if it, among other things, doesn't ultimately cohere with happiness, or perhaps even militates against or otherwise precludes it? Moral faith on this score isn't a bad response, we think, as long as such faith is rational and not fideistic. This, however, demands an explanation of where the full rational authority of morality comes from. Kant was wont to locate its source in God. This isn't the most direct route, perhaps, from morality to God, but it was a significant and thoughtful attempt at forging such a connection that, in our estimation, carries considerable weight in light of the need to think of morality as fully rational.

A second way to talk about what's at stake here is in terms of *moral motivation*. John Hare offers a nuanced motivational interpretation of Kant on this point. On his reading, Kant maintained that we are capable of acting morally without doing so for the sake of our happiness. Still, Hare holds that Kant thought that unless we can have confidence that acting morally is compatible with our happiness, at least in the long run, we could not sustain our commitment to the moral life. So Hare has Kant claiming that we make compatibility with our happiness a condition of, though not our reason for, doing what morality demands.

Kyla Ebels-Duggan, however, offers this critique:

> Hare's approach, some argue, is implausible as a reading of Kant. In fact the moral psychology that Hare articulates more or less exactly describes the structure of the evil will to which Kant refers in the *Religion:* Instead of making morality (permissibility) the condition for acting to secure her happiness, the evil will makes her happiness the condition on which she is willing to act morally.

She continues,

> Kant thinks that human beings *are* like this, but also that we *ought not be*. This last thought goes missing on Hare's approach. The empirical world

may be much less hospitable to morality than it looks from the comfort and safety of the lives that most of us live. Those who act well may indeed make themselves vulnerable to those who do not. Kant holds that *even so* the moral demand is uncompromising.[21]

If Ebels-Duggan is right about this, this is an important point at which we find ourselves parting company with Kant. More than Kant, we are comfortable with staking the rightful claim of morality on our full moral motivation on the unbreakable connection between morality and happiness in the long term. Without this assurance, which we think theism is eminently qualified to provide, moral agents would, we think, be justified to find their moral motivation wane. For moral apologetic purposes, we can put the case disjunctively: a less-than-airtight case between morality and happiness detracts either from moral rationality or from moral motivation (inclusive disjunction). Either way, it would detract from the moral enterprise. Classical theism can, without reducing virtue to happiness or happiness to virtue, ensure the airtight connection between virtue and happiness, thereby vindicating the rational stability and authority of morality.

A third way to articulate what's at stake here is in terms of *moral hope*. Arguably, this is more deeply consistent with Kant's own approach than the motivational point is. Ebels-Duggan makes this case. We find this a fitting way to draw our discussion of Kant to a close for now, because with it several interesting threads converge. Ebels-Duggan discusses the tension that arises in ethics between deplorable actions and deplorable consequences. Such a tension often operates at the heart of excruciating dilemma cases where the choice is between choosing an abhorrent action or allowing an abhorrent consequence. As a deontologist, Kant would consistently assign primacy to avoiding the abhorrent action, even if such a choice results in awful consequences. On his view, not only are we incapable of ensuring an ultimate correspondence between virtue and good states of affairs (happiness writ large), but sometimes our actions will actually work against those states of affairs coming to pass. But Kant knew that we are also obligated to pursue those good results, though not at the expense of neglecting our duty.

In light of this, moral agents on occasion will be tempted to despair. In fact, some have succumbed to the temptation, thinking that our ethical dreams will inevitably come to ruin. Kant's answer, instead, was one of hope—hope that ultimate reality is good, that the good will win, that tragedies will be redeemed, that life will turn out to be a comedy and not a tragedy, that injustices will eventually be fixed and the world set right. Theoretical reason can't ensure or guarantee that such hopes won't disappoint, he thought, but nor can it preclude it. Satisfaction of such hopes is at least possible, and morality itself requires such hope. So Kant thought this hope was well grounded for powerful practical reasons. Its very possibility ensures that it's no mere wishful thinking for something we know can't happen.

Hope, rather than moral motivation, is another answer about what's at stake in this discussion, and requires no departure from Kantian principles. And hope is needed by everyone, not just by the weak-willed who might all too easily lose moral motivation in circumstances of ethical difficulty. Indeed, hope is needed for the strongest-willed and most consistently virtuous, for they are often the ones most acutely aware of the potential tension between virtue and good temporal consequences for oneself or others.

This leads to three final points, all of them directly relevant to moral apologetics. First, most typically moral arguments start with clear ethical deliverances on which most everyone would agree, like the wrongness of an action type like torture of children for fun. Its obvious wrongness calls for an explanation, and the argument proceeds from there. Far less typical is starting with hard dilemma cases; but this discussion has yielded an interesting result—namely, starting with dilemma cases can be a useful starting point for moral apologetics after all.

For all of us, strict Kantians or not, will likely one day find ourselves in situations where doing what we intuitively sense is our moral duty gives us no reason at all to think that doing so will produce good consequences, much less the best ones, yet we still feel like the virtuous action is morally required. Robust faith in a good God in such situations can provide the needed assurance that those temporally bad consequences aren't the end of the story. Such hope means that even the most difficult moral dilemma cases won't prove intractable after all, at least on classical theism, and that hope rather than moral despair is the rational response.

Second, hope for a world redeemed and restored certainly speaks to the social dimensions of the argument from providence. Earlier we went from the individual to the social; now the discussion is moving in the opposite direction. Rational hope for a world set right isn't merely hope for the aggregate—it is also hope for the individual. On various consequentialist readings, hope for the aggregate might suffice; but robust hope demands more. It demands hope for every individual, nobody falling through the cracks. On Kant's view, every person is of inestimable value; each and every one is precious, has dignity and worth. Redemption is available for all.

And in light of some of the unspeakable tragedies persons have endured in this life, hope would require something incommensurably awesome posthumously to make those lives worth living. In this way, Kant, on this interpretation, would be echoed later by Marilyn McCord Adams in writing about how God himself will be that incommensurably great good who can redeem every life: "If Divine Goodness is infinite, if intimate relation to It is thus incommensurably good for created persons, then we have identified a good big enough to defeat horrors in every case."[22]

The moral orderer must be powerful enough to bring about the highest good, loving enough to will it, and involved with the world in such a way as to enact it. The being that Kant thought that we must rationally hope for is an omnipotent, benevolent, and providential agent, very like the God of the religious tradition on which he draws. Kant thus argued that, though we cannot know that there is such a God, the person committed to morality is rationally committed to the hope that there is. So the virtuous person hopes that there is such a being, one who can and will bring moral order out of apparent chaos. So, once more, morality leads to religion.

Thirdly, again in a Kantian spirit, perhaps indeed we have an *obligation* to hope. If we care about the tragedies of this world, if we have cultivated a life of virtue and holiness and love, might it be altogether rational to insist that hope is much more than a luxury or eliminable prerogative—no, instead, might it not be our binding duty? Hope for a world redeemed, for gratuitous evils to be defeated, for the loveless to be embraced, for injustices to be healed?

Here is how Richard Creel makes just such a case:

> As long as it is logically possible that evil be defeated, that innocent suffering is not meaningless and final, it seems to me that we have a moral obligation to hope that that possibility is actual. Therefore we have a moral obligation to hope that there is a God because, if there is a God, then innocent suffering is not meaningless or final.... To be sure, the Holocaust was enormously tragic—but without God it is even more tragic. Indeed, a far greater evil than the evils of history would be that the evils of history will not be defeated because there is no God. This seems to me a terribly important point that Dostoyevsky's Ivan failed to consider.[23]

Once more, on our reading, we take the import of the Kantian argument from providence to suggest rational warrant for believing in God for the sake of rendering the moral enterprise *rationally stable*; the sort of *moral motivation* able to sustain us in any and all circumstances in which we might find ourselves; and for *moral hope* rather than despair in light of our inability to ensure a world set right. We can hope that, though setting the world entirely right and making justice and peace embrace isn't *our* job, it is the solemn, sacred undertaking of *Someone's*, who will be faithful to do it.[24]

Synopsis: Better than anyone, Kant recognized the power and authority of the moral law. On that foundation he constructed two variants of the moral argument. His *argument from grace* pertains to whether or not the moral life is *possible*. Morality requires us to achieve a stand too demanding to meet on our own. Divine assistance is needed to close the resulting gap. So rationality dictates that we postulate God's existence. Kant's *argument from providence* pertains to the aforementioned rational need for happiness and virtue to cohere. Full rational commitment to morality requires that morality is a rationally stable enterprise, which entails the ultimate correspondence between virtue and (both individual and corporate) fulfillment. Without God's existence there's no particularly good reason to think such correspondence obtains. So rationality dictates the postulation of God's existence.

3

A Contentious, Contemplative Cardinal

John Henry Newman

My wife, Marybeth, and my right-hand-man and managing editor at MoralApologetics.com, Jonathan Pruitt, settled into our chairs in my basement. The computer was hooked up, we'd made contact via Skype with our amiable host, Cameron Bertuzzi, and, for the first time ever, I said hello to my interlocutor of the evening, the outspoken atheist Matt Dillahunty. He was in Texas, and I was in Virginia, and moments after a few quick pleasantries, we would be having an exchange on God and ethics. I had hoped a dialogue would be less contentious than a debate, and it probably was, but the evening still left me disappointed. I didn't know Matt, nor he me, and yet there we were—within confining time constraints and the nerve-racking dynamic of knowing a slew of onlooking partisans on both sides were hoping for fireworks—engaged in conversation about some of life's biggest mysteries as if it were the most natural thing in the world.

There was no personal history, no shared memories cementing our past, no common context, just two people who didn't know each other and who saw the world in rather incommensurable ways trying to make sense of morality and whether God has anything to do with it. Such dialogues have their place, no doubt, but the experience left me profoundly dissatisfied. I walked away enjoying Matt and wanting to get to know him more, in order to understand him better, and him me.[1] However, I couldn't help but fear that most viewers were likely to go away simply bolstered in the conclusions they brought with them. Rather than forging connections, despite the generally friendly tone, I felt like we did little to advance the dialogue, to build any meaningful bridges, or to provide much illumination.

The most substantive and fruitful conversations aren't usually achieved in a synchronic, artificial, awkward environment like that—much less in animated and acrimonious debates or social media conflicts treated as zero-sum games with participants gunning for their opponents' jugulars. Rather, they thrive in the richly relational context of committed colleagues or friends who treat one another with respect, good faith, and cordiality; who sense they have as much to learn as to teach; who are willing to invest the requisite time; perhaps who even care for one another; who, in some real sense, are rooting for their opponent in a collaborative effort to apprehend the truth. So far Matt and I haven't been able to find such a connection, but this chapter will provide a colorful illustration of just such a fertile friendship.

Our next significant figure to discuss is the Anglican-turned–Roman Catholic John Henry Newman.[2] Born February 21, 1801, Newman was a poet, theologian, intellectual icon, and an all-around complex figure, by turns an empathetic counselor, biting polemicist, and brilliant epistemologist.[3] First an evangelical, then Anglican, and later a Roman Catholic priest and cardinal, Newman was an important and controversial figure in the religious history of England in the nineteenth century, becoming nationally known by the mid-1830s.

He was also a literary figure of note, writing the popular hymns "Lead, Kindly Light" and "Praise to the Holiest in the Height." Major writings included the *Tracts for the Times* (1833–1841), *The Idea of a University* (1854), his autobiography *Apologia Pro Vita Sua* (1865–1866), *Grammar of Assent* (1870), and the poem "The Dream of Gerontius" (1865), which was set to haunting orchestral music in 1900 by Edward Elgar.

The Oxford academic and priest would eventually be drawn to the high church tradition of Anglicanism, becoming known as a leader of and able polemicist for the Oxford Movement. In 1845, joined by some but not all of his followers, he officially left the Church of England and his teaching post at Oxford and was received into the Roman Catholic Church. He was ordained a priest and continued as an influential religious leader based in Birmingham. In 1879 he was made a cardinal by Pope Leo XIII in recognition of his services to the cause of the Roman Catholic Church in England. He was also instrumental in the founding of the Catholic University of Ireland that evolved into University College Dublin, today the largest university in Ireland.

Newman's Epistemology

Newman's contributions to moral apologetics pertain mainly to his insights on the need for an expansive epistemology (a recurring feature among most major moral apologists) and the formative role played by guilt and conscience[4] as evidentially significant for theistic foundations of morality.

A primary, though not the only, source we will use below is his magnum opus *Essay in Aid of a Grammar of Assent* (1870), a book notorious for having taken him twenty years to complete.

Overcoming the challenges and persisting through various fits and starts of the project paid off handsomely, as *Essay* finally came to fruition and culminated in what has come to be known as a seminal classic in religious philosophy. The book was written against the background of British empiricism, particularly that of Locke, Hume, and Newman's contemporary John Stuart Mill, all of whom insisted on, for Newman, too restrictive a range of evidence in their theorizing.

Despite the technical, theoretical, and scholarly nature of Newman's book, what also helped inspire it was something profoundly personal. He was originally encouraged to write this treatise by a dear friend by the name of William Froude, a distinguished scientist and the younger brother of Newman's closest friend at Oxford. Many of the main themes of *Essay* were fleshed out in personal correspondence and sustained dialogue with Froude. Topics contained in the *Essay* weren't the only subjects covered in their lengthy correspondence; theirs was a rich, full friendship. But time and again they would return to its themes, iron sharpening iron, friends who often failed to see eye to eye yet who valued one another and what they had to say. Froude repeatedly tried persuading Newman to develop his views on certitude, for example. Froude would die before receiving Newman's final comments on the long letter he had written in March of 1879, but Froude did live long enough to receive Newman's brief note of acknowledgment agreeing that "truth sinks slowly into the mind, and that therefore paper argument is most disappointing—indeed this is one of the 'morals' of my *Essay on Assent*."[5]

Newman distinguished between *real* and *notional* assent, and perhaps this is a good place to begin by getting clarity on a distinction that is one of Newman's most important epistemological contributions. He dubbed it as a distinction between two modes of the operation of assent. A "real assent" is the form of assent that we give to concrete realities or the truths of religion independent of any abstract inferences from which they may derive. A "notional assent" is the form of assent we give to an abstract inference, whether deductive or inductive. Crucial to grasp is that Newman didn't intend the distinction to be between two kinds of assent but rather between two modes of a single operation of the mind.

Their difference lies in their object. The object of a notional assent is the inferential pattern of, say, a theological deduction. The object of a real assent is, for example, a truth of religion. More generally, real assent is assent to realities, whereas notional assent is assent to concepts, but the truths remain on a par. Real assent does admittedly feature a sort of relative strength and vividness, simply because ideas can't compete in effectiveness with the experience of concrete facts. We could point to a theological affirmation of God's omnipotence, on the one hand, after reflection on philosophical theology, as an example of a notional assent, versus a more experiential sense of God's abiding faithfulness as an instance of real assent.

This distinction helped Newman anticipate and structure much of what he would write about in his *Essay*. The book has two parts; in its first part the object is to show that one can justifiably believe certain things not fully understood, like the doctrine of the Trinity. The second part aims to show that one can justifiably and firmly believe what can't be absolutely proven by a chain of reasoning. At the end of each part is a chapter (chapters 5 and 10, respectively) in which Newman applied the ideas he's been discussing to certain religious questions. In both of those chapters Newman broached his moral argument for God's existence, but a few preliminary points are worth emphasizing before turning to that argument.

First, interestingly enough, the focus of his moral argument—conscience—was one among other options from which he could have chosen. Selecting conscience was strategic, however, largely attributable to the nineteenth century, as he claimed in a letter to William Brownlow. It was a potentially persuasive starting point in his argument, tactically chosen in order to get the argument off the ground, since he figured conscience was something most would admit.[6] Newman desired to make an impact and be persuasive, and he didn't think it would be effective to offer evidential considerations that were nonstarters.

Second, although Newman thought it was altogether rational to believe in God, he wanted to show that the sort of evidence on offer doesn't necessarily lend itself to a discursively inferential pattern as much as a more holistic apprehension of the truth—allowing for more of a real assent than a notional one, something more akin to literary and aesthetic cognition than the linear rationality characteristic of theoretical deduction. His concern was more with "persuasive illustration rather than formal proof," as Nicholas Lash puts it in his introduction to the 1979 edition.[7] Recall that his second purpose in the book was to argue that one can justifiably and firmly believe, even know, what can't be absolutely proven by a chain of reasoning.

Before exploring Newman's application of his epistemological resources to moral apologetics, let's first delineate more explicitly a few more of his central insights about how it is we often come to the conclusions that we do. Newman gave his endorsement to a broader construal of rationality than that of classical rationalism. Truth, he thought, sinks slowly into the mind, and strict premise-conclusion forms of arguments often play, and rightly so, a smaller role than people imagine. We are more than logicians; we're complex conative, emotional, intuitive, relational, imaginative creatures who are able to come to principled convictions and conclusions by considering, explicitly and implicitly, a wide range of available evidence. Departures from scientific forms of the quest for truth don't necessarily, for Newman, represent fits of irrationality or flirtations with fideism, but rather they are a privileging of a different and more expansive mode of rationality, predicated on a richer epistemology attentive to a broad scope of evidential considerations, not all of which lend themselves to pithy premises in a discursive analysis. Recognizing this didn't make Newman anti-reason; he was simply opposed to a myopic construal of rationality that irresponsibly ignores evidence that's really there. A benefit of this broader approach is that it allows the unlearned just as much warrant for religious belief as it does the scholar, which was an important priority for someone with Newman's bent as a practitioner.[8]

Newman's life spanned most of the nineteenth century (he died in 1890), and, despite his lack of training in analytic philosophy (largely predating it), Newman's gestures in epistemology proved remarkably prescient—anticipating insights ranging from William James's notion of precursive faith to Thomas Kuhn's *Structure of Scientific Revolutions*, from H. G. Gadamer's *Truth and Method* to W. G. de Burgh's reticence about ratiocination, from Lewis's logic of relations to Plantinga's proper function and notions of warrant to Karl Polanyi's *Personal Knowledge*. Newman's originality and innovation was at least partially a function of consistently and courageously refusing to accept as sacrosanct prevailing rules of engagement conditioned by perspectives at odds with the truth as he understood it.[9]

Lash conjectures that Newman's assignment of primacy of "religion" (in some sense) over "theology," "faith" over "reason," and "action" over "reflection" had its roots in his participation in the complex tradition of British empiricism.[10] As Lash puts it,

> It is in the life of the spirit, in the "interrogation of our hearts," in the practice of loving obedience, that we are brought to a "real apprehension" of those

symbols of transcendence which serve, analogously to sense-experience, as the "starting points" for Christian reflection. The mode of rationality appropriate to such apprehension is—in its concreteness and irreducible complexity—closer to "personal knowledge," or to literary and aesthetic cognition, than it is to the "linear" rationality characteristic of theoretical deduction.[11]

A commitment to prioritizing logic generally seems like a solid way to go, but Newman retained reservations, writing that logic is *loose at both ends*, by which he meant that, especially when it comes to answering certain questions, assumptions can be too restrictive at the front end, resulting in conclusions at the back end that don't adequately track or map onto reality.

Logic then does not really prove; it enables us to join issue with others; it suggests ideas; it opens views; it maps out for us the lines of thought; it verifies negatively; it determines when differences of opinion are hopeless; and when and how far conclusions are probable; but for genuine proof in concrete matter we require an *organon* more delicate, versatile, and elastic than verbal argumentation.[12]

It is useful to lay this foundation before examining Newman's moral argument because readers expecting a tight discursive format will be disappointed. Newman would suggest that such disappointment is instructive. It provides an opportunity to subject to critical scrutiny a prior assumption—specifically, that an argument has to conform to that particular pattern or that evidence has to be explicable in propositional terms and thereby imitate scientific inquiry. Newman simply didn't see this as true to life. What's appropriate in one context isn't appropriate in every context; the scientist doesn't act like the historian, and vice versa. Their reasoning patterns are different, and rightly so.

When it comes to the reasons for why we finally give our assents, concerning religion and other concrete matters, Newman used a series of analogies to depict the nature of the nonlinear and often complex process involved. He wrote that "proof in concrete matters does not lie (so to say) on one line, as the stages of a race course (as it does in abstract) but is made up of moments converging from very various directions, the joint force of which no analytical expression can represent."[13] Or: "An iron rod represents mathematical or strict demonstration; a cable represents moral demonstration, which is an assemblage of probabilities.... A man who said 'I cannot trust a cable, I must have an iron bar,' would, in certain given cases, be irrational and unreasonable."[14]

Newman likened the "proof of Religion" to "the mechanism of some triumph of skill, tower or spire, geometrical staircase, or vaulted roof, where ... all display of strength is carefully avoided, and the weight is ingeniously thrown in a variety of directions, upon supports which are distinct from, or independent of each other."[15] Perhaps the most illuminating metaphor is a mathematical one from *Essay*, involving the movement by which "a regular polygon, inscribed in a circle, its sides being continually diminished, tends to become that circle, as its limit."[16]

For Newman we give our assent with firm conviction because of reasons that taken separately are mere probabilities. It isn't a leap as much as an organic growth into our considered beliefs, and pregnant with risk. If our goal is both to avoid error and to acquire truth, however, logical certainty is an unrealistic demand. A measure of risk is worth it. It unavoidably involves a discernment process, one that requires tenacity, attentiveness to evidence, hard thought, and rigorous intellectual honesty. Cutting to the chase too soon will likely short-circuit and sabotage the process, leaving out important details not responsibly ignored.

In short, Newman would have likely concurred with Owen Barfield when Barfield would say, a century later, that the trouble today is that we have all gotten very clever, no longer capable of thinking deeply because we think too *quickly*. It takes patience to feel the force of a disparate collection of reasons whose cumulative force is considerable, and patience requires intentional cultivation.

It is worth quoting Newman himself on these points. Extending the informal inference pattern of limits, he wrote,

> In like manner, the conclusion in a real or concrete situation is foreseen and predicted rather than actually attained; foreseen in the number and direction of accumulated premises, which all converge to it, and as the result of their combination, approach it more nearly than any assignable difference, yet do not touch it logically ... on account of the nature of its subject-matter, and the delicate and implicit character of at least part of the reasonings on which it depends. It is by the strength, variety, or multiplicity of premises, which are only probable, not by invincible syllogisms—*by objections overcome, by adverse theories neutralized, by difficulties gradually clearing up, by*

exceptions proving the rule, by unlooked-for correlations found with received truths, by suspense and delay in the process issuing in triumphant reactions— by all these ways, and many others, it is that the practiced and experienced mind is able to make a sure divination that a conclusion is inevitable, of which his lines of reasoning don't actually put him in possession (emphasis added).

To Newman this was what "as good as proved" means, a conclusion as undeniable "as if it were proved," reasons "amounting to a proof." A proof, by his lights, is the limit of converging probabilities.[17]

Conscience and Imaginative Apprehension of God

Turning now to his *Essay*, its first part discussed *assent* and *apprehension*. Apprehension is an intelligent acceptance of the fact that a proposition reveals. The words of the propositions used to explain an idea may be clear and intellectually accessible, making the sort of apprehension requisite for assent possible even if there's a lack of complete understanding. The second part of Newman's book contrasted *assent* and *inference*. Assent is unconditional, whereas inference is conditional. Inferences involve drawing conclusions based on premises, so they're dependent on other propositions or ideas in a way that assent is not. Let's consider now chapters 5 and 10 of the *Essay*, by turns, to see how Newman applied his ideas to religion by using conscience as his touchstone and test case.

Chapter 5 is the culmination of Newman's discussion of apprehension and assent, as applied to the matter of religion. Real assent to a religious proposition is an act of religion; notional assent is a theological act. Not that this demarcation is meant to vitiate the ability to do both. His main topic here was assent, especially real assent, of God's Being (and also the Trinity, but we'll focus our attention on the former). Why "Being" rather than existence? Because Newman's focus was more (though not exclusively) on assent than inference, his primary discourse concerned the religious act of real assent to God, and this, to his thinking, meant he was "not considering the question that there is a God, but rather what God is."[18] A theological affirmation of God in his various exalted classical attributes is surely possible, but Newman asked if we can attain to a more vivid assent to the Being of a God than that which is given merely to notions of the intellect?[19]

Are we capable of an imaginative apprehension of God? Can we believe as if we saw? Newman thought so. Here there is no substitute for adducing Newman himself. So much of the felt power of the argument is only experienced as its implications are explicated and drawn out, carefully delineated and expounded on. To reduce the presentation to a syllogism would be rather dramatically to miss much of Newman's whole point, and the import of the underlying epistemology on which the argument is based.

Regarding other human persons, we know instinctively they are more than impressions on our senses: they are real beings; we know them by the quality of those impressions. Analogously, our experience of God is not reducible to sensory impressions but to relevant mental phenomena that reveal his Being. "Those phenomena," Newman wrote, "are found in the sense of moral obligation." From our faculty that identifies intimations of conscience and their source in an external admonition, we "proceed on to the notion of a Supreme Ruler and Judge."[20] Although Newman wasn't aiming to prove God's existence, he couldn't help but identify where he would tend to look for evidence—namely, a first principle, which Newman was willing to assume and not attempt to prove: that we have by nature a conscience. Unlike other proponents of the moral argument, Newman didn't accentuate the *content* of the moral law so much as the existence of our *faculty* of conscience. This has a dialectical advantage of evading the potential criticisms that the conscience of some is malformed or corrupt or dysfunctional. Newman could freely concede such a point without its detracting from his case.

Next Newman described what we might call the *phenomenology* of the conscience. When Newman examined moral experience, he found there a functioning conscience, as legitimate as other mental faculties like memory, imagination, or a sense of the beautiful. The faculty of conscience excites in us approval or blame, and a sense of right and wrong. As we experience this operation, it kindles in us "that specific sense of pleasure or pain, which goes by the name of a good or bad conscience." Once he's done laying out the contours of moral phenomenology, he would argue how in this special feeling (though not *merely* a feeling) that follows doing right or wrong lie "the materials for the real apprehension of a Divine Sovereign and Judge."[21]

Newman analyzed the feeling of conscience as twofold: "it is a moral sense, and a sense of duty; a judgment of the reason and a magisterial dictate." Its perceived deliverances aren't infallible, but the conscience has both a critical and a judicial office. Even if one loses her sense of the deformity of acts of dishonesty, for example, she shouldn't therefore lose her sense they are forbidden. That it can be mistaken or become warped lessens neither its testimony that there is a right and wrong nor its sanction to that testimony conveyed in the feelings that attend right and wrong conduct.[22] Newman put it this way: conscience isn't so much a *rule* of right conduct as it is a *sanction* of right conduct: "This is its primary and most authoritative aspect; it is the ordinary sense of the word."[23]

Newman then wrapped up his appraisal of the phenomenology of conscience:

> Conscience has an intimate bearing on our affections and emotions, leading us to reverence and awe, hope and fear, especially fear. Wrongdoing generates a lively sense of responsibility and guilt. These various perturbations of mind which are characteristic of a bad conscience, and may be very considerable—self-reproach, poignant shame, haunting remorse, chill dismay at the prospect of the future—and their contraries, when the conscience is good, as real though less forcible, self-approval, inward peace, lightness of heart, and the like—these emotions constitute a specific difference between conscience and our other intellectual senses—common sense, good sense, sense of expedience, taste, sense of honour, and the like.[24]

That's the raw moral data, and then Newman inquired as to what it implies. The way he put it, it's more than a moral sense, because it's paradigmatically emotional. That it is characteristically an emotional matter implies that it involves the recognition of a living object toward which it is directed. "Inanimate things cannot stir our affections; these are correlative with persons. If, as is the case, we feel responsibility, are ashamed, are frightened, at transgressing the voice of conscience, this implies that there is One to whom we are responsible, before whom we are ashamed, whose claims upon us we fear."[25]

The argument is somewhat analogical here, for we recognize the parity between a guilty conscience and the tearful, broken-hearted sorrow that overwhelms us on hurting a mother. We have within us "the image of some person, to whom our love and veneration look, in whose smile we find our happiness, for whom we yearn, towards whom we direct our pleadings, in whose anger we are troubled and waste away."[26]

Why an *intelligent* being? Because we aren't affectionate toward a stone, "nor do we feel shame before a horse or a dog; we have no remorse or compunction on breaking mere human law." Yet conscience "excites all these painful emotions, confusion, foreboding, self-condemnation; and on the other hand it sheds upon us a deep peace, a sense of security, a resignation, and a hope, which there is no sensible, no earthly object to elicit." If the cause of such phenomena doesn't belong to the visible world, "the Object to which his perception is directed must be Supernatural and Divine, and thus the phenomena of Conscience, as a dictate, avail to impress the imagination with the picture of a Supreme Governor, a Judge, holy, just, powerful, all-seeing, retributive, and is the creative principle of religion, as the Moral Sense is the principle of ethics."[27]

Note that Newman's claim was that such an appeal to conscience, at this point, is altogether a matter of general, not special, revelation. This vivid apprehension of religious objects is independent of the written records of alleged revelation; rather it exists in the twilight of natural religion. Newman went on to discuss special revelation and distinctive Christian teachings at length, but we will confine our focus here to general revelation.[28]

Inference, Assent, and the Argument from Conscience

The penultimate chapter of *Essay* introduced another distinctive of Newman's analysis, the so-called illative sense. Let's briefly outline what Newman meant by this central idea before looking at chapter 10. Newman himself connected it with Aristotle's notion of *phronesis*, the ancient Greek word for a type of wisdom or intelligence, particularly relevant to practical action. It implies both excellence of character and good judgment, and it can go by the names *practical virtue, practical wisdom*, or *prudence*. By Newman's account, the illative sense is the perfection or virtue of the reasoning faculty by which we potentially attain to a mental state of certitude.[29]

Certitude, in Newman's sense, is the mental state that accompanies the *limit* achieved by the accumulation of enough evidence. Newman consistently maintained that in concrete life incontrovertible proof isn't possible and that the best one can achieve is converging probabilities in favor of a conclusion. To close the gap between such probabilities and full assent, one needs the aid of the illative sense, which Newman once dubbed a grand word for a common thing, though something too subtle and spiritual to be scientific. In this way certitude, though not logical certainty, is within our grasp.

Here's how Andrew Greenwell characterizes the illative sense:

> The illative sense is what allows us to take our concrete human experiences—whether they be of nature's beauty, of the demands of conscience (the feeling of guilt, the pangs of remorse, the search for forgiveness), of the sense of the contingency of life, of the peaceful joy elicited by the shallow breathing of your sleeping child beside you in bed, of the honor given to a soldier who sacrificed his life for his fellows, of the haunting beauty of the second movement of Schubert's Piano Sonata in A major, of the pathos of G. M. Hopkins' poem "Spring and Fall," of indeed any created good or beautiful thing—and come to the conclusion that there must be a transcendent reality behind it all, ultimately, He whom we call or know as God.[30]

In the last chapter of his *Essay*, Newman again invoked conscience in his application of the ideas discussed in the second part of the book (including, most importantly, the illative sense). Interesting to note is how Newman began this chapter, by suggesting that in religious inquiry each of us can speak only for ourselves. We can share what we personally have found convincing and persuasive, but we should be hesitant to insist that others should be similarly satisfied. In this way, it would seem, Newman was quite committed to respecting the intellectual autonomy of others.[31]

The focus of what Newman discussed here will be, once again, general revelation most broadly, conscience more particularly, but it bears emphasis again that Newman had much to say about special revelation and its connection with natural religion. Special revelation, on his view—Christianity, he was convinced—was the completion and supplement of natural religion, and of previous revelations. He adduced the case of St. Paul at Athens appealing to the "Unknown God," saying that "He that made the world" "now declareth to all men to do penance, because He hath appointed a day to judge the world by the man whom He hath appointed."[32] To enhance appreciation of the supplement of special revelation, Newman thought it worthwhile to inquire into the chief doctrines and grounds of natural religion and the implications, once more, of conscience.[33]

When it comes to natural religion—that is, what we can come to know about God on the basis of general revelation alone—Newman thought there were three main *channels* available: our own minds, the voice of mankind, and the course of the world. The most authoritative of these, he thought, is our own mind, and the "great teacher of religion is, as I have said in an earlier part of this *Essay*, our Conscience." Conscience is nearer to us than any other means of knowledge, he asserted, teaching us not only *that* God is but also *what* He is; it provides for the mind a real image of Him, as a medium of worship; it gives us a rule of right and wrong, as being His rule, and a code of moral duties. "Moreover, it is so constituted that, if obeyed, it becomes clearer in its injunctions, and wider in their range, and corrects and completes the accidental feebleness of its initial teachings. Conscience, then, considered as our guide, is fully furnished for its office."[34] Note Newman's point—which will be echoed later by de Burgh and others—that one of the powerful distinctives of the moral argument is the way moral phenomena yield insights not just about God's *existence* but also about his *character*.

What in particular does *conscience* suggest about God? Newman thought its most prominent teaching, its cardinal and distinguishing truth, is that God is our Judge. Newman was unequivocal on this score, and it is worth quoting him at length:

> In consequence, the special Attribute under which it brings Him before us, to which it subordinates all other Attributes, is that of justice—retributive justice. We learn from its informations to conceive of the Almighty, primarily, not as a God of Wisdom, of Knowledge, of Power, of Benevolence, but as a God of Judgment and Justice; as One, who, not simply for the good of the offender, but as an end good in itself, and as a principle of government, ordains that the offender should suffer for his offence. If it tells us anything at all of the characteristics of the Divine Mind, it certainly tells us this; and, considering that our shortcomings are far more frequent and important than our fulfillment of the duties conjoined upon us, and that of this point we are fully aware ourselves, it follows that the aspect under which Almighty God is presented to us by Nature, is (to use a figure) of One who is angry with us, and threatens evil. Hence its effect is to burden and sadden the religious mind.[35]

Conscience for Newman is not individuals interpreting their own reality and creating their own version of God. Instead it is the true voice of God within our human understanding of reality. God was for Newman *the unknown known* and the basis for the moral law of the universe that was not known from human reason alone (or logical processes) but rather was known from our experience as human beings. It is our conscience that helps lift the veil between humanity and the transcendent and tells us whether an action is right or wrong.

Newman next discussed what can be gleaned by *the voice of mankind*, especially in light of this sense of having somehow fallen short.

What Newman found remarkable is the ubiquitous evidence of notions of atonement. From Greece to Rome, from India to Britain, from Africa to the islands of the South Seas and the natives of Australia, we find similar ideas and practices of atonement—a substitution of something offered, or some personal suffering, for a penalty that would otherwise be exacted. Why, Newman queried, should men adopt any rites of deprecation or purification at all unless they had some hope of attaining to a better condition?

What about the third source of natural religion, *the system and course of the world*? Here what struck Newman was a large measure of God's "hiddenness." "Are then the dim shadows of His Presence in the affairs of men but a fancy of our own, or, on the other hand, has He hid His face and the light of His countenance, because we have in some special way dishonoured Him?" For an answer Newman turned once more to conscience:

> My true informant, my burdened conscience, gives me at once the true answer to each of these antagonist questions: –it pronounces without any misgiving that God exists:–and it pronounces quite as surely that I am alienated from Him; that 'His hand is not shortened, but that our iniquities have divided between us and our God'. Thus it solves the world's mystery, and sees in that mystery only a confirmation of its own original teaching.[36]

Newman insisted on the "severe aspect" of natural religion first because this is the typical order of general revelation—its foundation is our sense of sin and guilt—and "without this sense there is for man, as he is, no genuine religion. Otherwise, it is but counterfeit and hollow; and that is the reason why this so-called religion of civilization and philosophy is so great a mockery."[37]

True religion, Newman was convinced, took sin seriously, recognizing the need for forgiveness and ultimate justice to be done. Interesting that in Athens, though generations apart and heralding from disparate and distant cultures—one Hebraic and the other Hellenistic—Socrates and St. Paul were both convinced of a coming reckoning, perhaps evidence to suggest that such a notion is at least intimated in general revelation. One more interesting feature of Paul in Athens, incidentally, was this: recall Socrates's recurring claim of ignorance; then, when Paul addressed the crowd, he declared that, because of the resurrection of Jesus, the hour of ignorance is over, which seems hardly a coincidence transpiring at Mars Hill.

As a Christian, Newman was convinced that general revelation prepared the ground for special revelation. Conscience is the aboriginal Vicar of Christ, and special revelation amplifies and augments the truths at which natural religion had already hinted. If the dominant tone of natural religion is stern, more bad news than good, and hope of a good God its minor theme and only remote hope, in the fullness of time the final revelation of God, Newman believed, effected a glorious inversion, making the possibility of forgiveness, prospect of moral transformation, and hope for salvation the *main* theme.

Our sinful condition before a holy God is but the necessary backdrop, making news of liberation all the more marvelous; the good news is that, though religion may start with sternness, it doesn't end there. God is not only Judge but also loving Father. The Holy is not just, to use Rudolf Otto's later language, *mysterium* and *tremendum*—dark, mysterious, unapproachable—but it is also *fascinans*: lovely, beautiful, gracious, charming.[38] By Newman's lights, the moral argument thus functions impeccably as a prelude and prolegomenon to proclamation of the gospel of Christ. From first to last, Newman's apologetic, forged in the fertile context of friendship, manifested a logic of dynamic relations.

> Synopsis: Newman exemplified the fact that the history of apologetics is very much a story about epistemology, a theme that will recur throughout this book. His rich epistemological insights served as the foundation of his moral argument. His broad epistemology and expansive empiricism recognized that we're more than narrow logic choppers. He likened the quest for truth to a vaulted ceiling that ingeniously throws its weight in a variety of directions. We gradually come to the conclusions we do through a complicated process of considering a great number of evidences, not just through tight discursive analyses. The phenomenology of conscience, in particular, he thought, can prove telling as we have direct experience of One to whom we're responsible, before whom we're ashamed, whose claims on us we fear, making possible what he called a *real assent* and a sense of deep assurance.

4

An Agnostic Moralist

Henry Sidgwick

The argument of this chapter has the distinction of being the only one we will consider that was not endorsed by its author. The Cambridge philosopher Henry Sidgwick only reluctantly acknowledged the force of a certain kind of moral argument, but he rejected it, despite recognizing it as a powerful resource to resolve a glaring problem in his own moral philosophy. Indeed, this moral argument was the only solution to his difficulty that he was aware of, but as we shall see, he rejected it anyway, despite the cost that exacted for him.

Sidgwick was born May 31, 1838, in Yorkshire to Mary Crofts and the Reverend William Sidgwick, an Anglican minister, who died when Henry was only three. He was educated at Trinity College Cambridge, where he graduated in 1859, and he became a fellow the same year. He remained in Cambridge the rest of his life.

Like many intellectuals of his era, Sidgwick faced a crisis of faith in the face of challenges to Christian orthodoxy from contemporary intellectual currents, especially from the new biblical criticism. The 1860s as a result were a tumultuous time for him, which he described as his years of "storms and stress." This was not just a personal crisis that was compartmentalized and sealed off from him academic work. To the contrary, his struggle over whether he could keep his fellowship bled deeply into his work. Indeed, he reported "that it was while struggling with the difficulty thence arising that I went through a good deal of the thought that was ultimately systematised in *The Methods of Ethics*."[1]

Sidgwick eventually came to the conclusion that he could no longer subscribe to the Thirty-Nine Articles of Religion of the Church of England, which his position required, and he resigned his fellowship in 1869. Although he lost his Christian faith, he retained theistic sympathies and remained attracted to the idea that the universe is morally meaningful and governed by a good God even though he was no longer confident he could rationally defend such a belief.[2]

His resignation from his fellowship was one of the events that led to a change of policy at Cambridge regarding subscription to the Thirty-Nine Articles of Religion; he was elected an honorary fellow in 1881 and resumed his full fellowship in 1885. He was a lecturer in classics at the beginning of his career, a position that evolved into a lectureship in the moral sciences in the late 1860s. His career at Cambridge culminated in his being named Knightbridge Professor of Moral Philosophy in 1883.

In 1876 Sidgwick married Eleanor Mildred Balfour, who was the sister of one of his former students, Arthur Balfour. Balfour's book *Theism and Humanism* was named by C. S. Lewis late in his life as one of the ten most influential books he had ever read.[3] Although trained as a philosopher, Balfour had a political career rather than an academic one, serving as prime minister of the United Kingdom from 1902 to 1905, among other posts and offices. Balfour was not Sidgwick's only powerful relative, however. His sister Mary was married to her second cousin, Edward White Benson, who was later chosen to be archbishop of Canterbury. Sidgwick was something of an activist himself, particularly in his advocacy for women's education, and he played an important role in the founding of Newnham College, Cambridge, which was among the first colleges for women in England. His wife, Eleanor, took the position of principal of Newnham in 1892.

One of the somewhat curious but fascinating aspects of Sidgwick's life is particularly pertinent to the argument that shall be our primary focus in this chapter. For many years he and Eleanor were actively involved in the Society for Psychical Research, which Sidgwick had helped to found in 1882, and often led, serving as president of the group from 1882 to 1885 and again from 1888 to 1893. Indeed, so prominent was their involvement that it was often called "The Sidgwick Group." Their interest in the paranormal was no mere hobby, however, nor a fixation on the strange and the esoteric. Rather, this mattered to him and his wife because they saw it as essential for a moral view of reality.

Writing in 1887, Sidgwick drew the connections as follows:

> Some fifteen years ago, when I was writing my book on Ethics, I was inclined to hold with Kant that we must postulate the existence of the soul, in order to effect that harmony of Duty with Happiness which seemed to me indispensable to rational moral life. At any rate, I thought I might provisionally postulate it, while setting out on the serious search for empirical evidence. If I decide that this search is a failure, shall I finally and decisively

make this postulate? Can I consistently with my whole view of truth and method of its attainment? And if I answer "no" to each of these questions, have I any ethical system at all?[4]

Despite years of intensive research and investment, his investigations never provided the solid evidence for survival after death that he was seeking. After Henry's death from cancer in 1900, however, Eleanor was convinced that her husband had communicated with her from the world beyond.

Sidgwick's academic interests and accomplishments were rich and varied, and he had a number of distinguished students in addition to Balfour, including G. E. Moore and Bertrand Russell. His most famous work, however, is *The Methods of Ethics*, which was first published in 1874 and went through five editions in his lifetime. It is recognized not only as the culmination of classical utilitarianism but also as a philosophical classic in its own right. It is this book we shall focus upon, particularly the moral argument of the concluding chapter.

Exclusive Humanism and the Moral Order of Mutual Benefit

The transition from the Victorian loss of faith to a secular worldview that had no place for God was not an easy or seamless one. Charles Taylor has told the story of the rise of secularism in great detail, and one of his key points is that secularism does not come about just because people learn more about science and become more educated. Nor is the story a simple one of subtraction, a narrative of rejecting the beliefs and practices of the supernaturally enchanted world of earlier times and places. To the contrary, secularism can take hold and become deeply rooted only when it can provide alternative moral sources that can plausibly claim to give our lives meaning and direction and secure our most important values.

The resources of Christian theism are not easily replaced. Taylor contends, however, that there was an "anthropocentric shift" in the eighteenth century that moved in this direction, generated by the "providential deism" that was ascendant during that era. A couple aspects of this shift are particularly pertinent, he suggests: "The first was that the plan of God for human beings was reduced to their coming to realize the order in their lives which he had planned for their happiness and well-being. Essentially, the carrying out of the order of mutual benefit was what God created us for."⁵ With this shift, the idea that there is anything beyond human flourishing in this life began to wane. The second follows naturally enough from the first: "Once the goal is shrunk, it can begin to seem that we can encompass it with our unaided forces. Grace seems less essential. We can see where exclusive humanism can arise."⁶ With supernatural grace fading into the background and eventually ignored altogether, the only moral and spiritual resources are of the immanent variety. The highest reaches of moral achievement and spiritual fullness are now understood in terms that make no reference to God or his assistance.

Taylor particularly emphasizes that in order to make this credible, the project of exclusive humanism needed a functional replacement for Christian agape or the disinterested benevolence of neo-Stoicism. Without a plausible replacement for agape, he does not think the transition to exclusive humanism would have succeeded. He is worth quoting at length on this point:

> This means that it had not only to incorporate the confidence that we can actually re-order and reshape our lives, but also the motivation to carry this out for the benefit of all. The locus of the highest moral capacity had to be a source of benevolence, and of the aspiration to universal justice. Now benevolence and universal concern are precisely the hallmarks of eighteenth century exclusive humanism, or perhaps we might say, of the humanism which turned exclusive; of utilitarianism, or the theory of Kant; or the Enlightenment proponents of the rights of man, and of a new dispensation based on general human happiness and welfare. As Bentham famously put it: "Is there one of these my pages in which love of humankind has for a moment been forgotten? Show it me, and this hand shall be the first to tear it out."⁷

What this requires is successfully making the case that the sources to motivate and practice benevolence can be found within human nature, apart from grace or other forms of divine assistance. Taylor distinguishes three strategies to accomplish this. One is through the idea that "disengaged reason" can free us from our narrow, selfish perspective and give us a vision of the larger whole that will inspire a passion to serve the whole. Disengagement can liberate us from the mass of our petty concerns and absorptions, our confused desires and cravings, and draw us to universal benevolence. Another way to internalize moral power is by way of a Kantian awe before a universal law and our freedom to acknowledge the authority of that law and to obey it.

The moral law within inspires us and fires our desire to meet the demands of universal justice and benevolence. A third way aims to awaken a sense of universal sympathy. Such sympathy, it was believed, lay deeply rooted in our emotional and volitional nature but has been distorted and overlaid by a number of historical and social forces. The task is to reawaken it and liberate it so it can fully flourish.

The ultimate aim here is not only to rehabilitate human nature but also to bring about a sort of revolution in how self-love was understood. Instead of seeing it as an impediment to universal love and benevolence or as a deep form of corruption that required supernatural regeneration, it was construed either as innocent or (even better) as a positive force for the good. Self-love, rightly understood and ordered, serves universal love and benevolence.

Exclusive humanism, Taylor emphasizes, is not just something we fell into once ancient ways of thinking had lost their power for many people. Rather, it represents an achievement because getting to the point that we are sufficiently inspired and motivated to universal benevolence requires developing our sense of sympathy, deepening our insight, and hard work on ourselves and our habits. In this respect, it is very similar to being moved and shaped by more classic moral sources, like the Platonic idea of the Good or the Christian account of God's agape.

Taylor also points out that it is a mistake to assume that the modern moral order lacks what he calls an "ontic component" that grounds or anchors it. Premodern morality, of course, located this ontic component in the will or nature of God, the structure of the cosmos, the Platonic forms, and the like. "The modern understanding of the order of mutual benefit central to the exclusive humanisms which arise out of the Enlightenment has indeed such a component. The difference is that it is now intra-human. This order is appropriate and realizable by us, precisely because we are, under certain circumstances, capable of universal benevolence and justice."[8]

Granted, materialists have often seen the natural world as "red in tooth and claw," and the massive universe may seem indifferent to us and our ideals, if not hostile and destructive. Moreover, it must be acknowledged that human beings do more terrible things to each other than the world of nature can ever do. Still, the idea can remain that the building blocks are intact to achieve our ideals. With the right training, the proper awakening and cultivation of our capacities for sympathy and justice, we can liberate our potential for universal benevolence and build an order of mutual benefit.

The Intractable Dualism of Practical Reason

Sidgwick's moral philosophy carried these ideas forward in the next century and attempted to secure them by resolving the conflicts of the previous century. In particular, as Alasdair MacIntyre observes, "For Sidgwick the history of moral philosophy in the preceding century had centered on the clash between utilitarianism and what he called intuitionism."[9] Sidgwick was a utilitarian who believed the "ultimate good" was "desirable consciousness." This is the happiness we naturally seek to maximize by the utilitarian calculus. By contrast intuitionists appeal to self-evident first principles that are morally binding apart from hedonic calculations. One of Sidgwick's major aims in *The Methods of Ethics* was to show that these two methods are not at odds but are in fact perfectly consistent. More central to our concerns, Sidgwick also wanted to show that egoism (also called egoistic or rational hedonism or rational self-love) is consistent with utilitarianism (also called universal hedonism or universal happiness).

To bring the latter objective into focus, let us consider Sidgwick's account of "ultimate good." He offered this definition in the context of affirming rational self-love while also arguing that is an unsatisfactory mark for our highest good. Individual happiness is too narrow, fleeting, and insecure to hold such a lofty status. Universal happiness, however, is a worthy target for our highest aspirations. "But Universal Happiness, desirable consciousness, or feeling for the innumerable multitude of sentient beings, present and to come, seems an End that satisfies our imagination by its vastness, and satisfies our resolution by its comparative security."[10]

It is worth emphasizing here the exalted terms by which Sidgwick described universal happiness. Indeed, so elevated was his language here that it is hard not to think he was extolling some sort of a deity, especially when he described universal happiness as "an End that satisfies our imagination by its vastness." Its moral gravitas was underscored by the claim that it "satisfies our resolution by its comparative security."

And yet, as powerful as this moral source appears to be, Sidgwick went on immediately to acknowledge that it cannot claim our absolute allegiance. Indeed, even though rational self-love is not of sufficient value to qualify as the ultimate good, its claims may nevertheless trump those of universal happiness. Immediately after the passage above in which he extolled the exceeding value of universal happiness, Sidgwick went on to write as follows,

It may, however, be said that if we require the individual to sacrifice his own happiness to the greater happiness of others on the ground that it is reasonable to do so, we really assign to the individual a different ultimate end from that which we lay down as the ultimate Good of the universe of sentient beings: since we direct him to take, as ultimate, Happiness for the Universe, but Conformity to Reason for himself.[11]

Notice the odd result that seems to follow if we demand of an individual that he sacrifice his own personal sacrifice for the sake of promoting the happiness of others, on the ground that reason requires him to do so—namely, that we produce a profound divide in the human race with respect to what is ultimately good, a divide that is hard to justify on rational moral grounds. For some, the ultimate good is happiness, for others it is conformity to reason.

It is important to make clear that this does not deny that it may be perfectly reasonable for an individual to choose to sacrifice his individual good for the greater happiness of others. If he wants to do so, that is surely a reasonable choice. At the same time, however, it would be no less reasonable to take his own happiness as his ultimate end. And he may not be able to do both, so he has to choose which way to go since both choices can be defended as reasonable. It is precisely the conflict between these incompatible courses of action that generates what Sidgwick called "the Dualism of Practical Reason."[12]

This dualism was a major problem for Sidgwick, and he wrestled with it until the end of his life. To get a sense of how large this issue loomed for him, consider his account of the development of his thought that resulted in *The Methods of Ethics*. This account appears in his notes for a lecture that explained how his thinking evolved and changed over the years. These notes are included as part of the preface to the posthumously published sixth edition of his famous book. In those notes, Sidgwick indicated that his first adhesion to a definite ethical system was to Mill's utilitarianism. He was, moreover, attracted both to the claim that every man seeks his own happiness and to the claim that each ought to seek the happiness of others. He did not, however, have any initial awareness of the incoherence of holding both of these claims. Indeed, he reports that the persuasiveness of Mill's exposition veiled for a time the discrepancy between the natural end of seeking personal happiness and the end of duty to seek the general happiness. If doubts ever assailed him, he "was inclined to hold that it ought to be cast to the winds by a generous resolution."[13] Throughout these lecture notes, Sidgwick referred to this problem several times, noting how it bedeviled him, and not surprisingly, the issue surfaced numerous times throughout the book.

One of the more interesting of these passages is in his chapter on "The Proof of Utilitarianism," where he offered a proof of sorts, in a modest sense of that word. In particular, this "proof" was directed at those egoists who defend their right to make their own happiness their primary pursuit by taking that right as self-evident, contending that egoism is good from the point of view of the universe itself. That is, the egoist may claim nature has designed him to seek his own good, so he is merely following the direction of nature in his rational self-love. If he takes this line, Sidgwick argued, it can be pointed out that there is no principled reason why his own happiness should be a more important part of the universal good than the happiness of any other individual person. For if nature has designed him to pursue his own happiness, then nature has designed the same for other persons as well. So his own principle may be used to support universal happiness as the ultimate good.[14]

Of course, this is not a proof strictly speaking, as Sidgwick recognized, and obviously enough the egoist might well reply that, yes, others too are designed to seek their own happiness, and they surely have a right to make this their primary goal. However, it does not follow that *I* am therefore obligated to pursue *their* happiness or to make the general good my overriding goal.

A Resolution Rejected

Sidgwick came back to this issue and faced it head-on in the final chapter of his book, where he discussed the relations between the various methods of ethics that he had compared and assessed, and stated his final conclusions. There he stated with confidence that he had successfully shown that the alleged conflict between the intuitional and utilitarian methods can be dissolved. Indeed, he affirmed that self-evident moral principles of the sort intuitionists defend are required to provide a basis for a utilitarian system of ethics. Among the self-evident truths he cited is the principle of universal benevolence, which holds that the happiness of all other persons is no less worthy of our pursuit than is our own happiness. The problem of resolving the conflict between self-love and universal benevolence remained, however.

> Indeed, if an Egoist remains impervious to what we have called Proof, the only way of rationally inducing him to aim at the happiness of all, is to show

him that his own greatest happiness can be best attained by so doing. And further, even if a man admits the self-evidence of the principle of Rational Benevolence, he may still hold that his own happiness is an end which is irrational to sacrifice to any other; and that therefore a harmony between the maxim of Prudence and the maxim of Rational Benevolence must be somehow demonstrated, if morality is to be made completely rational.[15]

Here Sidgwick employed the phrases "maxim of Prudence" and "maxim of Rational Benevolence." For the sake of consistency of terms, let us use "rational self-love" for prudence, and let us now spell out the form of his argument:

1. Morality can be made completely rational only if a complete harmony between the maxim of rational self-love and the maxim of rational benevolence can somehow be demonstrated.
2. A complete harmony between the maxim of rational self-love and the maxim of rational benevolence cannot be demonstrated.
3. Therefore, morality cannot be made completely rational.

This is the disappointing conclusion that Sidgwick embraced in the final pages of his book.

To be sure, Sidgwick made the best case he could to establish a complete harmony between self-love and benevolence, and to show that the second premise is false. He pointed out that in any tolerable society, performing duties toward others and practicing the social virtues largely coincides with one's personal happiness over the long run. Still, it cannot be empirically demonstrated that performance of duty and personal happiness always coincide, and this is all the more true if we take into account the variety of sanctions that are involved. General coincidence is the most that seems plausible even in the best of societies, let alone the many societies that are intolerable for many of their citizens.[16]

Sidgwick also acknowledged the value of sympathy for our lives, and the paramount importance many utilitarians ascribe to it in the calculus of happiness, and he readily agreed "that its pleasures and pains really constitute a great part of that internal reward of social virtue, and punishment of social misconduct."[17] The sacrifices we make out of sympathy are not for an impersonal law but rather for persons with whom we share some measure of fellow feeling. Indeed, some of Sidgwick's most eloquent writing was devoted to extolling the humane pleasures of sympathy. Still, it comes up short of the goal the utilitarian is aiming for. "But allowing all this, it yet seems to me as certain as any conclusion arrived at by hedonistic comparison can be, that the utmost development of sympathy, intensive and extensive, which is now possible to any but a few exceptional persons, would not cause a perfect coincidence between Utilitarian duty and self-interest."[18]

To make matters worse, not infrequently our utilitarian duty with respect to the general happiness calls upon us to make hard and painful sacrifices to relieve the distress of other persons, and sometimes to sacrifice the happiness of those we love most. Indeed, we may even be called to sacrifice our very lives for the greater good. There is no denying, Sidgwick thought, that regardless of what sort of elevated satisfaction we may take in such sacrifices, we are less happy on the whole than we would be if engaged in other kinds of activity. We must conclude, Sidgwick conceded, "that the inseparable connexion between Utilitarian Duty and the greatest happiness of the individual who conforms to it cannot be satisfactorily demonstrated on empirical grounds."[19] Thus far then, premise two in his argument seems clearly to be true as Sidgwick saw it, and he was stuck with the unhappy conclusion that morality cannot be made completely rational.

At this point in the discussion Sidgwick turned to the possibility of religious sanctions as a way to show the complete convergence between rational self-love and rational benevolence. If God is conceived to act for some end, that end must be the universal good. And if that is God's end, then no rational person could consciously act against what he perceived to be universal happiness. With this in mind, Sidgwick reasoned as follows:

> If, then, we may assume the existence of such a Being as God, by the consensus of theologians, is conceived to be, it seems that Utilitarians may legitimately infer the existence of Divine sanctions to the code of social duty as constructed on a Utilitarian basis; and such sanctions would, of course, suffice to make it always every one's interest to promote the universal happiness to the best of his knowledge.[20]

Here then are the makings of a moral argument, reluctant though Sidgwick was to acknowledge or embrace it. We can spell the argument out as follows:

4. If God exists, we may legitimately infer Divine sanctions such that there is a complete harmony between rational self-love (one's interest) and rational benevolence (universal happiness).
5. If we can legitimately infer that there is complete harmony between rational self-love and rational benevolence, morality can be made completely rational.
6. Therefore, if God exists, morality can be made completely rational.

Given Sidgwick's moral sympathy for theism, and his recognition that if God exists, he has legitimate grounds to demonstrate consistency between self-interest and universal happiness, and thereby make morality completely rational, we might think that he would embrace the existence of God, and think he was rationally justified in doing so.

He did not do so, however. The question he thought we must answer is how far the assumption of God's existence can be supported exclusively on ethical grounds, and what was at stake is the larger question of whether ethical science can be constructed independently of premises from theology or other sources. To carry out this examination, he proposes to reflect on our most certain intuitions. As he saw things, it is as clear and certain as any axiom of geometry that it is right and reasonable to treat others as we should like to be treated in similar circumstances and to do what we believe will promote universal happiness. "But I cannot find inseparably connected with this conviction, and similarly attainable by mere reflective intuition, any cognition that there actually is a Supreme Being who will adequately reward me for obeying these rules of duty, or punish me for violating them."[21]

Nor could he find, apart from the assumption of God's existence, any clear or certain intuition that such reward or punishment shall obtain.

> I feel indeed a desire, apparently inseparable from the moral sentiments, that this result may be realized not only in my own case but universally; but the mere existence of the desire would not go far to establish the probability of its fulfillment, considering the large proportion of human desires that experience shows to be doomed to disappointment. I also judge that in a certain sense this result *ought* to be realized: in this judgment, however, 'ought' is not used in a strictly ethical meaning: it only expresses the vital need that our Practical Reason feels of proving or postulating this connexion of Virtue and self-interest, if it is to be made consistent with itself.[22]

Kant, of course, postulated God's existence, along with freedom and immortality. Indeed, he discerned the sort of inseparable connection between morality and these postulates that he thought it practically necessary to assume them. Sidgwick, by contrast, left the matter of freedom aside,[23] and though he sought for empirical proof of survival, he never found evidence that convinced him. And even though he retained theistic sympathies, he was confident enough in the truth of our clearest moral convictions on intuitive grounds alone that he saw no rational necessity to affirm the existence of God.

In so thinking, Sidgwick continued the trajectory of the exclusive humanism emerging in the eighteenth century, with its confidence in a moral order of mutual benefit that could be constructed from purely human resources. Indeed, Sidgwick saw no reason to think morality should falter, despite the unresolved contradiction represented by the "dualism of the practical reason." Quite the contrary. "I do not mean that if we gave up the hope of attaining a practical solution of this fundamental contraction, through any legitimately obtained conclusion or postulate as to the moral order of the world, it would become reasonable to abandon morality altogether: but it would seem necessary to abandon the idea of rationalising it completely."[24]

Giving up the idea that morality is completely rational is obviously a rather high cost that Sidgwick was not happy to pay. But nor was he willing to admit that morality might ultimately depend on God. He apparently thought morality was better secured by relying only on premises that he took to be intuitively obvious than by admitting a controversial theistic premise, even though that would provide him resources to eliminate what he acknowledged to be a glaring contradiction in his system.

The subsequent history of moral philosophy does not support this. As Alasdair MacIntyre has pointed out, the intuitionist view gave way to the emotivism of the twentieth century.[25] The optimism of the eighteenth and nineteenth centuries with respect to the moral order of mutual benefit construed in exclusively humanist terms has been severely undermined.

Here it is worth noting that Sidgwick showed little concern for addressing the nature of our moral faculty or concerns that this faculty, as a product of the process of evolution, might not reliably produce true beliefs.[26] Again, later developments in moral philosophy, together with sociobiological accounts of our moral beliefs, have undermined this sort of confidence that naturalistic evolution, which aims at survival, can be counted on to produce true beliefs, especially in such rarefied areas as metaphysics and morality.[27]

Rather than taking our moral intuitions as foundational in such a way that no further questions can be profitably pursued about the ultimate source and explanation of our moral faculties, it is worth asking whether a theistic account of the origin of our moral faculties gives us better reason to trust them and their deliverances.[28] In short, a serious case can be made that theism is better equipped not only to explain why we have moral knowledge but also to resolve Sidgwick's quandary that led him reluctantly to embrace the disappointing conclusion that we may not be able to make morality completely rational. So ironic though it is, Sidgwick can be added to the important historical figures who have shown us the force of the moral argument.

Synopsis: Sidgwick's *dualism of practical reason* is a problem confronting the ethical enterprise. It's the tension between one's own happiness and the happiness of others, or between rational self-love and rational benevolence. Sidgwick thought each impulse was equally legitimate, yet on occasion they encounter an intractable tension. The full rationality of morality requires the resolution of this dualism, but Sidgwick didn't see such a rapprochement as forthcoming. The only potential solution he could see is a theistic one, according to which a providential God ensures their harmony, but Sidgwick himself refused to follow this path. Nevertheless, his writings include the seeds for such a moral argument, predicated on the full rationality of morality.

5

That Adorable Genius and a Prime Minister

William James and Arthur Balfour

William James: That Adorable Genius

The American pragmatist and radical empiricist William James (1842–1910) and his famous novelist brother, Henry James, once had the following exchange: Henry announced one day, "I believe in God; but I have no use for the church." To which William replied, "If you believe in God, you have got to believe in the church because God is the church."[1]

Such intriguing declarations tended to stagger Henry, which one can't help but think William rather enjoyed doing. For present purposes, the anecdote accentuates William's incredibly relational side. By reputation James, whom Alfred North Whitehead once described as that "adorable genius," was eminently ebullient, with a big heart and lots of dear friends. Although he wasn't exactly a moral apologist, he made several relevant contributions to the discussion. How most of this discussion will be structured is by way of comparing and contrasting James with John Henry Newman, covered in chapter 3. The comparisons will strike a major key, the contrasts the minor. First, though, a few words about James's life are in order.

Early in life William James aspired to be an artist; he later moved into the discipline of psychology. Studying at Harvard, he was undeniably brilliant and ended up writing a landmark work on the basic principles of psychology. Eventually, though, he came to see that philosophical questions were raised in his investigations that couldn't be avoided, and he ended up becoming as distinguished in the field of philosophy as he was in psychology.

The first point of resonance between James and Newman has exactly to do with the importance of relationality in their work. Recall the way Newman's *Essay* grew out of his friendship with his close friend William Froude, who was also a longtime skeptical interlocutor. Their differences only deepened their friendship and served as the catalyst and crucible for rich reflection and investigation. James similarly, far from being threatened by those with whom he disagreed, often intentionally cultivated close relationships with them.

For example, Charles Sanders Peirce renamed his own view "pragmaticism" to distinguish it from the variant of pragmatism James endorsed, convinced that the ugliness of the moniker would keep James from co-opting it. Lest someone think this humorous episode implied there was bad blood between the two, however, they were actually dear friends. In fact when Peirce experienced recurring financial struggles later in life, it was James who handsomely subsidized him for years.

Another example is Josiah Royce, adherent of the sort of "absolutist" conception of God that James vociferously rejected. James wrote in jocular and hyperbolic terms about the way Royce was the pole of his mental magnet whose system he was determined to destroy. Yet at Harvard they got on swimmingly, taught classes together, and formed a lifelong friendship. James would have hardly called himself an apologist of any sort, but apologists of all stripes could learn a great deal from his irenic example in this regard.

Relationality was such a priority for James it even made its way into his philosophy and refutation of agnosticism. Inextricably linked to his view of rationality, in fact, was relationality: the relation between person and person and between person and the universe. In his battle against the agnosticism of W. K. Clifford and T. H. Huxley—agnosticism motivated by the strongly evidentialist view that it is always wrong to believe anything on insufficient evidence—James was famous for offering examples in which believing on insufficient evidence is not only right but necessary. Self-fulfilling beliefs and social coordination cases are well-known counterexamples.[2]

He also brought up another category of cases: personal relations and the peculiar dynamics they manifest. The actualization of mutual affection often depends on trust that certain actions will be returned in kind, will be positively reciprocated. James then made it clear that, for the religious, the universe itself is no longer a mere It, but a Thou—with the consequences that "any relation that may be possible from person to person might be possible here."[3] That the dynamics of a personal relation may be at stake where the religious hypothesis is concerned makes the agnostic's demand that we veto our active faith all the more illogical.

As James understood the religious hypothesis to be a species of the relational cases, it is not surprising that he believed that openness to friendship per se can enhance one's ability to grasp truth. "I merely point out to you that, as a matter of fact, certain persons do exist with an enormous capacity for friendship and for taking delight in other people's lives; and that such persons know more of truth than if their hearts were not so big."[4]

Of a piece with James's own large heart was a creative mind, which brings to mind another point of resonance with Newman who, recall, likened the religious imagination to something in the vicinity of artistic, aesthetic, or even literary acumen. James had seriously considered becoming a painter, and he once wrote to his novelist brother that he felt that the aesthetic connections between things constitutes the truest reality. It seems likely that this ability to grasp connections at an artistic level enhanced his ability to appreciate relations between persons as important features of the seamless panorama of life, features not to be neglected in the construction of a worldview or in the practice of philosophy. Daniel Bjork notes that James believed that to describe experience was to visualize it as a "canvas of felt relationships"; accordingly, "important Jamesian metaphors such as 'stream' and 'field' were indispensable elements of verbal-visual landscapes in which the sensible action of relating took place—continually and naturally."[5]

Relationality with the divine is not an eisegetical imposition on James's views; rather, it was a central thrust of his vision of reality. Indeed, whereas he considered "rationality" to be often used as a eulogistic term lacking definitive meaning, he considered the extent of intimacy and relationality made possible with the divine to be the considerably better measure of the quality of any particular worldview. As David Lamberth writes, "'Intimacy' is in some sense the central criterion for James's distinctions among the types of philosophic thinking."[6] To the extent some particular vision of reality fails to demand or provide some sense of intimate relations with the universe, James considered it a sign that something is wrong with that conceptualization of ultimate reality. His own conception of deity was less monarchical and sterile than what he considered the impersonal magistrate of Anselmian theism, more immanent and intimate than the dualistic God of scholastic theology, more organic and particular than the transcendent and unapproachable God of absolutistic monism, more limited and finite than the all-enveloping God of Baruch Spinoza or G. W. F. Hegel, and more humane and civil than the sovereign cosmic lord of theological determinism.

Now, James admitted that the ordinary faith of orthodox religious believers features a strong emphasis on an intimate relationship with the divine, but he identified this as one of the differences between religious practice and theology. Here James both agreed and disagreed with Newman. Recall Newman's distinction between religion and theology (echoed in real versus notional assents, respectively); both Newman and James recognized such a distinction. But unlike Newman, James was quicker to dismiss the importance of theology, sensing certain intractable tensions between it and fervent religious practice. He was eminently open to the evidence contained in vivid religious experience—thus his Gifford lectures, *The Varieties of Religious Experience*—but less so the speculations of theologians. This probably made him read more into Anselmian theology, for example, than Newman likely would have. Newman was not nearly as suspicious of theology as James was. In at least recognizing the distinction between religious practice and theological reflection, though, they were sympatico.

Another important and related parallel between Newman and James manifests in their expansive epistemology. Both were radical empiricists of a sort, not in the sense of delimiting the range of genuine evidence to the deliverances of our senses, but to a radically enlarged conception of allowable evidence. For James, not unlike Newman, intimations of beauty, steps of precursive faith, discernment about proper evidential fits, sympathetic attentiveness to the experiences of others, satisfaction of moral and aesthetic criteria: all of these features and more characterized his expansive epistemology. Whereas metaphorical knights of Occam's razor feared superstition, James said he feared desiccation, reductionist and deflationary accounts of reality that fail to do justice to its rich relationality. In response to an evidentialism perpetually teetering at the brink of skepticism out of a fear of being wrong, James recognized the risks it takes to be right—just as Newman recognized our best epistemic efforts to discover the truth are pregnant with risk. A rule of reasoning that precludes finding truth if it's really there to be found, James emphasized, is an irrational rule that fails to recognize some risks are well worth taking.[7]

Both James and Newman took morality as a veridical indication about the nature of reality. For example, James offered a moral critique of naturalism by pointing to the phenomenon of moral regret. Some tragic elements of this world—dehumanizing, horrific mistreatment of innocents, for example—make for a "crop of regrets." However, in a determined world—at least an approximate likelihood if naturalism is true—"nothing else had a ghost of a chance of being put into their place."[8] Regarding the moral phenomenon of regret, in other words, he thought naturalism lacked the resources to provide much of a principled explanation.

If there is any nagging doubt about James's verdict on naturalism, examine the following telling passage from his justly lauded *Varieties of Religious Experience*:

> For naturalism, fed on recent cosmological speculations, mankind is in a position similar to that of a set of people living on a frozen lake, surrounded by cliffs over which there is no escape, yet knowing that little by little the ice is melting, and the inevitable day drawing near when the last film of it will disappear, and to be drowned ignominiously will be the human creature's portion. The merrier the skating, the warmer and more sparkling the sun by day, and the ruddier the bonfires at night, the more poignant the sadness with which one must take in the meaning of the total situation.[9]

That James didn't think the case against naturalism and for theism was decisive didn't mean he thought they weren't strong—even if making the case was a complicated matter. As the James scholar Hunter Brown argues persuasively, for James among what is constitutive of the delicate idiosyncrasy and labyrinthine character of the intellectual life are included a great number of intertwining historical, cultural, linguistic, temperamental, neurological, and volitional influences, rendering irredeemably simplistic those appeals to evidence per se or the deliverances of a dispassionately judicial intellect.[10]

Ideally this recognition should lend itself to a large measure of epistemic humility in discourse with those of divergent opinions on various matters, which James's enduring friendships with ideological opponents show he practiced. As James once wrote,

> We ought . . . delicately and profoundly to respect one another's mental freedom: then only shall we bring about the intellectual republic; then only shall we have that spirit of inner tolerance without which all our outer tolerance is soulless, and which is empiricism's glory; then only shall we live and let live in speculative as well as in practical things.[11]

Whether in their expansive empiricism and epistemology, the value they placed on friendship and a logic of relations, the risks they were willing to undertake to secure the truth, or their confidence that morality offered a window of insight into reality, James and Newman offered compelling companion contributions to the unfolding chronicle of the moral argument.[12]

Arthur James Balfour: A Prime Minister

Winston Churchill won the Nobel Prize for Literature, primarily for his historical writings, but only one British prime minister had the honor of giving the prestigious Gifford lectures in natural theology: Arthur J. Balfour.

Tim Madigan writes that

> In many ways, Balfour was a sort of anti–Bertrand Russell. Both were related to British Prime Ministers (Russell's grandfather served in that post from 1846–1852 and 1865–1866). Both wrote works in philosophy and religion, came from aristocratic backgrounds, attended Cambridge (where they studied with the famed Utilitarian philosopher Henry Sidgwick, later to become Balfour's brother-in-law). And both were noted for their biting sense of humor and skill as debaters. But unlike Russell, Balfour was a strong supporter of Christianity, an arch-traditionalist, a defender of the British Empire, and president for many years of the Society for Psychical Research, something the skeptical Russell would have had no tolerance for.[13]

Madigan continues his Balfour-Russell comparison:

> Russell and Balfour knew each other, and although never friends, had a cordial relationship. Russell puckishly remarked that whenever a crank contacted him with a desire to talk about supernatural matters, he would tell them that Balfour was the expert on that topic and would be a better person to consult—a very convenient way of getting rid of annoying people! And when Russell was arrested in 1918 for opposing the First World War, Balfour, then the powerful Foreign Secretary, helped to arrange for better prison quarters for him, including having access to books and writing materials (which among other things allowed Russell to compose his books *Political Ideals: Roads to Freedom* and *Introduction to Mathematical Philosophy*).[14]

Balfour seems an unlikely moral apologist. Born in 1848 (and living until 1930), he served as British prime minister from July 1902 until December 1905, and later as foreign secretary. By training he was a philosopher, having read moral sciences at Trinity College, Cambridge. Though known for saying "nothing matters very much and few things matter at all," much of his life of service and scholarship seemed predicated on a rather different sentiment.

In 1914, he delivered the first of two Gifford lectures in Glasgow, published the next year as *Theism and Humanism*; and the second course in 1922–1923, published in 1923 as *Theism and Thought*. *Theism and Humanism* was, as noted in chapter 4, one of the ten books C. S. Lewis would later identify as the most formative in his own life. Balfour's involvement in the war effort as the first lord of the admiralty was the cause of the significant gap between his Gifford lectures. Knowing his audience would widely differ because of the protracted delay, and in light of the continuity of argument, he reiterated a fair amount of material from the first volume in the second.

By most accounts, Balfour inhabits a relatively minor place among the luminaries of moral apologists, largely because of what many considered his inordinate deference to authority and custom. Certitude, he thought, is found in custom, not reason, and on that basis some have dubbed his view one of "Tory metaphysics." On that account, what one finds in Balfour is too deferential and expedient to qualify as anything like the most penetrating example of the moral argument. We are inclined to think this reading a bit harsh and somewhat mistaken; but whatever the merits of his central argument, a quick examination is worthwhile, for there are several suggestive nuggets to mine and arresting sights to see along the way.

Mindful that his charge as a Gifford lecturer was to traverse the path of natural theology, he confined himself to the topic of God—setting aside those other timeworn favorites of freedom and immortality.[15] As to his operative theology, he began by noting that the highest conceptions of God tend to approximate one of two types, which he called the *religious* and *metaphysical*. The latter, as Balfour depicted it, emphasizes God's all-inclusive unity—the "logical glue which holds multiplicity together and makes it intelligible." The former focuses on God's ethical personality, turning away from speculations about the Absolute, "to love and worship a Spirit among spirits."[16]

As to which conception he favored, he broached the possibility (not unlike Newman) that they are not mutually exclusive but, rather, compatible and harmonious. He didn't claim to have fused or harmonized the two conceptions to his own satisfaction, but he wasn't content with their separation. As for Balfour's argument, references to God were to mean "something other than an Identity wherein all differences vanish, or a Unity which includes but does not transcend the differences which it somehow holds in solution."[17] Rather, "I mean a God whom men can love, a God to whom men can pray, who takes sides, who has purposes and preferences, whose attributes, howsoever conceived, leave unimpaired the possibility of a personal relation between Himself and those whom He has created."[18] Unlike William James, Balfour saw such a religious conception of God as reconcilable with a more metaphysical conception, but while attributing the latter to "the conclusion of our intellectual labours," it was "hardly (as it seems to me) their motive or their reward."[19]

In laying out an argument from values, anticipating an argument from reason that would come later (in the third chapter of C. S. Lewis's *Miracles*, not to mention more recently in works by Victor Reppert and Alvin Plantinga), Balfour distinguished between reasons and causes and noted that certain sorts of explanations of beliefs are tantamount to their refutation. If the origin of a belief shows that it is held for reasons unrelated to its truth, for example, the belief has been shown at least to lack justification. This poses serious problems for our moral values, as Balfour recognized, and this is why he thought it's important to provide a broader explanation for their veracity than what naturalism can provide. Naturalism, he thought, undermines our moral convictions by providing a causal explanation for their emergence, an explanation inadequately connected to their truth.[20]

By explaining our moral convictions in the way naturalism does, naturalism explains them away. For moral (and aesthetic) values to be rational, they can't be rooted in unreason, but instead "must have some more congruous source than the blind transformation of physical energy."[21] Such values demand a design "far deeper in purpose, far richer in significance, than any which could be inferred from the most ingenious and elaborate adjustments displayed by organic life."[22] This is why Balfour looked inward (to ethics and aesthetics), not outward (to the order found in the universe), to the mind and soul of man rather than external nature, for what he deemed the best prospects for an argument from natural theology. To his thinking the moral order provided the more powerful apologetic resource.

Indeed, he seemed to find the naturalistic story for the emergence of ethical values implausible. "Can we be content to regard the highest loyalties, the most devoted love, the most limitless self-abnegation as the useless excesses of a world-system, which in its efforts to adapt organism to environment has overshot its mark?"[23] He deemed this impossible: "The naturalistic setting must be expanded into one which shall give the higher ethics an origin congruous with their character. Selection must be treated as an instrument of purpose, not simply as its mimic. Theistic teleology must be substituted for Naturalism. Thus, and thus only, can moral values, as it seems to me, be successfully maintained."[24]

It's important to note that Balfour didn't think God's existence could be *deduced* from moral values. The relevant inquiry is rather this: which worldview can accommodate our moral beliefs (and accompanying emotions) better, a naturalistic one or an essentially religious one? Naturalism, he was convinced, carried too high a cost in this regard, compromising beyond recognition our most cherished values, a loss to which we shouldn't be willing to acquiesce. By contrast, "in the love of God by the individual soul, the collision of ends for that soul loses all its harshness, and harmony is produced, by raising, not lowering, the ethical idea."[25]

In the very next paragraph, Balfour sketched Kant's moral argument, and drew a distinct contrast with his own approach:

> Kant, by a famous feat of speculative audacity, sought to extract a proof of God's existence from the moral law. In his view the moral law requires us to hold that those who are good will also in the end be happy; and, since without God this expectation cannot be fulfilled, the being of God becomes a postulate of morality. Is this (you may ask), or any variant of this, the argument suggested in the last paragraph? It is not. In Kant's argument, as I understand it, God was external to morality in the sense that He was not Himself a moral end. It was not our feeling of love and loyalty to Him that was of moment, but His guidance of the world in the interests of virtue and the virtuous. My point is different. I find in the love of God a moral end which reconciles other moral ends, because it includes them. It is not intolerant of desires for our own good. It demands their due subordination, not their complete suppression. It implies loyal service to One who by His essential nature wills the good of all. It requires, therefore, that the good of all shall be an object of our endeavor; and it promises that, in striving for this inclusive end, we shall, in Pauline phrase, be fellow-workers with Him.[26]

Balfour's main contention didn't pertain to the difficulty of harmonizing moral ends in a Godless universe but instead to the difficulty of maintaining moral values if moral origins are purely naturalistic. Balfour wasn't averse to risking a bit of rhetoric at this juncture: "That they never have been so maintained on any large scale is a matter of historic fact. At no time has the mass of mankind treated morals and religion as mutually independent. They have left this to the enlightened; and the enlightened have (as I think) been wrong."[27]

He felt they had been wrong by their failure to face the implications of their own theories. He was convinced that if morality is a causal product of nonmoral and ultimately of material beings guided by natural selection, then

> a sense of humour, if nothing else, should prevent us wasting fine language on the splendor of the moral law and the reverential obedience owed it by mankind. That debt will not long be paid if morality comes to be generally regarded as the causal effect of petty causes; comparable in its lowest manifestations with the appetites and terrors which rule, for their good, the animal creation; in its highest phases no more than a personal accomplishment, to be acquired or neglected at the bidding of individual caprice. More than this is needful if the noblest ideals are not to lose all power of appeal. Ethics must have its roots in the divine; and in the divine it must find its consummation.[28]

Synopsis: James offered several resources that a moral apologist can deploy. He saw it as irrational to embrace a rule of reasoning that precludes finding truth that's really there to be found. He argued that the category of moral regret is a bad fit with a naturalistic worldview. Like other philosophers we've considered, his was an expansive empiricism that included considering the evidential value of relational, aesthetic, and ethical deliverances. Balfour similarly recognized the moral deficiencies of naturalism, though, more so than James, he thought reconcilable the religious and metaphysical accounts of theism. Balfour was particularly intent on underscoring the ways in which deflationary analyses of moral values and duties are better at *explaining them away* than actually explaining them. He didn't think the moral argument was best thought of as a deduction; rather, he saw it as something closer to an inductive or abductive approach.

6

A Knightbridge Professor

William Sorley

In October of 1915 during World War I, a young man was killed in the Battle of Loos, shot in the head by a sniper. Found on his body was a sonnet, his last poem, which read like this:

> When you see millions of the mouthless dead
> Across your dreams in pale battalions go,
> Say not soft things as other men have said,
> That you'll remember. For you need not so.
> Give them not praise. For, deaf, how should they know
> It is not curses heaped on each gashed head?
> Nor tears. Their blind eyes see not your tears flow.
> Nor honour. It is easy to be dead.
> Say only this, "They are dead." Then add thereto,
> "Yet many a better one has died before."
> Then, scanning all the o'ercrowded mass, should you
> Perceive one face that you loved heretofore,
> It is a spook. None wears the face you knew.
> Great death has made all his for evermore.[1]

The poet, barely twenty, was one of the three great "war poets" of World War I, and the first of those poets to die. The other two were Isaac Rosenberg and Wilfred Owen, but Poet Laureate John Masefield considered Charles Sorley the greatest of the three. News of Charles's death hit William Sorley particularly hard, as the loss of a beloved son is bound to do.

William Sorley was born in 1855 to a Free Church of Scotland minister. First educated at Edinburgh and New College in philosophy, mathematics, and theology, he would then spend a year at Trinity College, Cambridge; subsequently, he lectured at Cambridge until, in 1883, he was elected a fellow at Trinity. In 1900 Sorley succeeded his old professor Henry Sidgwick at Cambridge, a post he held until his retirement in 1933. Interestingly enough, though not a Christian himself, Sidgwick said it was a relief to have a *Christian* philosopher replace him.

Like many of his contemporaries, Sorley developed an interest in philosophical idealism, but eventually he found it unable to provide a satisfactory account of evil. Sorley took the moral argument against idealism to apply to any nontheistic theory, and held that theism, in light of some Kantian considerations, was necessary to explain moral reality. Among his distinguished works were *A History of British Philosophy to 1900* (1920), *Recent Tendencies in Ethics* (1904), *The Moral Life and Moral Worth* (1911), and his Gifford lectures, which he gave in 1914–1915 and which were published under the title *Moral Values and the Idea of God* (1930). J. H. Muirhead wrote of this volume that he could remember the sense of freshness and power the book gave its readers at the time.[2]

In 1889 Sorley married Janetta Smith. They had four children, two daughters and two sons, including the eminently gifted Charles Hamilton Sorley. On November 11, 1985, Charles was among sixteen Great War poets commemorated on a slate stone unveiled in Westminster Abbey's Poet's Corner. The inscription on the stone was written by Wilfred Owen: "My subject is War, and the pity of War. The Poetry is in the pity."

A close look at the moral argument of William Sorley reveals an approach that, rather than being dated, remains a lively, instructive, and germane model to follow. Whether he's integrating or reconciling life and work, finite and infinite goods, the temporal and transcendent, the moral law and evil, philosophy and poetry, or morality and metaphysics, Sorley's was an expansive and integrative mind and an open and capacious heart whose prescient insights have proven the test of time. He demonstrated what long and intimate acquaintance with the world of ideas can generate, and his enduring example can serve as an inspiration and corrective to much of what passes for apologetics today. In short, in the approach and attitude of a thinker like Sorley can be found a model of excellence to emulate in *living with arguments* and *rigorously thinking through evidential questions about God's existence*.

This chapter will make this case by examining, by turns, five germane aspects of his work, as follows: (1) the seriousness with which he personally and professionally took ethics; (2) his assiduous resistance of the temptation to confuse moral and nonmoral goods, thereby not falling prey to domesticating the categories of morality and, in the process, vitiating their evidential power; (3) his adherence to "Lotze's dictum," privileging the deliverances of morality in the metaphysical quest rather than doing metaphysics first and relegating morality to a relative afterthought; (4) his integration of poetry and philosophy, thus effecting the kind of synthesis of the head and heart that the expansive epistemology of a practicable moral apologetic requires; and (5) his bold reconciliation—while enduring unspeakable loss—of the moral law with the problem of evil, insisting on neither trivializing this world's travails nor allowing them the final word.

First, though, let's quickly consider a cursory sketch of Sorley's moral argument.

Sorley's Moral Argument

Sorley had argued against naturalistic ethics in 1885 in his *Ethics of Naturalism*. Assessing a form of ethical theory founded on the basis of naturalism, Sorley built a case against an ethics of evolution that proceeded on the assumption that life is desirable, and that it has a value which makes its pursuit and promotion a reasonable moral end. Sorley's conclusion was that no appropriate end of human conduct can be derived from the nature of evolution in general. Whereas adaptation may be necessary for life, such adaptation cannot provide an end for *action*. Ethics is concerned with practical goals, and these do not coincide with the goals of natural selection. He developed in detail a set of potential defeaters for what may still be considered the most plausible strategy for founding a moral philosophy on the basis of evolutionary theory, and thus set the stage for *Moral Values and the Idea of God*, perhaps the most sophisticated development of the moral argument for God's existence before the present time.

Sorley thought that God provides the best and most rational and unified view of reality, the ground of both the natural and moral orders. Like other proponents of the moral arguments, Sorley embraced a broad empiricism that includes not just the deliverances of our senses but also our experience of moral value and obligation. Overcoming a false dichotomy between the causal and moral orders, or between is and ought, was a high priority for Sorley; he saw this dichotomy as contributing to the mistaken notion that value has little to contribute to metaphysics.

Kant served as inspiration for Sorley's quest for integration here. The special form Kant's moral proof had taken was a result of the distinction he drew between the two worlds of the sensible, or phenomenal, world and the intelligible world. The former is ruled by mechanical causation and is the world of natural law; the latter is the realm of freedom and in it moral ideas rule. But each is a closed system, complete in itself. Kant's own thought, however, pointed beyond this distinction, for his practical postulates were a demand for harmony between the two realms of physical causation and of moral ideas, while his third *Critique* exhibits a way in which this harmony can be brought about through the conception of purpose.

Sorley was convinced that we must regard the two systems, therefore, not as the orders of two entirely different worlds but rather as different aspects of the same reality. From this point of view the moral argument would require formulation in a way different from that of Kant. It would be necessary to have regard not to a connection between two worlds but to relations within the one system of reality, and also necessary to inquire into what kind of general view is justified when both moral ideas and our experience of nature are taken into account.

Sorley started by giving close attention to morality, arguing against both reductionist and subjectivist accounts of ethics, rejecting in the process Humean notions that moral judgments primarily concern mental states or emotions. Rather, Sorley argued, they are about a reference to something outside ourselves, the objective goodness or badness of what we're considering. Just as our empirical experiences give us good reasons to make inferences about our physical surroundings, our moral experience gives us justification to make moral inferences about objective realities. There's a parity between them; the realities of the moral and physical worlds are on an epistemic par, on the same footing. In each instance there are *givens* in our experience that warrant such inferences; and in the case of morality, among the central deliverances is the experience of *moral oughtness*.

In addition to moral obligations, Sorley also recognized the seminal evidential role of *moral goodness*, which is connected to reality in a particular way—namely, it's always instantiated in concrete situations. Moral ideals are always *in rebus*, exemplified in the particulars of the existing world—in contrast with Platonic conceptions of such ideals existing as universal forms. Ascriptions of moral value have a distinct sort of existential implication, for the ascription conveys that a particular morally desirable state of affairs in some sense *ought to exist*, whether or not it actually does. This renders moral goodness a unique predicate.

Another dimension of moral value is its delimited scope of application. Moral value resides specifically *only in persons*. The only bearers of intrinsic moral value are persons, because meaningful moral behavior requires purpose and will. For Sorley our very identity as persons is inextricably tied to our future purposes, especially our moral purposes. "The moral agent is thus compelled to regard his true personality as consisting not in the actual features of the passing moment but in an *is to be*—in something to which he should attain and to which he can at least approximate."[3]

People, however, are only approximately good; anything like an absolute moral ideal stands only as a limit as we morally mature and grow in moral knowledge and sensitivity. As a result, we can only realize the ideal partially, but the real extent to which we approach the good presupposes the ethical ideal outside ourselves. It's somehow a feature of the system or order of the universe itself, an objective fixture of reality transcending finite persons, yet manifested in persons, though only partially in finite persons.[4]

It is impossible to do justice to Sorley here, but with those features of morality identified, why did he gravitate to the hypothesis that theism could explain them best? An adequate explanation must explain the moral order as objective and as a part of reality, and the world process or history must be so structured as to realize the moral purposes, which requires that the causal and moral orders be properly synthesized. Sorley argued that theism does the best job satisfying these constraints, even if the problem of evil poses a challenge of its own with which theism has to contend, to which we'll return later in this discussion.

Sorley's positive argument for the adequacy, indeed superiority, of the theistic explanation has strong affinities with that of Hastings Rashdall, the focus of our next chapter. To put it briefly, moral ideals and obligations are part of an objective reality and are person-dependent. They are universally and eternally valid, yet the moral ideal has never been fully recognized by any finite person. Thus it's not grounded in finite persons. Unlike other objective truths, the moral ideal is presently valid (binding and obligatory for the finite world) without being wholly realized by any finite mind. If its validity implies an existing objective mind as its ground, then there must be such a Mind that presently realizes the moral ideal. Such a personal Mind, moreover, must be eternal, and it was Sorley's conviction that such an eternal Person is God himself.

Sorley then proceeded to refute the other two alternatives, pluralism and monism. Here's William Lane Craig's quick synopsis of the refutation:

Against pluralism, which holds that the moral ideal resides in a plurality of finite beings, Sorley argue[d] that the moral values are eternally valid and so cannot reside in temporally finite persons. Against monism, which holds that the universe is constituted by a single non-personal reality of which minds are mere modes, Sorley maintain[ed] that it leaves no room for purposeful endeavor or real freedom, because "is" and "ought to be" are identical and everything simply is as it is. Hence, concluded Sorley, there's reason to think that theism offers the most reasonable and unified explanation of reality. The moral order is the order of an infinite, eternal Mind who is the architect of nature and whose purpose man and the universe are slowly fulfilling.[5]

With the foundation of that cursory sketch in place, let's now consider some finer-grained observations and objections in an effort to elaborate and flesh out Sorley's character and context, ideas and ideals, traits and trials.

A Moral Philosopher

Sorley argued that there are good philosophical reasons to take belief in God seriously. This made him an *apologist*—someone who argues that belief in God is rational. Still, like A. E. Taylor in this regard, he wasn't likely to call himself an apologist, preferring instead to be known as simply a philosopher. Even then, it seems, apologetics carried unpalatable implications in certain quarters. Sorley wanted to be known more as a truth seeker than a partisan, and he saw arguments more as lifelong companions with which to live, or treasure troves of insights to mine, than as tools in an arsenal for purposes of persuasion or vanquishing ideological opponents. Because he took evidence and argument seriously, he was averse to seeing them reduced to divisive weapons of intellectual warfare. His aversion to a tendentious and divisive spirit was animated both by his intellectual honesty and his moral commitments.

What struck many who knew Sorley personally was how seriously he took ethical issues, not just as a theoretician but also as a practitioner. G. F. Stout depicted Sorley by descriptions of his vigor, his ability, his cordial friendliness, and his lively wit, calling him a "most loyal and devoted friend," a man of "strong and warm feelings." What struck Stout most in Sorley's character was "the consistent way in which he was guided both in his private and public life by moral standards and practices."[6] These qualities ensured a resonance between Sorley's life and work, because so much of his professional work revolved around issues of ethics and morality. For Sorley morality was evidentially significant about the nature of the world, and his life demonstrated that he took the moral project seriously, not merely investigating the argument but embodying it.

Sorley asked what it is that impels the philosopher to his unresting search for truth. Philosophy is not a passive, receptive attitude. "It is a life, an active process in which the soul realizes what is akin to its own nature—the vision of truth and reality."[7] Sorley concurred here with Plato, contra Francis Bacon's passive model that, even for purposes of scientific inquiry, struck Sorley as objectionably myopic. The quest for truth is more active than that, and all the more so when it comes to goodness, or moral value, which is recognized as having a claim on our allegiance and requiring activity to realize the ideal. Moral maturation is essentially active and dynamic, and involves a journey toward a destination.[8]

The phrase *moral philosopher* is rich with ambiguity. It may mean a philosopher who works in ethics generally or, more specifically, gives a moral argument for, say, God or the afterlife. Or it could mean, more straightforwardly, a philosopher who does his work and lives his life ethically, with integrity and character. Sorley is an example of a moral philosopher in both respects, which David Horner argues is a crucial ingredient for effective apologetics today.

Horner distinguishes between *credibility* and *plausibility*. Making theism and Christianity credible, he says, involves giving interlocutors reasons to think them true; making theism and Christianity plausible helps people to think of them as *possibly* true. If someone, for whatever reason, doesn't think Christianity is even possibly true, then no number of credible reasons to believe it will have much effect. Usually the forte and stock-in-trade of apologists is enhancing credibility, but some listeners with bad attitudes toward Christians may find Christianity implausible, not even possibly true.

This is where doing apologetics in the right way—with kindness, gentleness, winsomeness—can help render the gospel plausible. It can also vividly remind us that Christianity is not merely a set of propositions to espouse but a transformed life to be lived. Horner argues that, although there's important work for moral apologetics to do at the levels of both credibility and plausibility, the need for making plausible the Christian worldview is particularly exigent today to soften "the moral soil so that the seeds of the gospel may be able to penetrate."[9]

Sorley's model is worth emulation on this score: integrating life and work, and in the process facilitating the use of moral apologetics as a precursor to the Christian message.

What Is Good?

As we saw, much of what preoccupied Sorley's attention was the issue of moral values, and a question that arises concerning moral goodness is what sorts of things can be called "good." Nowadays, among our secular friends, a trend is afoot to explain morality by implicitly blurring lines between moral and nonmoral goodness. Sam Harris, for example, suggests that since we know pain is bad and pleasure is good, on this foundation we can construct our ethical systems. Erik Wielenberg, though a sophisticated philosopher, wishes to speak of how the intrinsic nature of intense suffering renders it "bad," offering us all the moral reasons we need to avoid it for ourselves and others. This way of explaining ethics, however, risks explaining some of its most important features away.

David Bentley Hart has written that among the mind's transcendental aspirations, the longing for moral goodness is probably the most difficult to contain within the confines of a naturalist metaphysics.[10] When we apply the notion of goodness to situations, things, or states of affairs, we risk domesticating moral goodness, reducing it to a matter of producing pleasant consequences or avoiding harmful ones, without coming to terms with the fact that it's people and their decisions, wills, and characters that are, by turns, morally good, bad, or some admixture of the two.

Pain, though unpleasant, isn't morally bad. Intentionally inflicting harmful and needless pain is a morally bad action, but note that it's the action of a person. When human beings are seen as the appropriate subject of ascriptions like "moral goodness" or "moral badness," the intriguing and revelatory nature of such predicates can emerge. Otherwise, the result is typically domestication, and the evidential power of this dimension of morality is obscured, narrowing the focus to material circumstances rather than allowing for talk of transcendence.

Sorley recognized with prescience the emerging tendency to confuse this matter. He saw that the category of intrinsic moral value rightly applies only to persons. Surely it's bad to experience excruciating pain, but it's not morally bad as such. The distinction here is between nonmoral badness and moral evil. Kant recognized this distinction, insisting that the latter is the more distinctively moral category, which is closely related to his insistence that the only truly good thing is a *good will*—a feature of persons—and also related to his point that morality is less about happiness per se than about deserving to be happy. To conflate nonmoral badness with moral evil contributes to quite a bit of confusion nowadays and is a real weakness in a number of contemporary efforts to construct a moral theory, however rhetorically effective such a theory may be at garnering adherents.

Sorley, to his credit, saw clearly the need to avoid this mistake, keep alive the vital organic connection between moral goodness and persons, and allow moral values in all their profundity and mystery to do their work.

Lotze's Dictum

William Lane Craig credits Sorley with the most sophisticated development of the moral argument prior to recent times. Much of what empowered Sorley's analysis was that he thought it incumbent to make the basis of our theory of reality as broad as possible and to realize that the theory will lack breadth and completeness if moral facts and ideas are excluded from the outset. The result is a truncated picture of reality. Sorley thus argued strongly for attentiveness to such data and a deep inquiry into its evidential significance. Such a methodology wasn't without important historical precedents. Plato's *Republic*, for example, featured an argument that examined ethical conceptions and terminated in the idea of the Good as the source of all reality and power.

The data of moral experience, though it may stand in need of correction by principled criteria, can't reasonably be summarily dismissed.[11] By Sorley's lights, the issue is which system can explain the greater number of facts and explain them well. Neither a moral system that vitiates the spiritual dimension of reality nor devalues the corporeal can do the job.[12] To his thinking, "At every critical turn the moral judgment pronounces for the superiority of the spiritual to the material in life, and recognizes the importance of social ends when confronted by the interests . . . of the self-seeking individual."[13]

In most systems of philosophy ethical inquiry gets postponed until questions of metaphysics are settled, but Sorley thought this to be a radical mistake. Instead he sided with "Lotze's dictum," which says that the true beginning of metaphysics lies in ethics. The gist of Lotze's conviction here is that ethical ideas about value or worth hold a certain primacy for the interpretation of reality—metaphysics ought to be founded on ethics, objectively construed.

On this point Sorley stood foursquare against the stance of one like Bertrand Russell, who warned against any strategy that aims to figure out the nature of reality by considering morality:

> Driven from the particular sciences, the belief that the notions of good and evil must afford a key to the understanding of the world has sought a refuge in philosophy. But even from this last refuge, if philosophy is not to remain a set of pleasing dreams, this belief must be driven forth. It is a commonplace that happiness is not best achieved by those who seek it directly; and it would seem that the same is true of the good. In thought, at any rate, those who forget good and evil and seek only to know the facts are more likely to achieve good than those who view the world through the distorting medium of their own desires.[14]

Of course we can appreciate part of Russell's point here—though Sorley would suggest the evidence morality gives us is no mere pleasing dream but often, instead, a disquieting sense that something is amiss. However, we suspect that Russell's dismissal of the evidential significance of morality was more than a little premature. The idea residing at the very foundation of moral arguments for God's existence is that morality provides a veridical window of insight into reality. Attending to its deliverances—rather than watering down its categories, domesticating it, or deflating it—can arguably prove evidentially significant.

The moral argument is based on this powerful idea: a close examination of morality in its distinctive features, its robust construal that's true to our rich and thick moral experiences, functions evidentially to provide reasons to think that the merely temporal and finite goods of this world are neither the only nor the most important goods there are to secure. To his credit, Sorley saw, rather than severed, the connections between morality and metaphysics.

An Imaginative Apologetic

As a philosopher, Sorley had a refined aesthetic and imaginative taste. His reading wasn't myopic or provincial; it included not only philosophy but also a wide range of classic literature, and he possessed prodigious literary ability himself, a trait he passed down to his son Charles.

Sorley knew that human beings aren't merely logic choppers, which likely contributed to his attraction to an argument that appeals to both the intellect and affective—the full range, in fact, of our relational, aesthetic, and imaginative faculties. Nor was he alone in this regard; the fertile history of moral apologetics is filled with profound thinkers who could see that our efforts to apprehend reality in all of its fecundity and fullness requires an expansive epistemology and keen, intentional attentiveness to the broad array of evidence at our disposal. This requires openness to an interdisciplinary approach.

A. E. Taylor later echoed this insight in this powerful passage:

> We all attach great weight to Shakespeare's interpretations of human life, or Dante's, or Pascal's, or Wordsworth's; even when we reject their testimony, we at least do not reject it lightly. I believe it would be safe to say that Plato is the only metaphysician whose verdicts on things human we ascribe anything like this significance, and the reason is manifest. It is that Plato was so much more than the author of a philosophical theory; he was one of the world's supreme dramatists, with the great dramatist's insight into a vast range of human character and experience, an insight only possible to a nature itself quickly and richly responsive to a world of suggestion which narrower natures of the specialist type miss. If I am found . . . appealing to the testimony of "moralists," I trust it will be understood that by moralists I do not mean primarily men who have devoted themselves to the elaboration of ethical systems, the Aristotles, or even the Kants, but men who have lived richly and deeply and thought as well as lived, the Platos, Augustines, Dostoevskys, and their fellows.[15]

Sorley, like Taylor, like John Henry Newman, like Clement Webb (as we will see), could see that the head and heart must come together, that philosophy and literature must converge, that an inquiry into truth requires the full panoply of our resources.

The Problem of Evil

When Sorley said we must be attentive to the moral evidence, he wasn't blind to the suffering of the world. He clearly saw it as a sign something was awry and in desperate need of fixing. There was nothing Pollyannaish about his approach. He wrote his Gifford lectures in the throes of World War I—the way Lewis would later write *Mere Christianity* during World War II—sending early chapters to his son Charles, who was in the middle of the fight. Sorley acutely recognized that ignoring the sufferings and evils in the world wasn't an option. He couldn't merely speak of the evidential power of the moral law; he had to acknowledge and somehow come to terms with the broken and dysfunctional (dysteleological) elements in the world, the sense in which the world clearly isn't yet what it ought to be.

Then something happened that brought the problem of evil home in the most personal way possible: the devastating news arrived that Charles had been killed. There was already inextricable connection between Sorley's work and life, but now it became a dramatic, dynamic collision of heartrending loss and his life's work. His grief over and abiding faith despite his son's untimely and tragic death resonates on every page of *Moral Values*. The problem of evil was no mere academic discussion for Sorley; it simply could not have been a more gripping existential reality. The moral law is real, he was convinced, but equally undeniable is evil. The moral evidence vividly contains both intractable realities.

Sorley came to see that this very recognition makes sense of a dispute between Immanuel Kant and David Hume. Kant's formulation of the moral argument suggests that the moral law (the inexorable fact of duty) requires us to assume the being of God as what he calls a practical postulate necessitated by moral reason. But of course the facts of morality have also been used to argue against theism, especially in the form of the problem of evil, a point Hume pushed forcefully in his *Dialogues Concerning Natural Religion*.

Sorley could see that the most serious objection to theism is the problem of evil, for it raises the dreadful possibility that the natural order and the moral order are working at cross-purposes with each other, locked in an intractable, irremediable conflict. The natural order, frankly, often fails to realize the good that ought to be realized. Hume argued that the amount of evil and suffering in the world implies that if there's a creator, then this being is either malevolent or limited in power. What evidence in our moral experience is there that the moral purpose will be realized, or is even capable of being realized in our hostile world?[16]

How could reflection on good and evil lead Kant and Hume in such opposite directions? Sorley came to realize they were approaching the question from different points of view. Hume directed his attention to the struggle of mankind, what men suffered, the cruelty of the world, and the havoc of life. Kant, however,

> was not looking upon outward performance, but upon the inward law of goodness and the power it reveals in the mind which is conscious of it. His reflexions were not based, like Hume's, upon the measure in which goodness is actually realized in the world—as to that he would have been willing to admit that it argues nothing for the goodness of the author of the world. It was the idea of goodness, which consciousness revealed to him, that formed his starting-point. He was aware of a moral law whose validity he could not question, and the recognition of which secured him a position above the play of merely natural forces.[17]

Might nature after all be regarded as a fitting field for the realization of goodness? The question Sorley was considering is not what a perfect world looks like but what a world might need to look like in order to make growth in goodness possible and likely. Real agents, rather than marionettes and automatons, require the possibility of missing the mark; only by this means might they come to have goodness and consciousness of the good—not to mention communion with God himself.

The objection to theism from evil, Sorley said, tends to confuse moral purpose with personal happiness. Because personal happiness is often not realized, it is assumed that moral purpose has been frustrated; but Sorley pointed out that the realization of moral purpose cannot be equated with the realization of personal happiness. Just because we are not happy about some situation does not imply that the situation ought not to be. In general, Sorley argued that suffering and evil are possible in a theistic worldview if finite minds are gradually recognizing moral ends that they are free to accept or reject.

On the evidential role of evil and the difference between Kant and Hume, then, Sorley agreed with Kant, and he used the very fact of evil as the foundation for a theistic argument. He argued that both the moral order and the order of nature belong to the essence of reality, and if it is synthesis and integration we seek, they can be harmoniously united in one universe only when nature is understood not merely in its present appearance but as working out the purpose of making moral beings. The problem of evil, Sorley thought, is often cast in a way that overlooks the creation of beings who will achieve goodness only freely, requiring experience of all sorts of circumstances that it may develop into secure harmony with the moral order.

It was the idea of goodness, not the extent of its actualization, that animated Kant's analysis. It was awareness of the absolute authority of a transcendent moral law that gave Kant such confidence in his doctrine of the postulates of practical reason. God, freedom, and immortality are all implied in the moral law (with varying levels of directness). Without God our moral ideas would be incapable of realization in the world.[18] On Kant's view God is the means of uniting two disparate systems of conceptions, reconciling nature and the moral order. Because such systems differ, and stand in rational need of harmony, God is necessary for there to be a "Great Reconciler." Neither system by itself proves God, but moral reason demands their reconciliation, and God is needed to effect it.[19] Sorley's argument wasn't a straightforward inference from morality to God; it was a bit more circuitous, with a wider range. But it was intent on taking the moral evidence of evil seriously.

When St. Paul counseled patience during trials and afflictions, he knew of what he spoke, having endured shipwrecks and brutal beatings, imprisonments and rapacious hunger. Sorley too was existentially acquainted with heart-wrenching loss and grief. Even while William was writing his Gifford lectures, siding with Kant rather than Hume, Charles's death broke his heart. The abhorrent news hit him and his wife hard, and though it undoubtedly changed them, it conditioned his reflections here with a measure of authenticity, pathos, and humanity that are simply undeniable. Readers can disagree with his analysis, but he can't be accused of evading the hard questions. Little surprising that Sorley's moral argument, forged in the crucible of unspeakable personal loss, refused to trivialize this world's travails. He drank of them to their dregs. Nor, however, did he allow them the final word.

An Integrative Mind

Sorley argued for a nondeductivist approach, something approaching a best-explanation methodology, predicated on an expansive epistemology structurally resembling verification theory in the natural sciences but intentionally inclusive of the evidential significance of moral values. Among the relevant pieces of evidence to be considered in assessing and appraising a philosophical theory, to his thinking, is "an immediate attitude of the individual mind to the meaning of things as a whole," inspiring "not only intellectual ideas but also the activity in which the individual shows himself as an agent in the world's progress."[20]

Sorley saw the ontological, cosmological, and teleological arguments for God's existence as efforts to explain the world, and he saw the moral argument in the same light. Morality, too, is part of what needs explanation. In this way Sorley viewed all four arguments as limited when taken in isolation, as each bases its inference along a single dimension of reality. He saw all of them as more effective at refuting naturalism than proving theism, their cumulative effect stronger than their individual effects; moreover, the moral argument is needed to have hope of showing not just God's existence but also God's goodness.

Charles Taylor writes that the secular age into which we've entered features *exclusive humanism*, a vision of life in which the immanent takes primacy, a humanism accepting "no final goals beyond human flourishing, nor any allegiance to anything else beyond this flourishing. Of no previous society was this true."[21] In contrast with this remarkable trend, such historical moral apologists as William Sorley gave extended arguments that morality functions semiotically by pointing beyond itself to eternal goods that, rather than trivializing or devaluing earthly or temporal goods, imbue them with sacramental significance.

Following a bout of pneumonia, Sorley died in Cambridge in July of 1935. A fully attended and impressive service was held in the majestic King's College chapel at Cambridge, concluding with eight lines from a poem by Charles. With the exquisite, sublime artistry of Charles, William had once modestly compared his own achievements: "He will be remembered when I am a dead and forgotten scholar—there is in his poetry the *truth* I sought, and beauty such as I have never found."[22]

> Synopsis: Sorley argued that God provides the best and most rational and unified view of reality, the ground of both the natural and moral orders. What a close look reveals is that Sorley's approach, rather than being dated, remains a lively, instructive, and powerful model to follow. Whether he was integrating or reconciling various pieces of natural theology—the causal and moral, is and

ought, reality and value, life and work, finite and infinite goods, the temporal and transcendent, the moral law and evil, philosophy and poetry, or morality and metaphysics—his was an expansive and integrative mind and an open and capacious heart whose prescient insights have proven the test of time. He demonstrated what long and intimate acquaintance with the world of ideas can generate, and his enduring example can serve as an inspiration and corrective to much of what passes for apologetics today.

7

An Edinburgher
Andrew Seth Pringle-Pattison

His Life and Work

Andrew Seth Pringle-Pattison (1856–1931; henceforth "PP") was born Andrew Seth, in Edinburgh, adopting the surname Pringle-Pattison at the age of forty-two as a condition of inheriting a family estate in Scotland. PP studied philosophy at Edinburgh University, under Campbell Fraser, and also studied for two years in Germany (a trip made possible by a Hibbert Traveling Fellowship). His brother James was also a philosopher; they taught together at Edinburgh for twenty-one years. Their father was the son of a farmer from Fife and a bank clerk in the head office of the Commercial Bank of Scotland; their mother, Margaret, was the daughter of Andrew Little, a farmer from Berwickshire.

Over the course of PP's career, he was a contemporary of D. G. Ritchie, William Sorley, and R. B. Haldane; he and Haldane became lifelong friends. From 1880 to 1883 he served as Fraser's assistant at Edinburgh and then took the chair of philosophy in the University College of South Wales at Cardiff. He became Balfour Lecturer in philosophy in 1883, and in 1884 he married Eva (who died in 1928), the daughter of Albrecht Stropp; they would have five children. Their youngest son was killed in action on the Somme in 1916, and their eldest daughter died in infancy.

In 1891 he achieved his ambition of succeeding his old professor, Campbell Fraser, to the chair of logic and metaphysics at Edinburgh. In 1919 he resigned, after thirty-nine influential years as a university teacher. He was Gifford Lecturer, University of Aberdeen (1911–1913), Hibbert Lecturer (1921), and Gifford Lecturer again, University of Edinburgh (1921–1923). PP saw philosophy as a sober and noble enterprise. He sought to advance his subject through critical interpretation of the great philosophers, especially Kant and Hegel.

Rebelling against the absolutism of Hegel and of such Hegelians as F. H. Bradley and Bernard Bosanquet, for whom the individual is merged in the universal, he insisted on the uniqueness of the individual person. It is only as knower that the self is a unifying principle. As a real being it is separate and distinct, impervious to other selves, even to God, who is also a Person. We cannot deny him self-consciousness, because this is the highest source of worth in ourselves. In such ways PP assigned primacy to personality—an influence that would later affect William James, George Santayana, Bertrand Russell, and George Herbert Mead.

Philosophy, PP held, cannot do justice to those memories, thoughts, and feelings that make each of us a separate soul. Our knowledge starts from experience of the concrete worlds of morality, of beauty, of love, or of the passion of the intellectual life, but it's a postulate of reason that the world is a *cosmos*, not a *chaos*, which we can gradually explore but never grasp in its entirety. He thought both British empiricism and Anglo-Hegelianism degraded the independence of the individual, and he described his philosophy as a "larger idealism" that reconciles the dictates of morality and religion with the findings of science, *purpose* being the supreme category.

Among his principal works were *The Development from Kant to Hegel* (1882), *Hegelianism and Personality* (1887), *Man's Place in the Cosmos* (1897), *Studies in the Philosophy of Religion* (1930), and *The Balfour Lectures on Realism* (1933). His book most relevant to moral apologetics, however, is *The Idea of God in the Light of Recent Philosophy: The Gifford Lectures Delivered in the University of Aberdeen in the Years 1912 and 1913* (1917).[1] PP's principal purpose there was to engage with the longstanding debate about the significance of Enlightenment philosophy and nineteenth-century scientific developments for the coherence and plausibility of Christian theism by setting these debates within the context of the idealist philosophy to which he was himself a major contributor. In what follows we will highlight some aspects of these lectures in order to emphasize aspects of the story of the moral argument that might otherwise not be accorded the attention they merit, as well as point out both certain resonances and dissonances with other leading moral apologists.

The Idea of God and the Problem of Evil

In this first set of Gifford lectures, PP's title was strategic, and it serves a useful reminder of a distinctive feature of the moral argument. The title is the *idea* of God—the *nature and attributes* of God, not merely the question of God's *existence*. This is a timely reminder that the moral argument, if it works, is ideally suited for revealing something about God's character and moral identity. Sure enough, by the time PP finished his analysis, he returned to this question and spoke specifically about how better to envision who God is.

As a native of Edinburgh, PP must have grown up accustomed to hearing quite a bit about his town's most famous philosophical son, the towering eighteenth-century philosopher, economist, essayist, and historian David Hume, whose *Dialogues Concerning Natural Religion* dealt primarily with *who God is* rather than *whether God exists*. In fact, PP's opening lecture focused on Hume's *Dialogues*, at the culmination of which Hume seemed to think that we could generate only a vague conception of the divine based on the evidence available. PP, however, argued in reply that Hume's conclusions were determined by the restricted nature of his premises. Hume looked to nature, not to the incessant hopes and fears that actuate the human mind. PP counseled instead that we look to the "sentient creation and the facts of human history," a broader array of evidence than Hume considered. To PP's thinking, though, such evidential factors constitute the very center and foreground of the whole picture, and for that reason they can't responsibly be ignored. PP, in this way, resonates with so many of the moral apologists in this volume who insisted on a broad empirical approach and expansive epistemology.

Like A. E. Taylor would do later, PP then contrasted Hume and Kant on this score, noting that, when it comes to what they say about God, their stark differences make it seem as if they're from different planets. Whereas Hume tended to accentuate the less-than-optimal conditions of this world, questioning why a good and loving God would allow these things, Kant, though mindful of such challenges, analyzed man's moral experience instead. When he did so, it yielded Kant's assurance of the existence of God, and it was God's moral attributes that he was primarily concerned to establish. Whereas Hume attributed to the Supreme Mind complete indifference to natural and to moral evil alike, Kant believed God to be primarily and essentially the author and maintainer of a moral order. The last word of Kantian philosophy is the universe as a moral system through and through.

PP was more drawn to Kant than to Hume here. If the world of time is really, as Kant held it to be, a training ground of the spirit, if "man's painful history is but the long discipline by which a moral being is shaped out of a merely animal creature,"[2] then Hume's points are not what's of central importance. The point of course is an old one, harkening back to Irenaeus and his notions of theodicy, for example. As PP's contemporary Sorley would argue just a few years later, during the throes of the First World War, if there's reason to think that the world is, as John Keats put it, a "vale of soul-making," or, as Gotthold Lessing put it, a "divine education," rather than a context aimed at maximizing hedonistic delights, there's no particular reason to think the world *shouldn't* feature a measure of evils.

In fact, there's a good explanation for why the world *does* contain such evils, for they furnish the necessary context in which we can mature emotionally, morally, and spiritually. In this way PP, like Kant, wasn't unmindful, ignorant, indifferent, or oblivious to the world's travails. These lamentable features of reality constituted part of the moral evidence in need of careful consideration and explanation, but Kant's assignment of priorities in his moral theorizing led to a conclusion radically different from Hume's. The moral argument and the problem of evil, PP seemed to be suggesting, are locked in a zero-sum game.[3]

The right analysis—whether Humean or Kantian—of this world's evils can only be rightly judged in the light of what we take to be the end in view. What struck PP was the way Kant fixed the idea of an ultimate End through the idea of *value* or *worth* that figured prominently at the forefront of his ethics. Of course, on Kant's view, only the good will is good without qualification, and indeed a good will, for Kant, appears to constitute the indispensable condition even of being worthy of happiness. This was the bedrock absolute value on which Kant constructed his moral system, and it was a feature of persons and their wills. PP took him to be suggesting that there's a sense in which making good wills possible is the very reason for the existence of the universe in the first place. Reasons demand not merely the "is" of bare fact, but the "ought-to-be," the "deserves-to-be" of absolute value. So for Kant this quality exclusively of the moral will becomes the one end-in-itself, for whose realization the cosmos exists.

PP argued that it is not intellectual coherence alone that the philosopher seeks—the fitting together, as it were, of the parts of some gigantic puzzle. The most perfect realization of unity in variety means little if there is nowhere anything to which we can attach this predicate of value: "We must be able to say that the world is 'good' in the sense of possessing intrinsic worth or value."[4] Whereas Clement Webb later critiqued Kant for not saying enough about value, PP, interestingly enough, seemed to accord Kant great credit for putting his finger on a central question of value focused on the good will, the intrinsically valuable end in itself by which the existence of the universe is explained or justified.

Naturalism and Idealism

In PP's time in Germany, among his teachers was Hermann Lotze, to whom he frequently referred in his writings.[5] In light of Lotze's influence on PP, Taylor, Sorley, and others, we are reminded that a history of predominantly English-speaking moral apologists is not untouched by the German-speaking world—Kant, of course, the most salient example of all. Among the words of Lotze's that PP found memorable was Lotze's lament of the way some show "sham heroism, which glories in renouncing what no man has a right to renounce."[6]

Among the deep values that PP thought ineliminable were Kantian notions of duty and moral freedom (which mutually imply one another), and the good will. Kant's formulation of his second and third postulates—God and immortality—left PP a bit dissatisfied, however, because of the fact that PP thought immanence of the divine was an idea too foreign to Kant's whole way of thinking. How to strike a better balance between transcendence and immanence will come up again at the end of the chapter when PP gets to the issue of what God is like.

So PP was a bit ambivalent in his assessment of Kant's work, taking some but not all of it. Quite importantly, in terms of positive contributions by Kant, PP believed that the conception of intrinsic values as the clue to the ultimate nature of reality was the fundamental contention of all idealistic philosophy since Kant's time. The great German idealists enlarged and completed Kant's conception of intrinsic value by making it include all the higher reaches of human experience.[7] PP was steeped in the tradition of idealism, and in fact he suggested that the entirety of the latter half of the nineteenth century was dominated, among philosophers, by a battle between naturalists and idealists. The crux of their debate was this: Is the universe the expression of a transcendent Greatness and Goodness, or is it, in ultimate analysis, a collection of unknowing material facts? Is the ultimate essence and cause of all things "only dust that rises up and is lightly laid again, or is it the Eternal Love with which Dante closes his vision, the Love that moves the sun and the other Stars"?[8]

The idealists were those, by PP's lights, who safeguarded the category of intrinsic values, which are much less at home in a mechanistic universe lacking final causes. Idealism took its stand on the essential truth of our judgments of value and the impossibility of explaining the higher from the lower. As he put it, "Beauty and goodness are not born of the clash of atoms; they are effluences of something more perfect and more divine."[9]

To represent the other hypothesis, PP quotes Balfour's poignantly beautiful passage describing the final run-down of the solar system in which

> man will go down into the pit, and all his thoughts will perish. The uneasy consciousness which in this obscure corner has for a brief space broken the contented silence of the universe, will be at rest. Matter will know itself no longer. "Imperishable monuments" and "immortal deeds," death itself, and love stronger than death, will be as if they had not been. Nor will anything that is be better or worse for all that the labour, genius, devotion, and suffering of man have striven through countless ages to effect.[10]

Such mechanical systems of time and space offer no reason to think that our moral aspirations are anything but wishful thinking. PP, who had a flair for appreciating dramatic erudition, quoted Martineau along these lines:

> Amid all the sickly talk about "ideals" which has become the commonplace of our age, it is well to remember that so long as they are a mere self-painting of the yearning spirit, they have no more solidity or steadiness than floating air-bubbles, gay in the sunshine and broken by the passing wind.... The very gate of entrance to [religion] is the discovery that your gleaming ideal is the everlasting Real, no transient brush of a fancied angel's wing, but the abiding presence and persuasion of the Soul of souls: short of this, there is *no object* given you.[11]

Answering Hume's Challenge

What PP tried to do in these lectures was to meet Hume's challenge to construct only those hypotheses to which the evidence pointed. Although PP accepted the challenge, he disputed its terms, rejecting Hume's artificial limitation of the argument to contemplation of nature. Here of course PP echoed sentiments similar to those from throughout the history of the moral argument—from Newman and Sorley to Taylor and Webb. The reason he preferred a more expansive epistemology that takes moral phenomenology seriously was because, contra Kant, he did not think the mediation of reality by various factors precludes our coming to know it. The mind is set in the heart of the world; it is itself the center in which the essential nature of the whole reveals itself.[12] If man's knowledge does not put him in touch with reality, how can his ideals be supposed to furnish a clue?

PP's contention has been that everything depends on keeping in view the whole range of germane accessible facts, if we are to form a true idea of the nature of the Being whom it reveals.[13] Instead of being excluded from consideration, the characteristics of human consciousness and human development must be the most significant of all facts for the solution of the question at issue. It was PP's view that the presence of the Ideal is the very reality of God within us, a view that bears more than a passing resemblance to Descartes's argument in the third of his *Meditations*.[14] At bottom PP tried salvaging the kernel of Descartes's insight. The idea of perfection is not mere negation; it's something more: the moving spirit of life within us. We don't possess it in terms of conscious experience or of thought until it's revealed to us bit by bit through time and in the travails of our souls.[15]

PP claimed that it's what we desire—what we are not, but what we have the power to become—that is the moving power in all advance, and he quotes Wordsworth to that effect:

> Our destiny, our being's heart and home,
> Is with infinitude, and only there,
> With hope it is, hope that can never die,
> Effort, and expectation, and desire,
> And something evermore about to be.[16]

PP thus claimed that the ideal is precisely the most real thing in the world and that those ranges of our experiences, such as religion, which are specifically concerned with the ideal, instead of being treated as a "cloud-cuckoo-land" of subjective fancy, may reasonably be accepted as the best interpreters we have of the true nature of reality.[17]

Anticipating Lewis's later distinction (in "Meditation in a Toolshed" from *God in the Dock*) between looking at versus looking along, PP wrote,

> Reverence for the moral law, the self-humiliation caused by failure to fulfill its demands, the sense of sin, the attitude of worship and utter self-surrender, are possible only if the subject feels himself in presence of a Reality beside which all else pales into insignificance. And it is to the moral and religious man himself that we must go, not to the philosopher weaving theories about him, if we are to understand his experience aright.[18]

"The fundamental presupposition of any experience must be accepted from the experience itself: they may be explained, but not explained away," he added. "On the evidence of the moral and religious life, therefore, we are bound to treat the ideals of that life not as devout imaginations, in which fancy has combined with desire to heighten and idealize certain features of the actual, but as having their authentic basis in the nature of the world."[19] He saw that philosophical criticism and historical research could serve a purpose to distinguish truth in religious experiences from fanciful accretions, but he took the evidence of religious experience with tremendous seriousness.

Finally, PP was convinced that carving out such space for authentic religious experience could serve as a corrective to what he considered Kant's neglect of God's transcendence. The very secret of Christianity, PP thought, was that there's no God that's

> existing in solitary bliss and perfect, but a God who lives in the perpetual giving of himself, who shares the life of his finite creatures, bearing in and with them the whole burden of their finitude, their sinful wanderings and sorrows, and the suffering without which they cannot be made perfect.... The divine omnipotence consists in the all-compelling power of goodness and love to enlighten the grossest darkness and to melt the hardest heart. "We needs must love the highest when we see it."[20]

Thus, PP ended on a note that addressed the original question of Hume's *Dialogues*. The God to which the moral argument points is not an amoral deity who is completely indifferent to us; rather, he is a God whose very nature is self-giving love.

Synopsis: Pringle-Pattison touched a number of chords similar to those of other notable moral apologists, while distinguishing himself in a few salient respects. He lauded Kant on the issue of value, tracing that line of argument to focus on the principled reason to side with Kant over Hume on the problem of evil, while being critical of Kant in other respects, particularly in paying God's immanence inadequate attention. He saw clearly various implications of the moral argument for the character of God, not just on the matter of God's existence, and he intentionally launched criticisms at Hume's narrow empiricism. PP's idealism was broad, his epistemology expansive, his empiricism generous. He took religious experience seriously, refusing to privilege the perspective of external bystanders who lacked its rich phenomenology.

8

The Theo-Philosopher of Carlisle

Hastings Rashdall

Anthony Thiselton writes that in the nineteenth and early twentieth centuries the most convincing advocate of the moral argument was perhaps Hastings Rashdall.[1] Rashdall (1858–1924) was the son of an Anglican priest and received a scholarship to New College, Oxford, destined to become an eminent English philosopher, theologian, and historian. After a stint at a few other colleges, he was made a fellow at New College.

Rashdall wrote a magisterial two-volume history of medieval European universities, treatments of the atonement and personal immortality, books on the conscience, and more, including his best-known work, the two-volume *The Theory of Good and Evil* (1907),[2] which he dedicated to his mentors Thomas Hill Green and Henry Sidgwick. The propriety of the dedication has been noted in light of the formative influence that each wielded on Rashdall. Joseph Butler, G. E. Moore, and George Berkeley also made their mark on Rashdall's thought, and Rashdall and Clement Webb were close friends, overlapping in their time at Oxford and sharing a strong interest in theology and philosophy generally, and matters of ethical concern particularly.

Rashdall was president of the Aristotelian Society from 1904 to 1907, a member of the Christian Social Union from its inception in 1890, and an influential Anglican modernist theologian of the time, being appointed to a canonry in 1909. He was dean of Carlisle from 1917 to 1924; he died of cancer in Worthing in 1924. P. E. Matheson wrote the biography *The Life of Hastings Rashdall, D.D.* in 1928.[3]

Rashdall did a great deal of reflection on moral philosophy, exploring its connections to theism, to the afterlife, and to conscience. Perhaps the best way to encapsulate Rashdall's main lines of argument is by looking at his *Theory of Good and Evil*. The main moral argument for God that this treatise contains can be found in the second volume, but there are some important and instructive preliminaries to canvas from volume 1 first. Before diving in, however, there's a matter of some importance to discuss.

Hastings Rashdall was, in important ways, a product of his time, and he fell prey to certain attitudes on race that were clearly wrong, even racist. He was, on this score, deeply inconsistent, affirming, for example, that the principles of justice require that we give equal consideration to the well-being of all those affected by our actions, even while proceeding to contradict himself by affirming that the social condition of the "higher races of mankind" is of greater importance than the social condition of the "lower races." He ended up attempting to justify a systematic and institutional form of racism in allocating wealth, property, and basic rights. In a 2011 study of discrimination and the law, Nicholas Mark Smith describes Rashdall as a racist thinker who did not agree, as a matter of fact, that "we are each other's equals."[4] In a volume of his Gifford lectures published in 2017, Jeremy Waldron discusses Rashdall's anti-egalitarianism at length.[5] (Rashdall, incidentally, was himself invited to give Gifford lectures.)

Rashdall's views on these matters were eminently unfortunate and flat wrong, but two points are worth making. First, Rashdall's views on race were distinct from his moral argument. In fact they were, as mentioned, radically at odds with his claims about equal consideration elsewhere. To the contrary of there being anything inherently tying his racist views and moral argument, they are diametrically opposed—here the herculean resistance to and categorical rejection of slavery by such examples as Frederick Douglass, William Wilberforce, and Dr. Martin Luther King, Jr. are the much more representative normative Christian models. Aristotle, recall, held simply hideous views about slaves and women, but what most readers of him tend to do, and rightly so, is separate out those views from his many sound observations and insights, without in any way trivializing or excusing his significant errors.

Where there are organic connections and theoretical parities between disparate views of a thinker, of course, they are fair game to expound on and explicate; where there are not, efforts to make it seem otherwise don't serve to advance but rather to derail the discussion. Moreover, the very conviction that something like racism is categorically wrong assumes as axiomatic the nonnegotiable nature of moral objectivity. Such an obstinate fixture of reality and moral experience cries out all the more vociferously for careful examination and close scrutiny.

Second, Rashdall's example in this regard is an instructive, sober reminder that even otherwise quite intelligent people can confuse and conflate prevailing cultural views with the dictates and deliverances of objective morality, thus providing a cautionary tale to all of us, one applicable to the whole scope of the political spectrum and to our own cultural moment. Reigning plausibility structures are seldom sacrosanct. The purpose of this book has never been to chronicle the inspired ideas of previous thinkers who never got it wrong; it's a story, like every honest history, with warts and bumps and missteps, featuring the noble and ignoble, both beauty and ugliness, tragedy and comedy, and in between rife and riddled with a rich assortment of humanity. Our intent is neither to lionize nor demonize but to humanize and, if such echoes there be, to hear intimations of the divine and notes of redemption. Despite our hearts of darkness, feet of clay, penchant for bias, recurring epistemic limits, and chronic liability to error, hope remains that we fallible creatures nevertheless can not only avoid mistakes but gradually glean and garner wisdom and truth, effecting needed course corrections and sometimes radical changes in trajectory along the way. This should serve as deep encouragement to us all.[6]

Rationalistic Utilitarianism

After laying out his plan in the book to study human conduct and investigate the meanings of various moral terms, concepts, and realities, beginning with common moral sense and experience, Rashdall devoted a chapter to discussing psychological hedonism. For present purposes this treatment need not detain us for long, but he argued at length against the view of psychological hedonism, specifically the version that suggests it's the pain of a bad conscience or the pleasure of a clear conscience that guides our decision-making. Rashdall found this inadequate because deriving pleasure from doing good or feeling pain from doing bad reveals, in the person having such experiences, desires for something besides pleasure. This insight isn't unique to Rashdall, of course, but it's worth noting because of the frequency with which this variant of hedonism even still recurs.

Rashdall next explored rationalistic utilitarianism, discussion of which will give us the opportunity to extend our previous treatment of Sidgwick in an illuminating way. Sidgwick had been Rashdall's teacher, and recall Sidgwick's dualism of practical reason: man is made to promote the public good, but no less evidently he's made to promote private good. As Rashdall put it, "The fundamental question raised by Professor Sidgwick's position is the logical compatibility of a rationalistic theory of duty with a hedonistic conception of the true good or [telos] of man."[7] Rashdall suggested that Sidgwick's attitude toward *duty* was that of Butler and Kant, while his attitude toward the idea of *good* was that of the hedonist. Sidgwick admitted the aforementioned dualism—namely, that it can be reasonable for someone to desire something for oneself at the same time as seeing as desirable something good for others that may stand in variance with the first desire. The only way Sidgwick saw out of the dilemma was by positing theological postulates, which he wasn't willing to do; and in a previous chapter this provided resources for a variant of the moral argument.

Rashdall, however, didn't go in that direction. Actually, he resisted it, though we think that his point and the earlier points are quite consistent. Rashdall instead wanted to raise this question for Sidgwick: Isn't it the case that the point of view of the whole—the altruistic impulses we have—is the *right* perspective? Isn't it the reasonable perspective, rather than Sidgwick's claim that the self-regarding and altruistic perspectives are *equally* reasonable or rational? One's own pleasure and the general pleasure aren't equally important or valuable.

When one's personal pleasure is, as it sometimes can be, inconsistent with the general good, Rashdall was reticent to concede to Sidgwick that it's still reasonable to pursue one's personal pleasure. In fact, he attributed Sidgwick's willingness to dub it as such to a domesticated and defanged understanding of "rational" as meaning simply internally self-consistent or conducive to any particular end actually desired. Rashdall saw, rightly we think, such a notion of rationality as too myopic and watered down.

What troubled Rashdall was this: If someone chooses to behave egoistically rather than altruistically, even when reason declares the latter to be an altogether rational course of action, she does nothing wrong by Sidgwick's lights. She might have rationally chosen to go the altruistic route instead, but she's no less rational for opting for the egoistic path. This struck Rashdall, understandably enough, as a deficient analysis. There *would* be something wrong, he was convinced, with the choice to privilege oneself over others in that way.

If we really have duties to others, and the lives of others really are of intrinsic value and worth, egoistic tendencies are not, after all, equally rational options when there's a conflict between self-regarding and other-regarding desires. The latter trump. As a result, Rashdall wasn't inclined to rest content, even as a theistic ethicist, with merely assuming that Sidgwick's dualism of practical reason provides warrant for positing theological postulates. In fact he thought that it was a mistake, predicated on a defective understanding of altruistic duties.

Rashdall thought what was needed wasn't simply an ordering of the universe by which happiness and holiness cohere; needed was an account according to which other-regarding behaviors aren't optional but required, holding primacy over egoistic motivations. What's needed is not only the consistency of self-regarding and other-regarding actions and desires but also a more intimate organic connection between virtue and happiness. Rashdall put it like this:

> But if goodness be the end and without which the highest happiness is incomplete, if goodness be of the essence of the highest happiness, then it is not inconceivable that the voluntary neglect of a lower good in the pursuit of a higher may be intrinsically necessary to the attainment of that completed state of being, of a life which shall embrace both these concepts of goodness and happiness which Modern Philosophy has been accustomed to separate—the "Well-being" or [*eudaimonia*] of ancient Ethics.[8]

Rashdall thought what would make excellent sense of the need for self-sacrifice to equip people to be worthy of happiness is this: love, which is essentially other-regarding, constituting a vital part of earthly happiness. His critique of Sidgwick is that Sidgwick's effort to reconcile a hedonistic conception of the good with an intuitionist or rational basis of morality breaks down. "The 'dualism' of Practical Reason is not bridged over and cannot be bridged over without the admission of Virtue or character—at least the Virtue or character which consists in the promotion of general pleasure—as an element and the highest element of the 'good' which it is right to promote for the whole human race."[9]

Rashdall may have been inclined to think, therefore, that our earlier effort to draw a theistic lesson from Sidgwick's dualism of practical reason was misguided, but we think, if so, he would be mistaken. Rashdall's point and our earlier one, by our lights, aren't inconsistent. Rather, Rashdall's point can augment and nicely nuance the earlier case, and help avoid an objection to it that could easily arise. That objection goes like this: appealing to God to make altruism consistent with one's own happiness makes it appear that morality has to "pay" in order to be legitimate. There's something objectionably mercenary about such a depiction. The authority of morality doesn't derive from the way it corresponds with self-interest.

Now, we happen to think that this criticism is misguided, because we think there is nothing untoward about expecting morality to be a fully rational enterprise, and if morality and ultimate self-interest don't ultimately correspond, morality would lack full rational stability. Morality and rationality could in principle diverge, and we have argued before that, in fact, on most any naturalistic or secular ethical system on offer, this actually happens. The need for the rational stability of morality is bona fide, and so we think the "mercenary" charge is predicated more on appearance than reality. This is not to deny that some religious believers might think that the only reason to be moral is to earn a reward or avoid a punishment, but there's nothing about our view that entails such an understanding—we demur from aspects of Locke here.

However, having said that, we acknowledge that there is a reason why some would think that the insistence on the correspondence between happiness and holiness projects a mercenary impression, and the reason is closely related to why deductivist variants of the moral argument are similarly susceptible to criticism. In both cases, the concern is raised by a counterfactual: Suppose that God didn't exist, and that morality and happiness didn't ultimately cohere—then what? If the idea is that there would be nothing to morality, this seems to vitiate the intrinsic authority of morality. The operative conception of morality in that case would be more explicable in prudential terms than those of intrinsic values or duties.

Once again, though, a less deductivist approach can handily avoid anything legitimate about this objection—even if the objection is often predicated on mere appearances. Rashdall's points enable us to gravitate toward a more abductive analysis. Take a step back, we suggest, and approach all of this from a different angle—including a richer sense of rationality than Sidgwick employed and a recognition of objective value and a more expansive conception of goodness than Sidgwick's hedonism allowed. Even if the full rational stability of morality requires an unbreakable connection between happiness and virtue—which we agree with and have argued at length that classical theism accounts for impeccably—another point is needed—namely, that altruism does trump self-interest in a very real sense. Egoism and altruism aren't equal rational options. Though the connection between happiness and holiness is airtight, such an affirmation remains too coarse-grained (after all, Stoics, Epicureans, and theists of various stripes can all agree on that).

A finer-grained analysis requires seeing that there remains a hierarchy, as Rashdall suggested. Sidgwick was wrong not to see it, leaving him with an intractable dualism (as a partial result of his misguided assumptions). Altruism does indeed have objective value, indeed primacy over self-interest, which needs explanation. What's the best explanation? Posing the challenge this way leaves behind the deductivism that, in this case, resides uncomfortably close to the mercenary accusation introduced when appearing to insist on morality to pay. What can explain both the legitimacy of self-interest and the objective, inherent, and superior value of altruism, effecting their perfect rapprochement?

An explanation emerges from not just *any* theism but from a theistic story featuring a God who effects ultimate justice and ensures resonance between happiness and holiness, ensuring that only the holy are ultimately the happy, but who also grounds the intrinsic and superior value of other-regarding behaviors. This is the God who's nothing less than perfect love, and such a God can indeed resolve the dualism of practical reason, making morality rationally stable but also satisfying the prior ontological need for grounding objective moral values and other-regarding duties, rendering egoism deficient. This approach makes Rashdall's critique of Sidgwick consistent with our earlier takeaway from Sidgwick, while neatly avoiding charges of reducing morality to prudence or putting self-interest on a par with altruism.

Of course this notion of a hierarchy is not original; Scotus and Anselm historically, and John Hare more recently, all spoke of the need for assigning a higher priority to the affection for justice over the affection for advantage.[10] Our natural impulses tend to get it backward, and there's no need to eschew considerations for advantage altogether. As Kant would say, our good requires the conjunction of happiness and virtue since we're not purely noumenal creatures. Still, what's needed is *more* than their *congruence*. We need to become the sort of people who *deserve* to be happy; the affection for advantage has to be subordinated to the affection for justice; altruism really does trump egoism, even if loving God and others perfectly coheres with our ultimate self-interest.

Intuitionism and the Categorical Imperative

Rashdall then delved into his assessment of certain prevailing views in the history of ethical thought. We think it worthwhile to accentuate just a smattering of his germane insights and reflections because it will culminate in a telling takeaway. Regarding intuitionism, the theory that actions are pronounced right or wrong a priori without reference to their consequences—either via reason or a moral sense—Rashdall was generally skeptical for various reasons. Among them was that moral notions that have seemed innate, self-evident, and authoritative to those who held them have varied enormously with different races, different ages, and different individuals (and even with the same individuals at different periods in life). Then again, Rashdall didn't think this the strongest argument against intuitionism, since we don't doubt the axioms of mathematics because someone untutored in math can't fathom them. Still, he saw that nearly all detailed moral rules have some exceptions.[11]

What Rashdall tried to do was effect a measure of reconciliation between consequentialist and deontological approaches to the questions of normative ethics. He could agree with utilitarians that the true criterion of morality is the tendency of an act to promote well-being, while insisting that this includes many good things besides pleasure, including virtue. All moral judgments, he could conclude, are ultimately judgments as to the intrinsic worth or value of some element in consciousness or life.[12] So, for example, he can agree with Kantians that some actions are so intrinsically bad that no calculation of their consequences could ever justify them—the character or disposition the acts show is just that bad. "There are acts so intrinsically repulsive that it strikes us as, on the face of it, impossible that any pleasure which they might yield could be worth the evil which they involve."[13] Indeed, Rashdall thought some pleasures to be intrinsically bad, like the pleasure of drunkenness.

So while Rashdall accepted the intuitional view of the imperativeness of duty and the supreme value of moral goodness, he also accepted the legitimacy of allowing consequences to figure into our calculations of the worth of various actions, along with the need for working to promote the general welfare. In accepting a simple, unanalyzable notion of duty, he recognized the importance of much of what Kant had to say, and in fact he devoted an entire chapter to the categorical imperative. In every ethical judgment, Rashdall was convinced, there's thought to be something that's intrinsically good and reasonable to do, something that ought to be done. The positions that the rightness of actions can be perceived by reason and is capable of motivating the will, Rashdall argued, are embodied in Kant's categorical imperative and the autonomy of the will.

Rashdall thought the value of Kant's ethical work consisted largely in supplying a metaphysical basis for ethics; more generally Kant insisted that all knowledge must be something supplied by experience and a formal a priori element. Rashdall argued that the Kantian categorical imperative occupies in ethics the same position that the law of noncontradiction does in logic. Kant's formal algorithm usually leaves underdetermined the content of the moral law, about the only exception being the few cases in which Kant showed an action to be internally inconsistent. This, though, leaves plenty of obviously immoral courses of action in the clear; and certain moral actions do seem to lack universalizability. Rashdall thus insisted that Kant's view left us still in need of the right ultimate principle in ethics.[14]

Rashdall raised several other objections to Kant, which we can set aside for now. The point for our purposes is this: although drawn to utilitarianism of a particular stripe at the level of ethical normativity, Rashdall distanced himself from hedonistic utilitarians and at times sounded more distinctly Kantian, despite his numerous reservations about aspects of Kantian ethics.[15] With Kant, though, he agreed that there are certain actions that should never be performed.

Much more could be said about Rashdall's ethics—his ideal utilitarianism, his thoughts on moral epistemology or retributive justice—but space constrains us to move on to his moral argument. Time has been spent spelling out a bit of his integration of deontological and consequentialist themes in order to make an important point, a significant takeaway from a detailed study of the history of the moral argument—namely, that theistic ethicists and moral apologists are far from agreed on some of the finer-grained debates in ethics. Moreover, there is little that's troublesome about this. Some are consequentialists, others deontologists, others virtue ethicists, and others are combinations of these theories. Others, either at the normative level or meta-ethical level, are divine will theorists, or divine command theorists, or natural lawyers, or divine desire theorists, or something else.

What moral apologetics requires is not a consensus about any one specific ethical account, or unanimity on any one particular way in which the phenomena of morality are rooted and grounded in God. Rather, what is required is that, in some nontrivial sense or other, there is principled affirmation of some such dependency relation. Different relations are explicated in different accounts. Most of such disparate relations are altogether consistent with one another, and likely mutually reinforcing; some may exist in tension, conflict, or even contradiction with a few of the others. For purposes of the moral argument, though, what its rich and fertile history reveals is that the core concept of important aspects of ethics existing in a dependence relation of God can be found among a wide variety of thinkers whose convictions, on this central score, are deeply consonant, even though the specific ways in which such a relation obtains may be conceived and explained in different—albeit usually consistent, mutually enriching, and informative—ways. Diversity at the periphery doesn't vitiate or even undermine the shared core; rather, it showcases its importance.

Metaphysics and Morality

Among the reasons why metaphysics matters to morality are these: an adequate account of morality involves metaphysical postulates, metaphysical conclusions affect our attitudes toward ethics, and moral philosophy involves consequences it's the business of metaphysics to interpret.[16] It is of course possible, Rashdall noted, to assume the existence of the moral consciousness, ignore metaphysics, and do analysis, but he added that those who do so have never done the most memorable work in the field.

> So long as he is content to assume the reality and authority of the moral consciousness, the Moral Philosopher can ignore Metaphysic; but, if the reality of Morals or the validity of ethical truth be once brought into question, the attack can only be met by a thorough-going enquiry into the nature of Knowledge and of Reality.... In practice it is hardly possible to write many lines about some very fundamental questions of Ethics from which some people would not dissent on metaphysical grounds.[17]

Rashdall was convinced that, since ethics deals with such a large and fundamental aspect of ultimate reality, it's practically impossible to deal with it thoroughly without taking a very important step toward figuring out the nature of reality as a whole. It's unrealistic to think that our views on the ultimate problems of ethics should not be influenced by our attitude toward reality as a whole, or vice versa.[18] The more that moral judgments are treated as an exception to the rest of our knowledge, the more difficult it is to explain their character and justify their validity.[19]

A narrow empiricism, for example, invariably detracts from confidence in our moral judgments, as would a deficient account of the self as a volitional creature. Indeed, something more than simply the existence of the self and its activity in knowledge is called for. "It is a presupposition of all Morality that the self is the cause of its own actions."[20] Denial of such selves is fatal to the conception of duty, of moral responsibility, of an objective moral law to which the individual self is subject.

This was why Rashdall thought it obvious why a materialistic metaphysics is at radical variance not only with the postulates of objective morality but equally with a spiritualistic metaphysics that would also vitiate meaningful agency. Morality assumes that in some intelligible sense actions may be attributed to the individual self as their cause and that actions are good or bad according to the extent to which the individual self is good or bad—"that is the starting-point and primary postulate of Ethics."[21]

That objective moral truth and meaningful agency are real and not illusory is a primary and essential presupposition of every system of ethics that can use the locution "ought," and "the very fact that this assumption is a postulate of Ethics is by itself a sufficient reason for declaring that it possesses metaphysical truth. It is implied in the idea of Morality, and the idea of Morality is a datum of the moral consciousness; and the data of consciousness are the only ground which we have for believing anything at all."[22]

As will become clear, Rashdall thought the conclusions legitimately drawn from ethics are in principle defeasible, but he was opposed to stacking the deck against them from the start by the premature adoption of questionable metaphysics. Like Sorley, Taylor, and most all the other major figures in moral apologetics, he thought it important to allow for the possibility of ethics shaping one's metaphysics. "We must not reject the deliverances of the moral Consciousness merely because they are inconsistent with some metaphysical theory which has been arrived at without taking those deliverances into consideration."[23]

So the existence of a significant self is a primary postulate of ethics, without which the language, logic, and phenomenology of ethical data are irremediably undermined, but are there other postulates? To this Rashdall next turned. Rashdall readily conceded that those indifferent to matters of metaphysics can choose, without inconsistency, to affirm the deliverances of ethics and follow the dictates of moral consciousness. "The truth is assented to, and acted upon, by men of all religions or of none, by persons who hold most dissimilar views as to the ultimate nature of the Universe, and by men who profess to have no theory of the Universe at all." And their use of the language of morality would not fluctuate considerably, despite these worldview differences. Rashdall thought this to be excellent evidence of the "independence of Morality," but he thought that such independence underdetermined the answer to the question of whether it made full sense without appeal to larger metaphysical matters. "So long as we refuse to bring any piece of our knowledge or experience into connexion with any other part of it, the particular piece of knowledge cannot be shown to be either consistent or inconsistent with such other parts of our knowledge."[24]

Rashdall then asked if there are any metaphysical positions about the ultimate nature of things that logically exclude the idea of an objective moral law. Interestingly enough, his first answer was a largely materialistic or naturalistic conception, for several reasons, among them an argument from reason that echoes Balfour and anticipates C. S. Lewis. On a naturalistic picture, the doubt arises "whether human thought in general may not wholly fail to correspond with Reality, whether thought *qua* thought may not be a delusion."[25]

Regarding morality, again, Rashdall went on to ask about its idea of an unconditional, objectively valid moral law or ideal. Does it in fact exist? Is it capable of theoretical justification? It's certainly part of what we mean by morality, but is it real? How could it exist? What seems obvious is that it is to be found, wholly and completely, "in no individual human consciousness."[26] Nor can an absolute moral law or ideal exist in material things. What follows?

> Only if we believe in the existence of a Mind for which the true moral ideal is already in some sense real, a Mind which is the source of whatever is true in our own moral judgements, can we rationally think of the moral ideal as no less real than the world itself. Only so can we believe in an absolute standard of right and wrong, which is as independent of this or that man's actual ideas and actual desires as the facts of material nature. The belief in God, though not (like the belief in a real and an active self) a postulate of there being any such thing as Morality at all, is the logical presupposition of an "objective" or absolute Morality. A moral ideal can exist nowhere and nohow but in a mind; an absolute moral ideal can exist only in a Mind from which all Reality is derived. Our moral ideal can only claim objective validity in so far as it can rationally be regarded as the revelation of a moral ideal eternally existing in the mind of God.[27]

Rashdall then had the foresight to imagine a response that has become commonplace more recently: watering down the categories of morality, its authority, and prescriptive force to such a degree that the postulate of God is no longer necessary. Rashdall admitted that this is possible, but he pointed out that it's a departure from what's actually meant by morality at its very heart in its "highest, more developed, more explicit forms."[28] Morality, at least in anything like its classically construed sense, must include the existence of an absolute, objective moral ideal; denying that is tantamount to an intolerable domestication.

At this point, we should note, Rashdall's point is entirely focused on the *explanandum*, that which is to be explained: in this case, the central, ineliminable core of morality. An axiomatic epistemic principle is that the right account of morality should have for one of its theoretical virtues a robust ability to explain what needs explaining without gutting it and denying or reducing its essence. Rashdall doggedly resisted sanguine efforts to do such things.

So he continued insisting that by his lights the evidence suggests that objective morality, freed from deflationary analysis designed only to avoid unpalatable results, implies the need for God. "The belief in God, if not so obviously and primarily a postulate of Morality as the belief in a permanent spiritual and active self, is still a postulate of a Morality which shall be able fully to satisfy the demands of the moral consciousness. It may conveniently be called the secondary postulate of Morality."[29]

What is it about God that can be inferred on this basis? Not merely, Rashdall thought, a Being of mere Thought and not Will. If morality is revelatory and veridical, it must represent not just an ideal for the Mind that is its ultimate source but also represent the nature of the end towards which that Reality is moving. The very idea of Morality implies action directed towards an end which has value. If the value of "good" has its counterpart in the divine Mind, the course of events is itself governed by the same Mind which is the source of our moral ideas, and must be ultimately directed towards the true moral ideal, disclosed however imperfectly in the moral consciousness of man.[30] What valid human judgments deem good must be part of the divine end.

Rashdall acknowledged that intense belief in a rational principle behind nature could be combined with vagueness about the personal, or even self-conscious, nature of that principle, citing Plato as an example. He thought this a theoretical deficiency, though, baldly offering his own considered views in contrast: to his mind the only form in which belief in the rationality of the universe is intelligible is the form that ascribes the events of its history to a self-conscious rational Will directing itself toward an end that presents itself to Him as absolutely good.[31] Among the implications of such a view is immortality of the soul, and Rashdall followed Kant in offering a moral argument for an afterlife.[32]

Such a picture would obviously mean that such a Being would have resources beyond this world to resolve putative problems of evil, and it would also do justice to the legitimate kernel of insight found in the ubiquitous crude testimony of the popular belief about reward and punishment in the afterlife. The salvageable core is that rationality demands an order of things in which goodness and happiness should go together, an insight, of course, we already saw in Kant and Newman and will see recur as the history of the moral argument unfolds.[33] If reality doesn't tend to promote the good, it can't be rational. What Rashdall and so many others saw clearly is that the full rational nature and stability of the moral enterprise demands an ultimate airtight connection between virtue and happiness.

Some suggest that belief in immortality is due merely to a defective appreciation of the intrinsic goodness of virtue or of the intrinsic badness of vice. Rashdall would demur. It's a belief usually held with an intensity proportional to that appreciation. It is a necessary corollary, he thought, of the rationality of the universe that "its course should be so directed as to bring about an ultimate coincidence between the higher and the lower kinds of good, which are both alike essential to the full and true Well-being of a human soul."[34] Belief in immortality is a postulate of ethics, by his lights, in the same sense as the belief in God. Again, he recognized that some will treat the fight against evil, say, as a sufficient motivation even if the fight is thought to be futile; in fact, this might make it all the nobler. But such pessimism, he answered, is not the belief best calculated to animate the highest energies of even the noblest souls. He thought the belief that the universe has a rational end is a postulate of ethics sufficiently obvious that it takes little speculative bent to recognize it.

How far can such postulates be reasonably grounded? Rashdall was convinced that the fact that the moral consciousness requires certain metaphysical postulates supplies reason for taking them as true and for accepting a view of reality that admits their truth. Newman, Rashdall recalled, had asserted that the existence of conscience provides sufficient reason for believing in the existence of God, but Rashdall found himself a bit skeptical of isolating just one feature of morality and resting so much weight on it. This is a departure from Newman, though on our reading the complexity of Newman's epistemology somewhat helps defuse the charge. At any rate, Rashdall took the opportunity to emphasize that his own moral argument found its grounding in a more extensive and less one-dimensional array of moral phenomena.

That said, though, he acknowledged a possible way to vitiate the moral argument. If morality were to point to God and nature did not, he admitted we might be obliged to admit that a postulate of ethics might not justify our turning it into a piece of speculative knowledge. His point here, then, seemed to be that the evidential significance of ethics isn't necessarily indefeasible—that the phenomena and postulates provided by the moral consciousness are part of a larger evidential picture. The examination of the universe as a whole might conceivably forbid us from accepting the view of things to which morality in isolation points.

Part of the import of this insight is something we saw earlier in this book: the moral argument works best in tandem with other evidential considerations rather than alone. Indeed, without elaborating further here, Rashdall then spent time showing why he was convinced that ethical and metaphysical deliverances dovetail and reinforce the conclusion that belief in God is eminently justified and rational. He saw them as mutually supportive of one another and, in the process, demonstrated his commitment to cumulative case-building, while retaining his conviction that the moral argument has distinctive contributions to make.

Religion and Morality

Having written at length on metaphysics, Rashdall shifted his attention to religion and various psychological considerations on these matters. Of particular interest to him was to explore the relationship between morality and religion in their developed forms. His primary concern was to estimate the ethical value and importance of religion in what he regarded as its highest form, the only form in which religion is fully in harmony with a sound reflective metaphysical analysis.

Rashdall recognized that the moral consciousness itself contains no explicit or immediate reference to any theological belief whatever. Nor does losing religious faith entail the loss of moral convictions. Still, the intellectual hold of morality upon his mind is weakened when he can give no account of it except that it is a way of thinking that evolution has somehow produced in creatures of his species.

Perhaps the language of defeaters can prove useful here; Rashdall's point isn't that loss or absence of theistic convictions provides a *rebutting* defeater to firm moral convictions but rather it provides something like an *undercutting* one. The psychological point here augments the earlier ones about metaphysics; considered in isolation the psychological point he's making surely doesn't entail theism. He did, however, think it an important point to bear in mind, one that helps flesh out the overall picture.

The metaphysics and psychology, though conceptually distinct, remain intimately intertwined. After all, rationality exercises influence over human conduct. When a belief is undermined, seen by its holder not to be as rooted in reality as previously thought, seen as nonrational if not irrational, a diminution of its influence on behavior should be expected. The alleged prescriptive power of such obligations often comes to be seen as epistemically indulgent and ontologically extravagant once the foundations are lost. As a result, such rich language as objective guilt, categorical obligations, and binding authority tends to be replaced with more domesticated notions of guilty feelings, instrumental obligations, and contingent reasons for action.

Adherence to a theistic picture instead "represents the form of belief about the Universe in which the intellectual hold of Morality upon the human mind tends to attain its maximum intensity."[35] Rashdall boldly asserted that theism is the creed that best secures the maximal emotional hold of human morality on the mind. Whereas motivation by nothing but the moral law itself is possible, it's rare even in the best people. Morality seldom excites the strongest emotion till it is embodied in a self-conscious Being; personal influence is the strongest of all moral motive powers.[36]

For this reason he thought it misguided when advocates of a purely "ethical religion" "expatiate on the additional purity which a nontheistic creed gives to moral aspiration. It is forgotten that the love of God means simply love for a Person who is the highest good and the source of all other goodness." Christianity, in particular, in its focus on God's essential goodness and Trinitarian essence of love, is especially clear on this relational aspect of morality, which is why Rashdall considered it peculiarly effective at stirring the highest moral motivations.[37] It's psychologically impracticable to expect to be motivated as strongly by an abstract principle or impersonal moral law than by an all-loving Person.[38]

For Rashdall, what most fills the prospect of an afterlife with significance is the highest form of religious reality: the love of God. The religious motive at its highest is the love of God for his own sake and not merely for any reward from him.[39] He wrote, "In the love of God the two strongest emotional forces which make for Morality in this world find their fullest and most harmonious satisfaction—reverence for the moral ideal and love of Humanity. . . .

Devotion to the moral ideal and to the true good of Humanity is, indeed, at bottom identical with the love of God."

Belief in the moral ideal attains its maximum momentum when it is identified with the love of a Person.[40] On a Christian view of ethics, the love of humanity can't degenerate into an otherworldly or antisocial pietism or mere sentiment; on the contrary, the transcendent goods invest the temporal goods with the deeper significance they were meant to bespeak all along.[41]

Synopsis: Rashdall critiqued Sidgwick's inability to see that rational benevolence has primacy over rational self-love, so while recognizing the dualism of practical reason, Rashdall underscored the strength of at least certain versions of theism to account for the priority of benevolence and altruism. As both a moral apologist and kind of utilitarian, Rashdall also demonstrated that agreement on normative ethical matters is not a prerequisite for proponents of the moral argument. What's needed more centrally is an essential dependence relation of morality on God, not agreement on the peripheral matter of fine-grained normative analysis. Rashdall argued that a generous empiricism won't domesticate morality but will instead insist on allowing the deliverances of morality, the binding nature of the moral law, and the transcendent implications and aspirations of the moral good to inform his metaphysics. Like others, he thought the moral argument works best when combined with other pieces of natural theology.

9

An Oxford Nolloth Professor
Clement Webb

At the apex of an impossibly narrow, very English spiral staircase atop one particular towering spire at Oriel College at Oxford University is a small archive room; it is there that a two-volume memoir of Clement Webb (1865--1954) can be found. The handwritten, never-published volumes include the wide-ranging musings of this long-time Oxford professor and Gifford and Wilde lecturer. Despite his distinguished career, Webb is not usually near the top of the list of notable moral apologists, but his work certainly contributed an important chapter in the history of the moral argument.

The charming narrative of his memoir includes this humorous anecdote. Sheepish in admitting he had met just a handful of famous people, he tried to compensate by recounting having met Charles-François Gounod, the famous French composer best known for his *Ave Maria*, based on a work by Bach, as well as his opera *Faust*. Gounod was a refugee from his native country at the time, and Webb's father was a great admirer of his music. In 1870 Gounod made an appearance at Webb's house. Webb recalled sitting on his father's knee looking up at the great man, and his father's words afterward: "An oaf had met a genius."

By coincidence it was the same year that Webb reports, in obvious retrospect, having been seized by "a sudden outbreak of metaphysical wonder like that which according to Carlyle is recorded of John Paul Richter, from which I date the habit of reflection that was to turn me at last into a professional philosopher."[1]

Webb was five years old. This may have been his first significant spiritual experience, but it wasn't his last.

A Short Biography

Webb was a fairly private man, reticent to share much of his personal history or individual testimony. Still, quite a bit of material is available about his private life because of the autobiographical information he shared in J. H. Muirhead's *Contemporary British Philosophy*, the memoir at Oriel, and several years' worth of daily journals he wrote that are housed at the Bodleian at Oxford.[2] What we will canvas here is just a small portion of this material, some of which has not been published before.

Webb was born in London in 1865, the youngest child of several children. Webb's father was a well-known London clergyman and a graduate of Cambridge, and his grandfather on his mother's side had been a Cambridge professor. Webb's older brothers went to Christ Church, Oxford, as would Webb. His childhood home featured a high standard of morality and duty, with little felt need for a personal conversion for young people raised as Christians who hadn't wandered from the faith.

This made it all the more surprising when, in Webb's first year at Christ Church, he experienced another formative spiritual episode, a significant "conversion" of sorts, and a turning point in his spiritual history. It left him with a profound conviction of the reality of God and of the duty of open-mindedness and intellectual honesty; "a belief that it was the first of religious duties to keep one's ears open to any voice, from whatever quarter, which might convey a message from God; a delightful sense of expectation of strange and wonderful things."[3]

Webb had always been religious and interested in religion. Early introduced to it in a clerical home full of books dealing with such subjects, he remained in close touch with the traditions of the Oxford movement and with the church life of London. By his own account, moods of premature *Weltschmerz* (melancholy) would eventually become familiar to him, leaving him "face to face with a dreary abyss of gray infinity." His unbidden conversion in 1885 came as an epiphany, but eventually he recognized its essential agreement with the "crisis" that evangelicals, of whom he knew little and on whom he'd been inclined to look down as intellectually inferior and theologically uneducated, held to be "the breaking in of God upon the life of his creatures." This gave him a new sympathy with them. "The grey infinity in the background of human life had been flooded with the light of a divine presence," as he put it.[4]

It was in this mood that he came to the study of philosophy. Bouts with melancholy were balanced by a strong affective and imaginative sense of the continuity of history, fostered by all his time at Westminster and Oxford with its traditions, customs, and venerable surroundings. He grew up into a man insatiably curious about ideas. At Oxford he typically read in the mornings, often in the Bodleian. For years and years he kept a careful daily log of his activities and observations. Consistency was an ingrained feature of his character, and it was evident in numerous ways—from his daily reading, faithful church attendance, regular journal entries, and reliable routine. Immersed in Oxford life, he often frequented Addison's Walk and was poignantly aware of nature. He had an eye for detail, a sense of the importance of the everyday, and a refined aesthetic taste for lovely views, the "glorious moonlight," and "rapid progress of thaw."[5]

He was deeply relational, always generous to colleagues, loyal, and ever careful to note and pay homage to lost companions. He wrote an important contribution to *The Life of Hastings Rashdall*, a close friend and colleague with whom, despite their differences, he enjoyed a warm relationship.[6] In his memoir and journals, Webb was fond of speaking of various dear friendships, and he had several quite longstanding ones. His was a giving spirit with a crackling good humor, and in light of his penchant for privacy, he had a surprisingly disarming willingness to share his vulnerabilities. He genuinely seemed to like people, which perhaps helps explain his affinity for reading autobiographies.

Webb was deeply devoted to his wife and enjoyed a strong marriage. Her health concerns in later life—fits of asthma and recurring collapses—created no small amount of consternation for both of them. Losing her, at long last, meant the savor of writing his memoir was lost, but he soldiered on.

Though an academic, he remained vitally engaged with current events. He noted the selection of a new pope, and he passionately cared about passage of a minimum wage bill, for example. He reported reading about the sinking of the *Titanic*, and he stayed preoccupied with the war, mentioning air raids intermittently. He followed World War I closely, beginning with the day it was declared, July 28, 1914. He was obviously very concerned about its extent and the lives lost. Although he rarely talked of personal feelings, he did say several times that the war made him anxious. Like Sorley, he gave his Gifford lectures in the midst of the war, which is a telling indicator of the relevance of his philosophical ideas—and the moral argument!—to the harsh realities of life.

In his undergraduate days at Oxford the influence of T. H. Green, whose death had taken place only a few years before, and whose posthumous *Prolegomena to Ethics* had just been published, was at its height.[7] He noted that for his own generation of Oxford men the starting point of their various philosophical developments was usually to be sought in the idealistic criticism of John Stuart Mill and Herbert Spencer for which Green stood.

The *Prolegomena to Ethics*, however, was not the philosophical book that most influenced Webb during his undergraduate days. His mind was, like that of all who are trained in the traditional "Greats" Oxford course, continually shaped by the intensive study of Plato's *Republic* and Aristotle's *Ethics*. Most significantly of all, it was a translation of Kant's *Groundwork of the Metaphysics of Morals* that triggered his philosophical imagination. Its presentation of morality as a "categorical imperative" made an extraordinary impression upon him, reviving the sentiments of his conversion of two years before, and leaving ineffaceable traces on all his subsequent thought. Turning now to his relevant work on moral apologetics, we will see that this is indeed the case.

Wilde Lectures: Studies in the History of Natural Theology

Webb's work on the moral argument can't be adequately expressed in tidy discursive format; it is more piecemeal and fragmentary than that. This is not for lack of coherence or orderliness of thought, but perhaps in part it owes to what he viewed as his role. He saw himself as a philosopher, first and foremost. For several decades he labored at Magdalen College, chiefly on the philosophy of religion, to which his interests in medieval studies greatly contributed. Religion provided him his primary motive to do philosophy, but he discerned a danger in becoming an apologist.

Echoing a sentiment we've heard before, he didn't see himself as out to promote an agenda or to proselytize. His temperament actually led him to refrain from sharing much about his personal spiritual pilgrimage. Perhaps what most bothered him about some popular apologists was the way he thought they were draping their work with the cloak of philosophy, and in the process underestimating the complexity and difficulty of significant philosophical questions. So visceral was his aversion to such a practice that he was adamant to be on his guard against it, thinking nothing less lovely than apologetic masquerading as philosophy. He saw himself first and foremost as a philosopher seeking the truth.[8]

As a philosopher, what he wrote about the moral argument was usually in the context of a sustained discussion of broader issues—like whether sacrifices to the divine are consistent with a moral religion or how we define the personality of God—and, as a result, these pieces need to be collected and stitched together. Rather than a single, sustained moral argument, what Webb offered, in various places, were contributions in each of the three main tasks of the moral apologetic endeavor: a defense of moral realism, a critique of naturalistic ethics, and a defense of theistic ethics (and, on occasion, specifically Christian ethics). Rarely did he treat any of his efforts as decisive arguments or his favored suggestions as the only possible solutions to the problems that arise. His epistemic humility shouldn't be mistaken, however, for lack of solid contributions to the discussion.

Examples of Webb's interactions with Plato and Kant and his contributions to various dimensions of the moral argument can be found in his Wilde lectures delivered at Oxford during the academic years 1911–1912 and 1912–1913. The relationship between morality and religion was a central preoccupation of his Wilde lectures, and Webb characterized Plato, more than anyone else, as taking great pains to establish the union of religion and morality. To Plato "an immoral religion was the worst form of blasphemy or irreligion, and an irreligious morality (such as the morality of the Sophists who grounded moral distinctions in merely arbitrary conventions that are not in the ultimate and eternal nature of the Universe) was twin with atheism."[9]

The relevant portion of Plato is the tenth book of his *Laws*, which is concerned with the religion common to man. Plato was concerned to combat three mischievous views: first, the view that there are no gods; second, that there are gods, but that they take no care for man; and third, that the gods take care for men but are easily persuaded by sacrifice. Respectively, this can be summarized as follows: (1) there are no gods; (2) there are indifferent gods; and (3) there are gods corruptible by sacrifice. Plato used moral criteria to assess these conflicting truth claims. That there are no gods, for example, was not a wholly bad choice when it was the morally deficient gods of the pantheon that were on offer, fostering "disgust felt at the stories told by the poets about the gods, such as that of the mutilation of Uranus by his son Cronos."[10]

Still, atheism wasn't much of a living option for Plato, for a few different reasons.[11] Indifferent gods, likewise, would be morally unacceptable. As Webb pointed out, "The canon laid down by Plato in the *Republic* that no evil is to be ascribed to God, would ... [make] almost a clean sweep of the Greek mythology, as well that contained in the Orphic literature as that related by Homer and Hesiod."[12] Webb contended that Plato's canon of theology "was the assertion that nothing but what was good should be ascribed to God."[13]

Plato was equally resistant to the notion of propitiating the gods, connecting such a possibility with manipulable and manipulating gods, unbefitting and unbecoming of supreme Goodness. What made this challenge by Plato particularly interesting to Webb is that the Christian faith, of which he was an adherent, makes propitiation for sins a cardinal article of its theology. Webb thus spent time exploring the question of whether the Christian doctrine of the atonement for sin effected by the death of Christ is as morally suspect as the doctrines associated with the mysteries of Orphicism. In the course of Webb's analysis on this matter, he made a detour through a central element in the ethical system of Immanuel Kant.

So the question before Webb was the moral status of the sacrificial idea in Christianity and whether it serves as moral evidence against its truth. Note that, in concert with Plato, Webb thought that moral evidence can count importantly, even decisively, in figuring out the nature of ultimate reality. But he would partially demur from Plato on this question of propitiation by arguing for morally relevant distinctions between Orphicism and Christianity.

It's in this context—that of assessing the moral status of propitiation in Christianity—that Webb looked to Kant. Recall how influential Kant had been in Webb's intellectual development. Webb considered Kant unparalleled on the matter of the urgency of the moral consciousness. Whereas Webb appealed primarily to Plato for a robust conception of Goodness, he looked to Kant for his equally powerful notion of duty.[14]

The salient feature of Kant's ethical system at this juncture of the dialectic, however, was (what Webb characterized as) Kant's reduction of religion to ethics, "to confine [religion] 'within the limits of mere Reason,' namely, of the Practical Reason, which expresses itself in the consciousness of moral obligations."[15] Webb was not uncharitable toward Kant in this regard. He was admittedly unhappy with this aspect of Kant's analysis, but his was an objective effort to interpret Kant correctly. Armed with neither an ax to grind nor an agenda to push, he was careful to accord Kant accolades for genuine insights. Nobody emphasized duty better and more clearly than Kant, Webb contended. Still, Webb thought, Kant was comparatively inattentive to other aspects of morality that Webb believed need proper emphasis—aspects helpful in discussing the issue of propitiation.

The central culprit in Kant's ethical system, according to Webb, was Kant's emphasis on the autonomy of morality, without which morality loses its essence. Such autonomy, Webb argued, severs morality from the true nature of Reality, precluding morality from reflecting such Reality. Here it's worth quoting Webb himself at length:

> Our recognition of the moral law as binding, though it waits for no ulterior sanction, cannot be reconciled with the rest of our experience without such a faith in the actual supremacy of the Good as Plato (we remember) holds to be involved in the procedure of our reason. Now this faith is just what Religion supplies to Morality. Kant did not ignore this consideration altogether, but it also made him uncomfortable.[16]

Now, what does the conviction of the actuality and supremacy of the Good have to do with a belief in a propitiatory sacrifice? On Kant's view, the only morally significant actions a moral agent can perform are those done out of respect for the moral law—not out of, say, delight in loving what God loves. But Webb insisted that this leaves something important out of the picture—namely, "any room for such a cheerful and even joyful performance of his duty by man as the sense of intimate union with God." Webb argued that Kant here made man "not enough God." In contrast, God's "holy will," on Kant's view, was thought of as wholly free from the "moment of negativity which is essentially characteristic of ours." This, however, "makes God not enough a man."[17]

It's here the doctrine of propitiatory sacrifice comes into view once more, for "this character of the moral life as involving a negative moment is just what we call by a metaphor, so deeply rooted in our language that we hardly think of it as such, the element of self-sacrifice in Morality."[18] Kant was profoundly cognizant of sin, yet the blood of bulls can never take sin away. On a Christian picture, the outward sacrifices don't suffice—the moral agent himself must be willing to be sacrificed. It's only in this way that the autonomous personality is realized. "That such a sacrifice should be seen as the principle of the good life, and therefore, for the religious faith that the good life is not only to be lived by us but is actually lived eternally by God, as involved in the life of God himself, this is the thought of the Christian doctrine of the Atonement."[19]

The sacrifices of which Plato spoke, offered from worldly wealth to bribe divine justice, lowered the conception of God as moral governor, fostered horror not of sin but merely its consequences, and facilitated a spirit of antinomianism. In contrast, "the Christian doctrine spoke of a sacrifice offered not by the wicked but by the righteous, the benefit of which the wicked could only receive if by a genuine repentance they alienated themselves in will from their sin. Such a doctrine heightened the conception of divine justice and was incompatible with a resolve to go on sinning."[20]

Gifford Lectures: "Divine Personality and the Human Life"

If there is an optimal place to look for Webb doing explicit moral apologetics, it's likely the fifth of his Gifford lectures, "Divine Personality and the Moral Life." H. P. Owen would later write, "For the argument from the moral law to a divine Lawgiver, see especially Clement Webb," and he pointed specifically to that chapter.[21]

In 1922, John Baille wrote,

> The last decade has witnessed several notable additions to the literature of that peculiarly English philosophical movement which seems to have appropriated for itself the name of Ethical Theism and which goes back very largely to the writings of Campbell Fraser and Martineau. We have had especially Mr. Balfour's *Theism and Humanism*, Professor Pringle-Pattison's *Idea of God*, Professor Sorley's *Moral Values*, and Professor Clement Webb's *God and Personality*—all of them Gifford Lectures delivered in the Scottish universities and representing, on a broad view, the same general tendency of thought. There seems no doubt that these volumes, and the very considerable literature of which they are but the most important examples, are indicative of a reaction against the very confident English Hegelianism so widely sponsored in the previous generation.[22]

It is worth recalling that the 1910s were the decade of the First World War. Indeed, Webb delivered his Gifford lectures in the very throes of that war. It's actually telling that, during such dark hours, moral discourse retains and perhaps regains its purchase. Morality reduced to and construed as superficially playing by the rules and projecting a mere impression of virtue is an emaciated domestication of its radical truths whose wildness becomes vivid once more when the niceties of polite company break down and are seen as the superficial displays they often are.[23]

Webb's lauded Gifford lectures were delivered at Aberdeen in 1918 and 1919. The overall motif of the lectures was the divine personality, which shows that Webb was interested in broader questions than merely God's existence. He also devoted considerable energy to thinking about God's nature, including God's personality, beauty, and goodness. The specific lecture of most relevance to the topic of this chapter and book is the evidential significance of our consciousness of the moral law.

Casting it that way, as Webb did, makes phenomenology directly germane to his analysis, assuming as he did that our moral experience can provide veridical insight into the nature of reality. As our empirical experiences give us good reasons to believe in empirical objects, likewise, he thought (reiterating Sorley), our moral experience gives us excellent reasons to think they point to moral realities. Moreover, morality is one of the pieces of evidence that helps distinguish between rival theologies—such as between personalist and impersonalist theologies.[24]

Webb recognized that there are a number of competing theologies on offer. Again, recall, he saw himself as less an apologist and more a philosopher, so it wasn't his design to challenge people to a debate as much as to invite them to a dialogue and a discussion, and to subject views to critical scrutiny. By inviting adherents of divergent theological traditions to ponder the questions raised in this chapter, he found one way to acknowledge, once more, the breadth and complexity of this discussion without pretending to have done all the work himself.

Once again he spent a fair bit of time in this lecture in dialogue with Kant, whom he again characterized as a reductionist, largely deflating religion to morality.[25] Webb admitted that temptations to reductionist analyses become stronger the more personalist theologies become. Christianity, for example, furnishes a stronger temptation to reduce religion to morality than, say, polytheism or pantheism, because of the morally exalted status of God in Christian theology. Recall Webb adducing Plato's moral concerns about the gods inhabiting Greek lore.

Webb acknowledged that sometimes efforts are made in the opposite direction, pointing to arguments that atheism provides the more robust ethical view of the world. He cited an American philosopher named Parker, who caricatured traditional religious belief in condescending terms. In reply, Webb wrote, "But who could recognize in [Parker's] picture of a sheltered, timid, unadventurous faith, unbraced by the discipline of real life, the religion of Paul or Augustine or Dante or Luther or John of the Cross or Bunyan or Pascal or Wesley?"[26] Webb was concerned Parker spoke of something about which he knew little; Webb was willing to call out sophistry or cheap shots, from any direction.

Still, in an interesting moment of personal transparency, he wondered if there was at least some merit in the generally discredited view that atheism and morality might prove on occasion to be at odds after all—for to eschew belief in a divine moral lawgiver is to reject the idea of the category of an ultimate moral reckoning. In John Milton's words, it would mean liberation from having to live "as ever in my great Taskmaster's eye." By his own admission he said there were times when he himself was tempted to entertain atheism for just this reason. He ended that passage, though, with a stirring analysis considerably more penetrating:

> Yet I do not think that we can without much loss welcome in this way the disappearance from within us of that consciousness which the youthful Milton described in the famous line quoted above; except indeed where it is not the surrender of our belief in God but the perfecting of our love for him which has cast out from our souls the fear of his severe inquisition.[27]

Whatever reservations Webb may have had about Kant's view of religion, he had few about Kant's confidence in a binding moral law. Recall that this was an influence from Kant's writings that never left Webb after college and that deeply shaped his work. We can see in this shared commitment with Kant Webb's firm moral realism, his strong belief in the existence of objective and binding moral obligations.

Nevertheless, Webb thought that Kant got himself into trouble by using the unfortunate word "autonomy" in describing the right moral attitude. Kant's bona fide insight here is one Webb concurred with—namely, that there are duties featuring an intrinsic oughtness, actions unconditionally good and right that ought to be done for their own sake; and we have to come to see their moral necessity for ourselves. However, Webb thought it equally obvious that our thinking it doesn't make it so. It is just here that Kant's locution of "autonomy" was unfortunate, he thought, for it makes him susceptible to a major criticism.[28]

By insisting that nothing extrinsic can be the ground of moral duty, but only something within ourselves, Kant's views led to a paradox at best, a contradiction at worst. It makes the judge of our wrong actions the same as the wrongdoer—ourselves. Kant himself seemed to recognize the paradox and in part tried to solve it by his distinction between our phenomenal and noumenal selves; on occasion he pointed to God to resolve it. On Webb's reductionist reading of Kant, however, what was denied is anything in the vicinity of God's genuine authority to function as the ground of moral obligation.

Webb wrote that, in Kant's

> anxiety to disclaim any knowledge, properly so called, of a Being who transcended what he took to be the conditions of any knowledge open to our intelligence, he missed, as it seems to me, the true conclusion to be drawn from that consciousness of moral obligation which few have felt more profoundly and no one perhaps described more accurately than he.[29]

So here is where Webb thought that Kant could have done better and tightened his moral argument, establishing a more direct connection between God and morality. Arguably it's just this inference, this case for theistic ethics, that was Webb's most explicit statement of his moral argument. In making the case for a theistic ethic, a divine foundation for the moral law, one can make such a case either positively or negatively. Here we will lay out Webb's positive case, and in the concluding section we will mention his defense against an objection that can arise.

Webb looked for inspiration at this stage of the dialectic to James Martineau, referred to earlier in this chapter in a quote from Baille. Martineau's works *Types of Ethical Theory* and *A Study of Religion* proved instrumental in shaping Webb's thought.[30] Here's how Webb articulated his debt to Martineau:

> The appearance of Martineau's two great works on Ethics and the Philosophy of Religion . . ., at a time when (especially at Oxford) the influence of Green was at its height made them, largely no doubt on account of their style which was that of their author's generation (he was in his eightieth year when the earlier of the two appeared), seem to some who, like myself, were then young students of philosophy, old-fashioned and lacking in profundity. In later years I have re-read them with greatly increased admiration, and have seen how well this writer deserved the commendation which I recollect my lamented teacher, Professor Cook Wilson, long ago

bestowing on him for his bold faithfulness to the facts of our common moral experience.[31]

Webb thought that Martineau's words contained the needed corrective to Kant's approach: "In the act of Perception," Martineau wrote, "we are immediately introduced to an *other than ourselves* that gives us what we feel; in the act of Conscience we are immediately introduced to a *Higher than ourselves* that gives us what we feel" (emphases added).[32]

To avoid identifying accused and accuser, we have to look to something beyond the self as the source of moral obligations, and moral experience and the logic of duties seem to bear this out. Webb cited Martineau to the effect that it takes two to establish an obligation; the person who bears the obligation can't also be the person whose presence imposes it. It's impossible to be "at once the upper and the nether millstone. Personality is unitary and in occupying one side of a given relation is unable to be also on the other."[33]

Webb conceded that Kant wanted to speak on occasion *as if* the moral law can be personified as something distinct from one's own personality; we are to live as though we were free, immortal, and under moral government, requiring we postulate guiding or regulative principles of conduct, but we must not assert them as a matter of knowledge.[34] Following Martineau, and departing from Kant, Webb thought the more principled and straightforward solution of the problem prescribed to the intellect by the putative fact of moral obligation is the frank recognition of a personal God.

Such a God, Webb insisted, is "not only immanent but transcendent, with whom a relation only to be described as personal intercourse is possible, and is, in the experience of Religion, actually enjoyed."[35] Such dynamic interaction with a living God, however, requires transcending Kant's epistemic limitations, and apprehending the real authority of the moral law requires recognizing the existence of "another than I . . . another greater and higher and of deeper insight."[36]

Webb thought moral duty posed a strong challenge to Kant's attempt to cordon off knowledge of God, because the moral law, by Kant's admission and insistence, is worthy of reverence. Yet elsewhere Kant had argued that it is only *persons* who are worthy of reverence. Once again Webb credited Martineau for discerning the theistic implications of the sentiment of reverence.[37] Webb wrote, "The frank recognition, which we find in Martineau, of the theistic implications of the consciousness of obligation is a step forward which we shall do well to make," although, in making it, Webb suggested we remain mindful of Kant's motives in resisting it.[38]

Among Kant's reasons for reticence here are included the tendency, common in his time, to reduce morality to something else, whether a consideration of consequences or something more distinctively religious. He also had a visceral aversion to sanction anything that would undermine human dignity, not to mention a haunting dread of religious dogma and fideistic fanaticism. Webb was sensitive to these worries and encouraged that they be taken seriously.

He thought this could be done, however, while departing from Kant in a few important ways that could salvage the authority of and reverence for the moral law, both the transcendence and immanence of God, and the possibility of living commerce with a personal God, while also avoiding identifying judge and accused.

Opus Postumum

Before drawing this chapter to a close, a word must be added about the whole book Webb wrote about Kant in 1926, especially in light of Webb's reductionist account of Kant. The last chapter of *Kant's Philosophy of Religion* examined a fragmentary work found after Kant's death among his papers that has come to be known as *Opus Postumum*. By then Webb had had the chance to examine that work and some scholarly descriptions of it, especially work by the German philosopher Erich Adickes.

In brief, here were some of Webb's most important conclusions. By the time Kant wrote this material very late in life (between 1800 and 1803), his sense of the manifestation of God in nature seemed clouded by a doubt of the *goodness* of the power thus revealed. Moreover, this divine origin is immediately revealed in the law itself. "In recognizing the Law we find ourselves in God's presence; and the language of personal intercourse is no longer forbidden us as involving an inadmissible severance of God from his Law; for the Law itself *is* the revelation of his Personality."[39]

This was at least how such Kantian passages struck Webb: "In the world considered as a totality of rational beings, there is also a totality of morally practical Reason, and consequently of an imperative Right (*Rechtsimperativ*) and therewith also a God."[40] Webb took Kant to be conceiving of God as revealed in the moral law "taken as a whole," in virtue of their common subjection to which all rational beings form a single whole or community such as Kant elsewhere had described as a kingdom of ends. The result, Webb thought, was intimation of the consciousness of a *personal* God.[41]

To illuminate why this is important in our study, we quote further from Webb:

> Without any knowledge of the *Opus Postumum*, Adickes's account of which was then unpublished, I observed in 1920 that Kant, while coming very near to, had notwithstanding never reached the conclusion which was, as I contended, legitimately to be drawn from that consciousness of moral obligation which no one has felt more profoundly and described more accurately than he; the conclusion stated by Martineau in these words: "In the act of conscience we are immediately introduced to the Higher than ourselves that gives us what we feel." In the *Opus Postumum* I think we may say that *he does reach that conclusion* (emphasis added).[42]

Although this concession is significant indeed, Webb still remained critical of Kant on two main points: Kant's unhistorical and inordinately individualist approach, and his making mathematical and physical science the sole standard of genuine knowledge. More positively, however, Webb accentuated three significant truths at the heart of Kant's thoughts on religion: the rationality of religion, the implicitly ethical character of religion, and the ethical or ethically rational character of the Christian religion "as the feature distinctive of it among the religions of the world, entitling it to stand apart from the rest as the true religion."[43] Webb retained an abiding appreciation of Kant's repeated and characteristic insistence that efforts to apprehend God "behind the back" of the moral law are altogether inconsistent with any religion in which an enlightened conscience can acquiesce.[44] Morality is too important not to play a role in understanding God.

Political Implications

One more point merits emphasis. It's been saved for last because it isn't the most central part of Webb's moral argument per se. Yet it's important to note because it highlights some of the broader significance of this discussion about the foundations of ethics. Webb finished his analysis of the moral life by drawing a parity between the authority of the moral law to which the individual recognizes he's subject with the principle of authority in the community of which he's a part. He claimed that the recognition of the consciousness of obligation as essentially a consciousness of God has important consequences in the sphere of political philosophy.

Recall Webb's agreement with Kant that at least some moral duties are intrinsically obvious; their authority should be obvious without having first to appeal to anything divine. Rather than undermining the moral argument, this is a necessary condition for it in order to avoid circularity. The line to God is then an inferential one. At any rate, he thought the historical case could be made for a close connection between Kantian autonomy and, in the political arena, "self-determination"—moral freedom as envisioned by Kant and political liberty as it developed under democratic governance. Now, remember Webb's reservations about the locution of "autonomy" because of its possibility of misinterpretation. Webb insisted that dangers of misinterpretation are *even greater* when we pass from the region of individual duty to that of political obligation.

Webb wrote,

> For while in the sphere of the individual's moral life the frequent incompatibility of duty and pleasure is obvious, and there is even a tendency—found, as is well known, in Kant himself—to exaggerate its frequency, in the sphere of Politics the pursuit of the general happiness may be so plausibly represented as the whole content of public duty, the sole end of public action, that it is especially easy here first to think of a "common good" rather than a "common obligation," and then to interpret this "common good" in terms which really in the end are terms of individual happiness or pleasure. In this way the principle of Authority comes to be dissolved, and of the two aspects of the political community which at one period obtained historical expression in the rival theories of the "social contract" and of the "divine right of kings" respectively we lose sight of the latter altogether. Yet I venture to think that both these aspects must be kept in view if we are to realize a social unity which will be satisfactory to our moral consciousness.[45]

Webb lived in a monarchy, of course, so some of his language strikes those who don't as, well, a bit foreign; but the point he was making is a profound one. The underlying concern is the diminution in priority of public goods and political duties, eclipsed by concerns for personal happiness and private interests. He was convinced that no other explanation of both the internal and external aspects of public morality "will be found in the last resort satisfactory but one which exhibits it as the presence of God to the soul which is made in his image, after his likeness."[46]

On his view,

> the legitimate authority in the community will have in the strictest sense of the word a "divine right" to the obedience of its members; but that authority alone can be described as legitimate which is established by consent, just as in the individual's moral life the only way by which I can know the command of God to be his is by the recognition that this and nothing else can I will, in Kant's phrase, "as law universal," that is to say disinterestedly, and as what it is not merely pleasant but *right* I should do.[47]

We end on this note simply to point out that a loss of transcendent foundations in morality is not merely an academic concern. It potentially has important repercussions in the political arena. Not only in England but in many other places of the world today, Webb's warning seems prescient and his worries vindicated; inadequate moral foundations will manifest in the public square with a compromised moral authority for amicably adjudicating conflicts between increasingly polarized personal commitments and identities. Questions about moral foundations have far-reaching implications in the arena of political philosophy.

> Synopsis: The work Clement Webb did on the moral argument often had for its context wider theological questions that he wished to explore. He primarily looked to Plato for inspiration about the nature of moral goodness, and he looked to Immanuel Kant on the nature of moral duties. Although he initially thought Kant had reduced religion to morality, he eventually softened on that conviction. As empirical experience justifies belief in an external world, he took our moral experience as solid justification for belief in moral realities. Inspired by James Martineau, Webb argued that the phenomenology of moral duties (that Kant explained so well) warranted belief in departing from an overambitious kind of Kantian autonomy that precludes belief in a "Higher than ourselves" (Martineau's words) that gives us the moral law. For Webb, sanction for belief in such an ultimate Source is found in morality, a Source both immanent and transcendent. Finally, Webb also saw some of the profound political implications of the erosion of moral foundations.

10

The Gregarious Aristocrat

W. G. de Burgh

W. G. de Burgh's friend A. E. Taylor supplied many of his basic biographical details:

> William George de Burgh, born at New Wandsworth on 24 October 1866, was the son of William de Burgh, a barrister holding a post at the War Office, and of his wife, Hannah Jane Monck Mason, a great-granddaughter of Samuel Whitbread, and granddaughter of the Lady Grey (great-grandmother to Viscount Grey of Falloden) who was well known in the Evangelical movement of her day. Of his paternal uncles, one, Maurice de Burgh, was Archdeacon of Ness, another, Hubert, became a priest in the Roman Catholic Church. Dean de Burgh, his paternal grandfather, was the builder of the church at Sandymount, Dublin. He was thus of mixed Norman-Irish and Northumberland strain, an "aristocrat" in the proper sense of a much abused word... his mother (who lost her own father early) was much attached to her uncle, Sir George Grey, Home Secretary, and to her cousins, in particular to Thomas Baring, Lord Northbrook.[1]

De Burgh was "tall, slim, bespectacled, and of aristocratic features," displayed a "religiously-grounded optimism which looked for the best in others, and could write off no one," and was known for his gregarious disposition.[2]

Educated at Oxford, de Burgh taught at the University of Reading, and his works included *Towards a Religious Philosophy* (1937), *From Morality to Religion* (1938), *The Legacy of the Ancient World* (1924, rev. ed. 1947), and *The Life of Reason* (1949). He strove to defend Christianity against fideism and logical positivism, and he is one of four noted thinkers in Alan P. F. Sell's *Four Philosophical Anglicans: W. G. de Burgh, W. R. Matthews, O. C. Quick, H. A. Hodges*.

For many years, both de Burgh's teaching and administrative duties proved absorbing. He taught classics and added philosophy to his curriculum and became professor of the subject in 1907. At Reading he guided the development of the college into a university. He was Gifford lecturer at St. Andrews in 1937–1938 and Riddell Memorial lecturer at Newcastle in 1938. His Gifford lectures were published as *From Morality to Religion*, the moral argument of which will be our focus in this chapter. In the summer of 1942, while walking on the Dorset downs, de Burgh suffered a stroke and died at his home, The Cottage, Toller Porcorum, Dorset, in August 1943. He was survived by his wife and was buried at Toller Porcorcum on August 30.

De Burgh sought to formulate a Christian philosophy by constructing a philosophical argument to the truth of the gospel, in many ways a countercultural project unpopular at a time of philosophical upheaval. Protestant theologians were disparaging reason, and few philosophers paid heed to religion. Sell's book fills in several other salient features of de Burgh's intellectual milieu. Idealistic metaphysics was under strong attack; science was held in high esteem by many; the scientific method was deemed by some to be the sole method of arriving at truth. The ideas of the German-born Swiss Reformed theologian Karl Barth—who lived from 1886 to 1968 and who, despite his aversion to natural theology, gave the Gifford lectures in 1937 and 1938—were much in the air. Barthian theology seemed to entail a "retreat from reason into a circle of revelation." Logical positivists were branding religious, aesthetic, and moral discourse nonsense.[3]

Ensconced in such a context, two major themes echo in de Burgh's work: One is the necessity of understanding that reason has to do with more than ratiocination (conscious deliberate inference), since it always includes an element of intuition of first principles. Second is the need of morality to find its *completeness* in religion. The points are related; the first is an epistemic point. Repeatedly in the history of the moral argument epistemological analysis has preceded and paved the way for the ethical, and here the pattern recurs.

A. E. Taylor wrote this concerning de Burgh's recognition of the limitations of reason narrowly construed:

> The point which [de Burgh] . . . makes with exceptional clarity, and on which I confess I completely sympathize with him, is that the whole position [regarding religion as a possible source of genuine knowledge] is bound up with the admission that truth, in the widest sense of the word, is not confined to the logical propositional form; there is a wider sense of the word in which we can speak of the truth not only of a religious insight, but of that of sense-perception or of *moral divination* or of *aesthetic intuition* (emphasis added).[4]

De Burgh's Moral Argument

Turning now to de Burgh's reflections on the moral argument: he devoted one chapter most particularly to it in his Gifford lectures–turned-book *From Morality to Religion*.[5] It's a rich chapter but in various respects derivative, depending heavily on Taylor, Sorley, and Kant. Rather than reiterating those aspects of the chapter, we wish here in rather short compass to highlight some of the other, more original, points. We don't pretend to cover all the important points, but we will endeavor to discuss at least several of the more central ones.

Consonant with his epistemic modus operandi, de Burgh acknowledged that faith in the *good* does not *necessitate* theism, but it does, he argued, *incline* toward it. Again we see a major moral apologist endorsing a less-than-deductivist account of the argument, not considering it a slam dunk, but more in the vicinity of a best explanation of relevant phenomena. De Burgh was convinced that when we think out the implications of the desire for good, the process comes to fruition in a *summum bonum* inclusive of all goods. He noted that history bore that out with the development of Buddhism into a metaphysical religion and neo-Platonists' gravitation toward more than a Platonic Form, something more like a soul as the primal source of being and of value.

For de Burgh, intrinsic to humanity is purposive activity that points forward to value; as teleological creatures humans are ideal-forming animals whose thought and conduct are guided by standards of truth and goodness. In this he found a link between Christianity and Platonism: "Widely different as are the knowledge of the Christian religion and that of the Platonic philosophy, they are at one in that for both (a) the supreme good is the supreme reality, (b) this supreme good is knowable, [and] (c) this knowledge is indissolubly bound up with love."[6]

The life of *duty* also points toward religion, he argued. First, negatively, because of our moral weakness: "No man of acute moral sensibility can be blind to the abyss that parts the austere requirements of the moral law from his unavailing efforts to satisfy them."[7] The result is one of nothing less than *despair* at the prospect of meeting the moral demand—reminiscent of Paul's words in Romans 7—which functions as a *praeparatio evangelica*, for it "brings with it a longing for release from bondage to the law and a readiness to find a refuge in divine grace."[8] More positively, though, the moral law inspires reverence, and "reverence for the law leads to reverence for its author." Few remain content with reverence for an abstract principle, even of moral obligation. "Reverence is naturally reverence for a person."[9]

Harkening back to an earlier point, de Burgh reiterated that the sort of evidence that natural theology provides for God is not a rigorous demonstration like that found in mathematics or pure logic; rather it is "a question of cumulative probability, for which religious and non-religious experience alike supply the evidence." Of special evidential and epistemic significance is *morality*:

> The more clearly we distinguish between morality and religion, the more need is there to test religious beliefs by their coherence with moral beliefs and moral practice. The supernatural would not be the supernatural, nor the transcendent the transcendent, were they not imaged immanently in the order of nature. And where is the image discernible, if not in man's consciousness of moral obligation?[10]

Regarding any particular argument for God's existence, de Burgh went out of his way to emphasize that, by itself, such an argument won't be enough because of the fact that "the evidences for theism are cumulative, and that none of the arguments carries its full weight without the others." Not only did de Burgh move away from *deductivism*, in other words; he also endorsed *cumulative case-building*. He lauded Dawes Hicks for having rendered a great service to religious philosophy by presenting in his Hibbert lectures "the cosmological, teleological, and moral arguments as grades in a hierarchical order, the first providing the groundwork for the second, and the second for the third."[11] De Burgh concurred, thinking the moral argument something of the capstone in rational theology.

De Burgh's explanation for the great interest in the moral argument in modern thought is that its fuller formulations required the idea of moral obligation to come into its own and be subjected to philosophical analysis. This took Kant. "The moral argument has been more fully discussed, especially in Britain, during the last hundred years than any of the other arguments to theism."[12] De Burgh also recognized, however, that it faced serious challenges, a few of which de Burgh wished to discuss. Before doing so, he elaborated a bit on Kant's formulation of the argument.

At first, de Burgh wrote, it looked as if Kant had brought God in to secure a connection between moral desert and happiness, which can't be otherwise conjoined. Kant made a concerted effort to focus on God's transcendence.

God's will is a holy will; man's will at its best can be but good. God is sovereign, while man is but a member in the kingdom of ends. Kant's zeal to vindicate the autonomy of morality from dependence on the sanctions of religion contributed to Kant's representation of God as though he were an external arbiter of human destinies.

However, de Burgh thought that this analysis could miss Kant's driving point—namely, that moral experience implies a morally ordered world. Kant's assumption was the experience of the *unconditionality of moral obligation* given as fact in the common moral consciousness. Such obligations aren't externally imposed, but, when properly discharged, they furnish the ultimate freedom. "It implies an ordered moral environment ... pointing to the concept of a kingdom of ends wherein finite rational beings are at once autonomous members and subject to the sovereignty of God." De Burgh added, "As the final step in the argument, Kant posits a transcendent Deity as the source alike of the moral order and of our obligation to act in accordance with its law."[13]

On de Burgh's reading, then, Kant's variant of the moral argument is that the consciousness of obligation, if it be not illusory, implies the reality of a moral order, and the reality of a moral order implies the existence of God as its author and sustainer. Rather than offering an alternative account, de Burgh instead decided to discuss a few salient objections to the argument, which will be briefly mentioned here. The first involves the inference from the reality of moral values to their source in God. Even admitting that if morality is not a delusion then it must have a status in reality, does such recognition entail or even render probable God's existence? Second, does ascribing moral attributes or even goodness to God implicate one in anthropomorphism?

On the first matter, de Burgh saw that a Platonistic conception according to which there are timeless Forms goes some way toward justifying the absoluteness that the moral consciousness discovers in the ideal source of obligation. Such a view would rule out naturalism, but it would prevent any entailment from morality to religion. But de Burgh still thought theism has the upper hand over Platonism, because an important moral phenomenon here in need of adequate explanation is what the rational ground is of the obligation to strive to realize in *this* world what's already real in *another*.

He thought the Platonist can only assure us that the ideal is a reality beyond the scope of our achievement, and "bid us do the best we can, in our own strength and that of our fellows, in the Sisyphus-labor of approximation to a goal that must forever elude attainment."[14] The moral argument, as advanced by Sorley and Taylor (on whose work de Burgh relied), provided a way out by claiming that "the reality of values and their relation to the reality of the temporal process is rendered more intelligible than on any other hypothesis if we conceive of values as possessed of reality, not per se, but in the mind of an actually existing God."[15]

On the second matter, anthromorphism, de Burgh shared an insight that's instructive to remember when thinking about the moral argument. Kant saw no difficulty in conceiving of God as a moral being endowed with moral attributes. But de Burgh wondered if the matter were that simple. "Does not the assertion that God is good involve an unwarrantable anthropomorphism?"[16] Whereas Kant held that the moral law, as the true expression of reason, is a principle of volition for all rational beings, including God, de Burgh demurred. "Holiness is not a moral but a religious attribute. Morality is something all-too-human to be ascribed to God. To hold that he is the ground of the moral law is one thing, to predicate 'moral' of him, even by way of analogy, is quite another."[17]

What de Burgh had to offer here was a bit off the beaten path, but since he was addressing an objection to the moral argument for God's existence, it's not irremediably off track. In fact, it provides a chance to emphasize a couple illuminating points. De Burgh recognized that Aquinas had taken up the challenge of how to predicate moral properties of God, particularly in light of human epistemic limitations and God's exalted status. The likeness between God and man is, by Aquinas's lights, unilateral rather than reciprocal; it's truer to say that "we image God" rather than "God images us," which would indeed be anthropomorphic. But since the order of being is different from the order of knowing, we can only rise to the knowledge of God indirectly from our sense-experience of created things. Further, from our judgments as to the relative value of created things there is implied an ideal of perfection, free from the defects that attach to its imperfect embodiments in the world of our experience.

"Hence, St. Thomas argues, we are justified in ascribing to God, who is the perfect unity of all perfections, such predicates, drawn from our experience, as express 'absolute perfection without defect ... such as goodness, wisdom, being, and the like,'" says de Burgh.[18] These must, however, be ascribed to God neither univocally nor equivocally, but rather analogically. De Burgh's query, however, was whether we are warranted in any application of the term "goodness" to God at all. He suspected that Aquinas, in his battles with pantheists, erred on the side of emphasizing God's *transcendence*, and that some of his statements could use to be balanced by a stronger sense of God's *immanence*. In particular de Burgh thought the place to look for an example of the inadequacy of analogical ascriptions to God is the relation of love between God and man.

Here de Burgh unapologetically (in both senses) explored implications of distinctively Christian theology. Between God's unbearable holiness and man's sin and corruption there's a bridge: the Incarnation.

> On the one side we have the infinite assuming finitude, in the perpetual re-enactment of the Incarnation in the souls of men; on the other side we have the finite, in process of regeneration and transformation by grace into a veritable participation in infinitude. "God became man"—we may add, and ever becomes man—"in order that man may be made divine."[19]

When de Burgh studied St. Bernard's *Sermons on the Canticles*, for example, he saw that in the twelfth century the love of God was the object of deep and constant study among the contemplative orders. De Burgh concluded that, had Bernard lived a century later, he would have regarded the distinction between univocal and analogical predication with mistrust. "His way to the vision of God was the inward way of introspection . . . rather than the outward way favoured by St. Thomas, that mounts upwards from things of sense."[20]

It would arguably be challenging to read Bernard's reflections on communion with God or the contemplative life without feeling that to interpret them in terms of analogies robs them of much of their meaning. Divine love deigning to man becomes human, making possible human love's transformation into something divine. "Herein is our love made perfect . . . because as he is so are we in this world," John wrote in 1 John 4:16–17. De Burgh thought the orthodoxy of such a view unimpeachable. Neither Bernard nor John would think of entertaining pantheism; still, de Burgh was convinced that the love of which we are capable is essentially univocal with God's love itself. Nor, he thought, is there anything merely analogous about the assumption of human nature by the Incarnate Christ.[21]

Of course such love is our destination, not our starting point; moreover, we might eventually *have* such love, whereas God *is* such love. This was de Burgh's final answer to the challenge of anthropomorphism. What warrants calling God morally good are his overtures of love expressed most paradigmatically and poignantly in the Incarnation. It's thus not a matter of conceiving God in our image but discovering the image of God in us.

Whereas A. C. Ewing (discussed in chapter 15) would insist that the source of goodness must be good, de Burgh thought that the moral argument alone isn't quite enough to make this case. The best philosophy on its own steam can do is affirm God's goodness analogically. The needed supplement is furnished, and the gulf closed, by experiential religious knowledge that God is good. This is how religion completes morality. "Thus our consideration of the moral argument bears out the truth of the principle set forth at the outset, that it is only by the conjunction of the witness of religious experience with that drawn from non-religious sources, that the foundation can be secured for a reasonable faith in God."[22]

A God of perfect holiness alone might wish to have nothing to do with sinful creatures. Religious sanctimony, stifling legalism, and separationist mentalities all represent distinct even if distant echoes of this divisive dynamic, when religious believers toot their own proverbial horn, think themselves better than others (rather than others better than themselves), and cordon themselves off from the irreligious. An emphasis on holiness without all-encompassing love to leaven and condition it is far from attractive.

Love and holiness are both needed, and they don't exist at odds with one another; de Burgh's point, though, is that emphasizing the latter in one's theology without an adequate focus on the former underplays God's immanence and makes the moral argument come up short. Since de Burgh thought Christian theology in particular provides this needed supplement, he recognized the potential for emphasizing how the moral argument is best construed not just generically for theism but also for an operative conception of God that's more specific and fine-grained: a God of perfect love.

The very limitations of morality itself suggest we should move from morality to religion. Beyond values of goodness, there are also values of truth and beauty that press on our allegiance. It's religion, de Burgh argued, that can integrate all these values, for it "embraces the whole personality of the worshipper, his mind and heart and will; and God, the object of worship, is the Alpha and Omega, the source of all being and of all value, compassing with His presence the whole universe of reality."[23] Whereas Plato's principle of goodness and Kant's moral law are abstract and impersonal, God is *personal*, and his loving reach extends to all his creatures.[24]

De Burgh's argument, like all the others considered in this book, is an example of the impressive body of work that's been done in this area, too often forgotten, neglected, or casually dismissed. But, again, it's eminently subject to criticisms. A fuller treatment of de Burgh's work, for example, would have considered reservations expressed about it by A. E. Taylor, H. P. Owen, A. C. Ewing, N. H. G. Robinson, and others, but we're reserving such a conversation for another stage in our ongoing research project. For now we leave de Burgh behind, though not forgotten, after this passage from the concluding sentences of his posthumously published book, *The Life of Reason*, in which he reflected on his long life:

> Believing as I do that in that faith alone lie the hope and promise for the world, I cannot . . . question the urgency of the obligation to use what strength remains to me in the closing years of life in drawing from it the materials for a constructive argument to the truth of the Christian [g]ospel, and for an answer to the speculative difficulties which, still after nineteen centuries, hinder so many acute and earnest thinkers from yielding to it their assent.[25]

Synopsis: For de Burgh moral evidence doesn't *entail* theism but does *incline* toward it. Such evidence includes both goodness and rightness, and de Burgh endorsed a cumulative case for God's existence. He thought it took Kant's work on obligations to give the moral argument its teeth and momentum. Consciousness of moral obligations implies the reality of a moral order, which then implies God as its author and sustainer. Likewise with moral values, which are better explained by a personal God than by an impersonal Platonic realm. When it came to God's love, he departed from the tradition of analogical predication, thinking it inadequate for a full appreciation of the Incarnation. He also argued that divine holiness without divine love would call into question God's goodness.

11

An Eminent and Erudite Platonist

A. E. Taylor

The World Is Not Enough, the title of a 1999 James Bond movie, could have served equally well for the title of A. E. Taylor's 1930 book, *Faith of a Moralist*. Taylor's premise was that the moral life and what it reveals shows that it needs more than this world to be completed. That's the short version; here we will strive to give a slightly longer version. Truth be told, however, Taylor's *Faith of a Moralist*—the main topic of this chapter—is a labyrinthine work featuring a plethora of moving parts in Taylor's architectonic system. It's virtually impossible to reduce it to a few pithy ideas, and the demand for such a reduction is impracticable, unfair to the breadth and texture of Taylor's expansive work. As readers we shouldn't insist that an author always answers our questions on our terms; instead, readers need to be willing to be patient and learn the artistic rhythms, systematic approach, and skillful dance steps of their author. This chapter will at least try to do that.

Biography

Alfred Edward Taylor, the son of Wesleyan Methodist parents, was born in the town of Oundle, Northamptonshire, in England on December 22, 1869. His father, the Reverend Alfred Taylor, was a minister in the Wesleyan Methodist Church in Oundle when Taylor was born and later served as a missionary in Gold Coast, Australia. The impact of Taylor's Methodist background would be felt strongly in his works.

Methodism historically is known for its focus on the role that faith plays in the formation of a Christian's character. In this connection, Methodists believe not just in *imputed* righteousness but in *imparted* righteousness—indeed the possibility of perfection through God's love.[1] Taylor would later join the Scottish Episcopal Church, a member of the Anglican Communion; however, his later theology—which focused on morality and faith, divine grace, perfection in love, and the authority of religion as a reflection of God's authority—deeply reflected his Methodist heritage.

Taylor received his early education at the Kingswood School in Bath, the oldest Methodist school in the world, founded by John Wesley in 1748 to educate the sons of Methodist clergymen.[2] As a child, Taylor was said to be a voracious reader and was in the habit of hiding under the bed with a book in order to avoid being sent outside by his parents to play. He was also a good storyteller and writer, making up long stories to tell his siblings. Taylor lost his mother while he was still young, after which his father alone raised him with his brother and sister.

Taylor was admitted to Oxford University's New College in 1887, where he read classics and obtained a first class in honor moderation in 1889 and in 1891 a first class in *Literae Humaniores*, colloquially known as the "Greats," an honors course in classics (Latin and Greek), philosophy, and the ancient history of Rome and Greece.[3] He preached in Methodist churches while attending Oxford's New College, but upon graduation, he became a member of the Scottish Episcopal Church.

In 1900, at the age of thirty, Taylor married Lydia Justum Passmore, the second daughter of Edmund Passmore of Ruggs, Somerset. She was an author who would eventually publish two novels (in 1914 and 1915). They had one son, Francis. Taylor and Lydia were very much in love, judging from his reaction after her death in 1938. Although he lived seven more years after she died, it was a life of loneliness, which he tried to ameliorate by fully submerging himself in writing: an endeavor he carried out even up to the last night of his life, when he was said to be preparing an English reader's companion to Plato's *Republic*.

According to a 1946 memorial essay by A. J. D. Porteous, Taylor had a striking personality. He was slightly shorter than the average height, and he had an intense contemplative face with thinning dark hair, which did not significantly whiten even as he advanced in age.[4] As Taylor grew older his "somewhat ascetic look increased his resemblance to some medieval scholar. He worked incessantly, with little recreation save reading, and whether at work or in conversation his pipe was his constant companion."[5]

Taylor was an inspiring and dynamic teacher who delivered his lectures in a free-flowing manner, which was enhanced by an erudition that made his lectures virtually come to life. He was also a great conversationalist and "a fast reader, with an unusually gifted memory; and his opinions on all kinds of subjects, political, historical, literary and theological, as well as philosophical, were voiced with such gusto as to make time spent in his company a delight."6

Taylor's professional career, which began with his being elected to a fellowship at Merton College of Oxford University in 1891 at the age of twenty-one, took him to various teaching positions in England, Scotland, and Canada. By the time he passed away in his sleep on October 31, 1945, Taylor had become an acclaimed authority in classical philosophy and moral apologetics. His vast and merited reputation rested on roughly twenty books for which he is highly honored in the academic world. He wrote with literary grace and philosophical perspicacity and profundity. His writings were inventive in terms of the reach and depth of his knowledge of the subject matter and his meticulous attention to detail. As a philosopher, theologian, and apologist for the Christian faith, his fame extended well beyond the Anglican communion of which he was a devout member.

Taylor's Work and Context

Taylor's writings demonstrated a variety of philosophical interests, especially Greek philosophy, ethics, philosophy of religion, and metaphysics. He was perhaps the most notable British idealist philosopher of his day and was noted as a Plato authority, having written *Plato: The Man and His Work*. He was also considered a leading scholar in moral philosophy and philosophy of religion, especially because of his 1926–1928 Gifford lectures and the resulting publication, *The Faith of a Moralist* in 1930, considered to be his most decisive work on the moral argument.7

For space constraints, the present treatment of Taylor will mostly draw from (the first volume of) his *Faith of a Moralist*, a book that H. P. Owen wrote deserves "to be placed among the classics of philosophy."8 Owen's book *The Christian Knowledge of God* identifies four dominant forms of the moral argument for theism, the fourth of which Taylor's represents: "This form of the argument is one to which A. E. Taylor gave classical expression in the first volume of his *The Faith of a Moralist*. It is based on the present discrepancy between value and fact, aspiration and achievement, potentiality and actualization."9

C. D. Broad noted that much of the value and interest of Taylor's book is "to be found in the long digressions which he constantly makes. . . . [T]hey contain many of Prof. Taylor's most original and ingenious reflexions on all manner of subjects, and they are replete with the astonishingly wide and deep learning which he pours into all his writings."[10]

Several philosophical strands of thought contributed to the particular ideological milieu in which Taylor operated. He was greatly steeped in such notable thinkers as Plato, Aquinas, Joseph Butler, and others. He was also a member of the Victorian Age, however, and as such he was well aware of prevailing trains of thought and the reigning plausibility structures of his day.[11] He was acutely cognizant of imminent shifts and incipient trajectories of dominant thought patterns in his native England and elsewhere, and so he recognized that strong challenges to a theistic picture of reality were emerging. Taylor embarked on his academic career in the late 1800s, a time that saw the publication of Friedrich Nietzsche's *Thus Spake Zarathrusta* and was described by some as the real start of the age of skepticism.

Before explicit nihilistic atheism developed more momentum in the twentieth century, however, a partially overlapping worldview development came to the fore. It was not so much the idea that because God does not exist, neither does objective morality. Instead, it was the idea that, even if God *does* exist, he is irrelevant to morality. Much of the import of the Enlightenment project was to make just such a case: that God is an extraneous hypothesis when it comes to morality. Even if natural theology retained some of its value, on this view, the most that could be inferred is the existence of an intelligent divine designer of some sort, nothing like a loving Heavenly Father or beneficent Being. The legendary Victorian moral sensibilities were perceived by increasing numbers as able to stand on their own footing, apart from the robust metaphysical foundations of theism (or even of a Socratic doctrine of the good and the ought).

Taylor thought that among the most significant and disquieting of all the social changes of the Victorian age was the "combination of universal state-enforced primary education with the transference of the work of the teacher to the hands of laymen under no effective ecclesiastical or theological control."[12] Challenges to authority were part of the air the Victorians breathed. This secularization of moral education inevitably raised the practical question of whether moral conduct does not form a self-contained domain and whether ethics is a "wholly autonomous science, neither requiring support or completion from religion, nor affording rational ground for religious convictions of any kind."[13]

Something of momentous import was at stake: the question of what the ideal of life is for the whole of humanity. In light of the significant claims of religion in answer to this question, Taylor wrote, "A wrong answer to the question about the relations of morality and religion, once generally accepted, is certain, sooner or later, to be made the foundation of an educational policy, and adoption of a radically vicious educational policy means shipwreck for the spiritual future of mankind."[14] For such reasons, Taylor saw the vital need to discuss the proper relationship between morality and religion.

Misunderstanding their vital connection, Taylor was convinced, yields huge problems, most importantly a misconstrual of what it is that is the good for man. We risk domesticating morality, robbing it of its revelatory power, underestimating its evidential significance, if we sever and unmoor it from God too hastily. We also run the serious risk, by too quickly dismissing God from the moral equation, of selling ourselves short as human beings, settling for paltry substitutes for what constitutes our ultimate good rather than the real thing. Eventually, we even risk losing morality itself, if by removing God as its ultimate source and authority we erode its foundations, rob it of its prescriptive power, and demote it to serve provincial purposes.

Taylor increasingly witnessed the relegation of theology to the proverbial backseat. Even where religious belief was retained, it was often seen as not particularly important or existentially central. Even Kant's famous variant of the "moral argument" in the second *Critique* took too circuitous a path from morality to God. At most it was an effort to address the first *Critique*'s denial of theoretical knowledge of God. Theoretical reasoning runs into its limitations where God's concerned, on Kant's earlier view; owing to our lack of empirical evidence, we cannot form theoretical knowledge about the contents of the noumenal realm, which includes God. Later Kant used morality to argue that we can and should practically postulate the existence of God to make sense of aspects of our moral experience, but such an approach was too tepid and indirect for Taylor. He thought the moral evidence for God was stronger and more direct than that, even if it did not attain to the level of a logical demonstration.

Coherence of Actuality and Value

So it was unsurprising that to Kant Taylor predominantly attributed the severing of fact and value. Of course Kant was a complicated figure whose ideas cannot be easily encapsulated, but there was at least a salient strain of Kantian thought, Taylor argued, that had the effect of tearing God and nature asunder, along with the Socratic doctrine of the Good from the Christian doctrine of God. Followed to its logical conclusions, this influence culminated in separating facts from values, making their conjunction seem at best accidental.

Taylor regarded it as "the most important problem in the whole range of philosophy" to examine this alleged lack of necessary connection between reality, actuality, existence, or being, on the one hand, and goodness or value, on the other.[15] It was his work in this area that led to the most important analysis he contributed to the history of moral apologetics.

Salvaging an intimate connection between fact and value was a crucial agenda for Taylor. What confronts us in actual life is neither facts without value nor values attached to no facts. The sufficient reason for a value-charged universe, he thought, must combine in itself both goodness and being, which assumes an organic connection between fact and value. Existence and value are also related in what "ought to be." The moral ideal stands as the goal of human purpose as it is realized in time by persons. Taylor was thus not the least averse to use moral values as a window of insight into reality.

In tackling questions about moral value, Taylor saw that if an absolute and rigid divorce between fact and value is maintained, morality would obviously, as a result, have nothing to say about eternal life conceived in the Christian sense, nor about an aspiration for total moral transformation and liberation from mutability. Bertrand Russell's essay about a free man's worship predicated on divorcing worth and fact left Taylor cold. Taylor would insist that Russell's dismissal of the evidential significance of morality was premature. Even Kant harbored reservations about *too* strict a severance of fact and value; and Taylor wanted to argue that, though we cannot move too quickly from actuality to goodness, a case can be made for a close connection between actuality and value, after all.

Taylor thought those implicated in a radical separation of value from actuality are often victims of a fallacy of diction, a false abstraction due to convenient but ambiguous habits of speech. He further argued that the ideals of good which in actual history move men to great efforts only move so powerfully because they are not taken to be an *addition* imposed on the facts of life but rather taken to be the very bones and marrow of life itself. "Serious living is no more compatible with the belief that the universe is indifferent to morality than serious and arduous pursuit of truth with the belief that truth is a human convention or superstition."[16]

To divorce facts and values is like trying to separate the sounds of a great symphony from its musical quality. If this is so, it is merely arbitrary to assume that while our physical structure and its history throw real light on ultimate reality, our moral, aesthetic, and religious being throws no light whatever on the nature of the real.[17] In fact, it may well be that it is just this knowledge which brings us most directly into contact with the very heart of reality.[18]

After arguing for the evidential significance of moral experience, Taylor emphasized that what is more important than *what we do* is *who we are*. What kind of people ought we to be? In answering this question, Taylor argued that the moral transformation we need involves gradual deliverance from our condition of change and mutability with which we begin. This shifting of interest from temporal to nontemporal good gives the moral life its characteristic coloring of struggle and conflict never finally overcome in this life. The moral life, robustly construed, involves people striving toward something yet unreached, but also something known only in a dim sort of way.

In pondering such realities, Taylor perceived an acute advantage for poetry as a medium of expression over "technical philosophy," because poetry conveys so well the epistemic need for tentativeness as we "grope our way in the half-light which is, after all, our 'master light.'"[19] Taylor was convinced that the closer we get to this Good, the more we find ourselves *closer to home*. Again, this is less a logical or scientific demonstration than an appeal to a shared moral phenomenology that provides an internal sort of evidence that such a Good is real and our proper telos.

In our moral experience, we find ourselves as striving and active beings. We aim at an ultimate goal that has yet to be achieved, and in the process moral maturation requires that we must turn away from those actions that don't conduce to reaching our destination. In this way, the moral life invariably involves both duration and succession and, most importantly, a contrast between "no longer" and "not yet." For this reason, Taylor argued, our moral experience of transformation involves us in temporality, in stark contrast with those experiences that, in a sense, seem to transcend time. Certain events in life offer a glimpse of such possibilities.

An example Taylor adduced of such transcendence came from music—like listening to a beautiful orchestral piece—which, though it features certain notes following others, doesn't feature the same contrast between "no longer" and "not yet" that most of ordinary living does. This is why, he thought, we can conceive of a whole musical performance as of a piece, an organic unity, which transports one, in some sense, beyond the constraints of time.[20] When listened to in the proper mood and with the right kind of appreciation, music offers a glimpse into the eternal, a transcendent realm in which the distinction between past, present, and future is vitiated.

As long as the moral struggle for transformation continues, however, such transcendence in the moral life remains but a goal to seek. Revealing the influence of Henri Bergson, Taylor characterized *time* as the characteristic form of the conative, forward-reaching life of which moral experience is a sort of paradigmatic example.[21] There is thus a dynamic quality to the moral life, perpetual novelty, "adjustment to the requirements of the moral ideal in a changing and unforeseeable environment."[22]

Even in our recognition of time, Taylor thought we are already beginning to transcend the form of temporality. Taylor used additional garden-variety examples to elicit such intuitions and illustrate his point. He invited readers to remember enjoyable times spent with congenial friends, which, while they last and our enjoyment is steady and full, "the first half-hour is not envisaged as past, nor the third as future, while the second is going on."[23] Or consider again aesthetic pleasures, or the enjoyment of unimpeded intellectual activity. The experience might involve a movement of some kind, but it takes place "within a conscious present, from a before which has not faded into the past, to an after which is not felt as belonging to the future."[24] Or, again, the apprehension of a musical score is "sensibly simultaneous" (and likewise with the enjoyment of drama and other forms of art), transporting us into a world of beautiful sound without bounds.[25]

How do such examples shed light on the moral quest? Taylor envisaged a kind of life in which all our various aims and interests should be so completely unified by reference to a supreme and all-embracing good that all action has the same character of completeness.[26] However, if the world is not enough, if merely temporal and secular good must inevitably fail to satisfy the moral aspiration, "we may fairly infer that there is a non-secular good to which moral endeavor is a growing response." Complete enjoyment of this transcendent good would swallow up time in its eternity.[27]

Just insofar as he takes life seriously, Taylor added, man's whole aim is to find and enjoy a good that is never left behind and never to be superseded. What his heart is set on is actually that simultaneous and complete fruition of the life without bounds of which Boethius spoke. As he grows more intelligent and moralizes his life more completely, the nature of this underlying ethical purpose becomes increasingly apparent.[28] Taylor found altogether inadequate mere futile attempts at temporal progression with no hope of final moral attainment. "Our experience must be something more than a progress in which the best we can say of every stage is only 'not yet good, but rather better.' "[29] He thought that morality demands there must be a sense in which we can really be "permanently established in a good beyond which there is no better."[30]

Taylor's conclusion at this point went as follows:

> The moral quest will be self-defeating unless there is an object to sustain it which embodies in itself good complete and whole, so that in having it we are possessing that which absolutely satisfies the heart's desire and can never be taken from us. The possession must be possession of a 'thing infinite and eternal', and this points to the actuality of God, the absolute and final good, as indispensably necessary if the whole moral effort of mankind is not to be doomed *ab anitio* to frustration.[31]

The Problem of Evil, Human Sinfulness, and Personal Guilt

Pivoting to an adjacent discussion, Taylor admitted that the biggest weakness of ethical treatises tends to be their inadequate treatment of evil. It is barely mentioned in G. E. Moore's *Principia Ethica*, for example. Taylor thought only Kant and Plato showed a keen sense of human sinfulness.[32] The contrition that makes itself heard in the "penitential" psalms seems almost unknown to philosophical ethics.[33]

Taylor protested the deflation of moral wrongdoing for its unsound moral psychology. Our human expression of wrongdoing and guilt is so singularly unlike anything we can detect in the prehuman world that we are bound to treat it as something strictly sui generis and human, not generically animal. Moral phenomenology when we do wrong makes us directly and intimately acquainted with moral guilt. Taylor specified five familiar characteristics that distinguish our human experience of guilt and wrongdoing from anything that is to be found in the infra-human world: First, it is characteristic of the human sense of guilt that it always involves condemnation of our own selves and our own doings and is thus radically different from any discontent with our surroundings.

Second, nothing is more characteristic of the human sense of guilt than its indelibility, its power of asserting itself with unabated poignancy in spite of all lapse of time and all changes in the self and its environment.[34] Old misdoings can haunt and torment us all through life. Rejecting the depiction of guilt as merely morbid, Taylor took at least characteristic instances of guilt as veridical. What is psychologically dysfunctional and unhealthy is someone blithely unworried about moral guilt while worried about trivial social blunders, rather analogous to becoming enraptured by abysmally poor music.[35] Nor are ascriptions of guilt a theological newcomer on the scene; the "poetry of Homer reveals there are some kinds of conduct regarded specially unpardonable and certain to provoke the anger of the gods, the unseen guardians of the moral law."[36]

Third, recognition of our guilt is regularly attended by a demand for punishment. The retributive character of punishment is a doctrine indispensable to sound ethics, and it has nothing to do with revengeful passion. We recognize the justice of a social penalty decreed on us only when and if we have already sat in judgment on ourselves. When people say God must punish wrongdoing, they are giving expression to a demand for punishment that they find in their own hearts. The gravity of forgiveness attests to this.[37]

Fourth, there is a recognition of the peculiarly polluting quality of moral guilt. All languages use the same words for what offends the conscience as language of what is defiling and loathsome to sight, touch, or smell. Wrongdoing is intuitively cast as filthy, dirty, stinking; it is the same specific emotional reaction characteristic of humanity in all ages and all levels of civilization. An occupational hazard of contemporary ethicists is thinking of morality only as obligations, and thinking too little about the association between "sin" and "uncleanness."[38] In the realm of senses, dirt is a vehicle for infection and danger.[39]

Fifth, what do we feel to be defiled and polluted by contact with what awakens our sense of guilt or wounds our sense of honor? The sense of both is itself a product of the moralizing process. Truly returning to nature would require giving up shame, honor, and chivalry.[40] What is amiss in all of us is not just what we have done but also that the fountain of our moral personality is poisoned. We are fallen creatures, and we know it. Our moral task is no mere business of canalizing or embanking the course of a stream; it has to begin higher up with the purification of the bitter waters at their source. We have not just broken a rule; we have insulted or proved false to a person of supreme excellence, entitled to whole-hearted devotion.[41]

If we are to think adequately of the shame of disloyalty to our best spiritual ideal, we have to learn to think of that ideal as already embodied in the living and personal God and of falsehood as personal disloyalty and ingratitude to God. Taylor was convinced that it is just because so many of our modern philosophical moralists are afraid to make the idea of God frankly central in their theories of conduct that their treatment of guilt is inadequate to the actual moral experiences of men with any depth of character.[42] "Thus once more I find myself forced back on the conclusion that, to be truly itself, the moral life must have as its last motive love to God, and so become transfigured into the life of religious faith and devotion."[43]

Belief in the absolute reality of God, and love for the God in whom we believe, are at the heart of living morally. The good of our fellow men is unworthily thought of when we do not conceive that good as a life of knowledge of God and transformation by the knowledge into the likeness of God. And the love that arises from our belief is the one motive adequate to secure the full and whole-hearted discharge of the duties laid on us by our ideal. Taylor insisted,

> If a man is seriously convinced that of all facts those of our own moral struggle are the most immediately sure and certain, that we have more intimate assurance of the reality of love and hate, virtue and vice, than of the reality of atoms or electrons, I do not believe he is in much danger of reducing Theism to the level of a metaphysical speculation or a "permitted" hypothesis.[44]

Taylor's Methodology

That all-too-cursory sample of Taylor's response to his cultural and theological milieu highlights a few important aspects of his apologetic methodology. First, he spent a great deal of time suggesting that a close examination of morality itself—moral goods that do not admit of deflationary analyses or merely temporal significance, binding moral obligations, genuine moral guilt for wrongdoing—points beyond itself to something more ultimate. This is the underlying logic of moral arguments for God's existence (and the afterlife): morality is taken to provide illuminating insight into the nature of reality.

What often happens instead—among, say, a certain stripe of naturalists—is this: they become convinced that reality is exhausted by the natural world, and then, predicated on that assumption, they presume to construct their ethical theory within the constraints and strictures imposed by their materialist assumptions. If they are not adamant in affirming metaphysical naturalism, they are often at least committed to methodological naturalism, which (at least in the realm of science) means they choose not to consider supernatural or transcendent causes, even as a remote possibility.

The result is largely the same either way: regarding ethical theory, they gravitate toward an analysis of morality that is amenable to naturalistic explanation. To do this, though, they often have to adopt a somewhat deflationary account of what morality is. They opt for a minimal analysis of what constitutes the operative arena of ethics. Morality, on such a view, is largely about promoting social harmony, effecting preferred consequences, or promoting happiness and minimizing pain. These are all, one might say, earthly or temporal goods, and there is something unassailable and, in today's "secular" context in which all of us are steeped, highly intuitive about affirming such goals. As long as morality gets reduced to rules for getting along and promoting a kind of overall utility, an exclusive consideration of temporal goods strikes many as fundamentally correct. The cultural momentum right now is on the side of the "immanentists," not the "transcendentalists." The latter get accused of exercises in obscurantism and ontological gluttony, but this is just where the force of *Faith of a Moralist* can be felt.

By rigorous examination of moral phenomenology, Taylor accentuated the ineradicable shortfall of secular goods, obtainable only under temporal conditions, inadequate to "evoke and sustain this aspiration which gives the moral life its specific character as moral." He asked bluntly, "Can a satisfactory morality be anything but what is sometimes called by way of disparagement an *other-worldly* morality?"[45] Taylor was convinced that all the greatest moralists have answered the same way. Secular goods are seasonal, come and go, and are always tinged with regret; the same can be said about the common, or social, good; whatever good civilization gains, a good is surrendered.

Second, Taylor's epistemology was laudably expansive. He knew that human beings were not merely logic choppers, which likely contributed to his draw to an argument both intellectual and affective—the full range, in fact, of our relational, aesthetic, and imaginative faculties. Like William Sorley, like John Henry Newman, like Clement Webb, Taylor could see that the cognitive and affective must integrate; that philosophy and literature must co-labor; that an inquiry into truth requires appeal to a wide range of resources.

Taylor's magnum opus is a model in this regard, generously peppered not just with tremendous erudition, ample references to Greek, German, Latin, and French vocabulary; detailed knowledge of the history of philosophy; and deft philosophical analysis but also with ubiquitous and adroit literary references. What the weighty questions under consideration most demand, he saw, is not mere information or even dialectical ingenuity as much as openness to the "whole wide range of suggestion with which all our active experiences are pregnant, combined with the sound and balanced judgment we popularly call common sense."[46] *Faith of a Moralist* is the book of a well-read genius with an expansive religious epistemology who had spent his whole adult life pursuing the life of the mind and living with the moral argument—not as an argumentative strategy but as a pulsating passion with which he wrestled and struggled.

A. E. Taylor's contributions and relevance are extensive. Two salient examples will suffice, outlined in the discussions that follow. First, though, it bears emphasis that Taylor wasn't simply appealing to the prejudices of his audience or exploiting the cultural momentum of his day. He had already begun to sense serious resistance to a classical theistic understanding of the world and account of moral truth. He was not just proclaiming his worldview (the terms of the Gifford lectures precluded it) but also meticulously arguing for its plausibility—by pointing, in this case, to the evidence that morality itself provides that there is more to reality than meets the eye. Like others we've considered, he did not claim to provide a "logical proof" of his position, but he still thought that the evidential significance of morality, rightly and robustly construed, weighed decidedly (1) against naturalism and (2) in favor of theism.

Critiquing Naturalism

The example Taylor provided in making his case in *Faith of a Moralist* is significant. His work helped reveal some of today's emaciated caricatures of morality and its reigning deflationary analyses woefully inadequate to do justice to distinctive features of morality that cry out for adequate explanation.

Taylor concurred with the sentiment once expressed by Hastings Rashdall, who wrote that so long as he is content to assume the reality and authority of the moral consciousness, the moral philosopher can ignore metaphysics; but if the reality of morals or the validity of ethical truth is once brought into question, the attack can only be met by a thoroughgoing inquiry into the nature of knowledge and of reality.

What makes certain thin conceptions of morality inadequate is not their fashionableness or lack thereof but their failure to come to terms with the implications and richness of our moral experience. Rather than deciding our metaphysics first and looking into ethics only later, thinkers like Taylor and Rashdall would suggest that a close study of ethical truth can itself yield insight into the nature of reality.

Two salient problems attach to reductionist analyses of morality.[47] First, a commitment to something like methodological naturalism is not neutral. It is problematically circular. So deflationary an account of morality is clearly more likely, in light of the powerful evidence that morality provides, on atheism than it is on theism. Most theists are not remotely tempted to adopt such a view. Second, and relatedly, it is an account that leaves too much out. By forcing morality into the procrustean bed of such sparse ontology, one simply has to ignore some of its most powerful and distinctive features least amenable to reductionist analysis.

Charles Mason has written,

> [Taylor's] major contention . . . is that man is in actual dependence upon a host of ideals, norms, presuppositions, and these enter into the warp and woof of his thinking and his acting. They are the ultimate rationales without which neither logical values, aesthetic values, nor ethical values have the slightest coercive cogency. The meaning of the fact is always in the universal . . . and it is for this reason that "all secular good" is declared defective.[48]

Taylor showed that the problem with privileging a thin metaphysics is that it precludes following where the evidence of morality may well lead. It is a circular, even if unwitting, example of domestication. Steven D. Smith writes that it may be that "we can do science well enough within the iron cage of secular discourse" but that such an approach does not work when we try to address normative matters; and morality is a paradigm of normativity.[49] In general, the closer we move to an effort to understand the human condition and ultimate reality, the more evidence a naturalistic set of assumptions tends to ignore.[50]

Moral Transformation and the Power of Theistic Explanation

Taylor not only modeled a substantive critique of naturalism; he also demonstrated the explanatory efficacy of theism generally, and even Christianity specifically, to which we can but gesture here. One of the most important deliverances of morality, beyond mere rules for behavior, is its insistence on moral maturation, growth, and transformation. This is one of the features of morality on which Taylor spilled quite a bit of ink. Recall that he did not think a deep understanding of morality could be exhausted by focusing merely on marginal moral improvement in this life, or even aspirations toward earthly utopias. Invariably such efforts remain thwarted and incomplete and, ultimately, temporary.

At root Taylor's concern was to recognize the challenging nature of the moral demand and the need for divine help if it's ever to be realized: "A man cannot receive the power to rise above his present moral level from his own inherent strength, because the process is one of rising above himself, and, in the moral as in the physical world, you cannot lift yourself by the hair of your own head."[51]

Morality, to Taylor's thinking, is not simply an expression of one's character. Its real job is rather "the task of reshaping and transfiguration of the inward personality itself, and the initiative to *such* an undertaking manifestly cannot come simply from within the personality which is to be remade."[52] Morality itself, then, involves the supernatural, in the proper sense of that word, as "its environment and daily nutriment."[53] To attempt the moral life on our own steam would be like continuing to breathe the same air, or living on one's own fat.

Yet except in the New Testament and in Plato, Taylor insisted, the indispensability of external help for the moral life seems never to have found adequate recognition. This is not to deny the need to work for moral progress, but if we are to grow into the likeness of the thing we contemplate, this can only be because the thing we contemplate is *not*, in the first instance, the thing we are.[54] We need to be radically transformed into something of which we have an inkling, but an inkling of the most valuable good there is. Or to alter the analogy, we need to be transported into a whole new country—though no strange land, but rather *home*.[55] Although the world is not enough, God *is*.

Not just any God, though. What the evidence of morality suggests, Taylor argued, was that God needs to be more than merely first cause or the god of deism. In fact, the moral life to which we're called is to be thought of as a response to God's initiative. And perhaps most importantly of all, the God to which morality points must be a God of nothing less than perfect love.

> Synopsis: Taylor argued at length against an artificial dichotomy between *fact* and *value*, in an effort to carve out evidential space for morality. Divorcing facts and values is like trying to separate the sounds of a great symphony from its musical quality. More important than *what we do* is *who we are*, and what's needed is an adequate account for the sort of external assistance we desperately require to be radically transformed (even transfigured)—after all, Taylor said, we can't pull ourselves up by our own hair—so we can enjoy a good never left behind and never superseded. The inherent features of moral guilt point in the direction of a personal and perfectly loving God as our first and final cause. Taylor counseled close and sustained attentiveness to the moral evidence and (as we've seen in others) modeled a laudably expansive epistemology.

12

Dean of St. Paul's
W. R. Matthews

Background

Walter Robert Matthews was an Anglican priest, theologian, and writer who taught at King's College, London, before becoming Dean of St. Paul's. He was one of the four thinkers highlighted in Alan P. F. Sell's comprehensive analysis *Four Philosophical Anglicans* (2010). Of those four Anglicans, Matthews had the highest national profile and, interestingly enough, was the only one of the four not to have been educated at either Oxford or Cambridge.

Sell describes Matthews's youngest years: "Matthews was born in a small house in Bushey Hill Road, Camberwell, London, on 22 September 1881 [he lived until 1973], and christened at All Saints Church, Blenheim Grove. He was deeply affected by the death on 24 March 1902 of his younger brother, Hubert, aged 18; twins, Olive and Edgar, completed the family."[1] His father was a Protestant with deep suspicions of popery; his mother fostered in Matthews a love of reading by encouraging him from his early childhood to talk about "God, freedom, and immortality" in childish parables and symbols.[2]

On leaving school Matthews worked at Westminster Bank, reading widely in his spare time, especially in religion and politics. He was grateful for Herbert Spencer's introduction to epistemology and for Charles Darwin for raising the questions of the authority of scripture and the nature of divine revelation. He went through a period of religious doubts until, as he reported, "I was taken hold of by a power, or Spirit, which filled me with joy and peace and courage. My doubts about God were transcended. He needed me and called me."[3]

At King's College, his greatest debt was to the professor of philosophy Alfred Caldecott, who left his students to guess what his own "system" might be. Matthews wrote several books, among them *Studies in Christian Philosophy* (dedicated to Caldecott), a 1921 published version of his Boyle lectures in which a chapter was devoted to a moral argument for God's existence.[4]

Less than fully committed to the Church of England's Thirty-Nine Articles of Religion, Matthews eventually overcame his scruples and was ordained in 1907. He was never invited to give the Gifford lectures, a source of no small amount of disenchantment for him and something that various biographers, like H. P. Owen, lamented.[5] Matthews seemed to particularly regret the selection of Karl Barth as a Gifford lecturer, someone who disbelieved in the subject of the lectures (natural theology) and who "held that the time spent lecturing on it was not only wasted but promoted a dangerous illusion."[6] In 1918 Matthews succeeded Caldecott as dean and professor of the philosophy of religion at King's College, and in 1930 he wrote *God in Christian Thought and Experience*.[7]

In his various courses of lectures given under the auspices of the Liverpool Diocesan Board of Divinity—*The Idea of Revelation* (1923), *The Psychological Approach to Religion* (1925), and *God and Evolution* (1926)—Matthews was said to show considerable ability in taking the deep questions posed by the person in the street with the utmost seriousness and addressing them fluently and with integrity. This trait would serve him well in subsequent years in his preaching, broadcast talks, lectureships, and written articles.

Sell delineates four general themes that underlie all of Matthews's writing: (1) the experiential basis of religion, (2) the psychological interest, (3) the relations between religion and science, and (4) the need of a viable apologetic.[8] Regarding apologetics, Matthews's diagnosis was that the gospel "does not appeal to people often because it answers a question which they have forgotten to ask." Yet these facts remain, he asserted: moral values are permanent, and the modern person needs salvation, and it's to these, he thought, we must appeal as we translate "the good news out of language which has grown archaic into words which speak directly to the man of today."[9] Sell characterizes Matthews's desire to *commend* Christianity to the people of his time as the deepest motive for his apologetic efforts.[10]

Boyle Lectures

In his Boyle lectures, Matthews observed the phenomena of the moral universe and asked which hypotheses among (to borrow a phrase from William

James) "live options" for us most adequately cover the facts? In accentuating the value of goodness, Matthews was careful not to assign it a priority over the other great values of truth and beauty, thinking them ultimately, though conceptually distinct, as of a piece. Together they form a whole, and there's no real tension between them—an idea rather at variance with contemporary postmodern trends but one profoundly resonant with robust and classical theism.

In dealing with the data of morals, he identified three methods to employ: historical, psychological, and ethical. The historical method considers the rise of moral ideas; the psychological method deals with the moral consciousness in the individual; and the distinctively ethical method the nature of the Absolute Good. In each case, Matthews was convinced, the consideration of the question yields theism. His approach was, therefore, threefold and cumulative. Like many others, Matthews explicitly disavowed attempting to show that the facts of morality could furnish premises that, by a necessary argument, deduce the existence of God. Still, he thought that moral evidence makes it highly *likely* that God exists.

Of course Matthews recognized that the efficacy of such an argument altogether depends on the weight that we allow to the moral aspects of our experience. A strict bifurcation of fact and value, for example, would undermine it. Once again we see that whether or not the moral argument is seen as persuasive depends on one's willingness to take moral evidence as revelatory of reality. Matthews was strongly of the view that this is a good idea and justified assumption, that morality provides a solid bet for providing a window of insight into what's real. He thought it would be a strange inference to deduce there is a certain type of fact that it's our duty to ignore. It is a patent fact, after all, that in this world are minds that form ideals and acknowledge themselves to be under moral obligation.

Matthews on this score thus stood foursquare with Plato, for whom the Idea of the Good was the highest reality, in the light of which alone we may see the whole as a rational order and the principle from which all objects of knowledge derive their reality. Of course there is no guarantee that following the moral evidence where it leads won't mislead us, if for no other reason than that reality may be less than fully rational. However, Matthews considered eminently irrational the proposal to rule out moral phenomena from consideration just because of that remote contingency,[11] agreeing with the likes of Newman and James on such a score.

Historical Method

Rather than seeing tension between theism and the development of moral ideas, Matthews was convinced we can find in a consideration of the evolution of morals evidence for the theistic hypothesis. How, though, are we to account for the development of our moral ideals without evacuating them of all *authority*? Naturalism, he argued, seems to have little to say on the question of why new moral ideals evolve. Even if evolution were able to account for the rise and development of ethical ideas, we should still be driven to seek some further ground for them on pain of divesting them of all authority.

Grasping an argument from reason (like Balfour before him and Lewis, Reppert, and Plantinga after him), Matthews argued that, just as with knowledge and truth, naturalism must end in moral skepticism, because if we can say of true judgments no more than that they are those that aid the survival of those who form them, the term *truth* has lost its significance. We are reduced to a skepticism in which all knowledge, including the theory of evolution itself, is ruined. If we can say of judgments no more than that they tend to preserve those who hold them, we have reduced moral authority to the level of mere convenience. There can be no categorical imperative, only a hypothetical imperative.[12]

He recognized that the defeat of naturalism isn't enough to establish theism, but he thought it could be argued effectively that no other hypothesis on offer is in so favorable a position to deal with the problem of accounting for our moral development without depriving our moral ideals of their authority. Although closed to naturalism, Matthews was open to evolution, and thought, in fact, that a theistic hypothesis is supported by the emergence and gradual elevation of moral and social ideals in the life of humanity.

> If we can regard the development of moral ideas as the more progressive expression of ... an imminent spirit, and if we have seen reason to believe that the moral ideals thus developed must be in a harmony, ... we have some ground for supposing that the developing moral consciousness is a revelation of the purpose of the world as a whole. At least it may be said that such a view would enable us to allow full weight to the undeniable facts of moral evolution, while maintaining undiminished the authority of our own moral ideals.[13]

Psychological Method

Matthews then proceeded to consider the moral consciousness as it exists in individuals: first, to discover if the moral life depends on any implicit assumptions about the nature of man and his relation with the world as a whole and, second, to inquire on what conditions those assumptions can be justified. He thought it sufficient for this purpose to call attention to two familiar principles: (1) the authority of moral ideals and (2) the objectivity that we naturally assign to the moral law. The authority of morality particularly manifests in moral obligations, the ought, the very "form of the moral life."[14] Joseph Butler was right, Matthews believed, in saying that a claim to authority is the fundamental character of the conscience.

What does the existence of moral obligations suggest about reality? Matthews made numerous observations here, but perhaps his most important was that this law of morality must be a law of our own nature. It can't be merely extrinsic or external to us; rather it must be something that reveals intimate truth about ourselves. He recognized that an objective and independent moral law must find some purchase in human nature if it is to have any authority, a necessity satisfied by theism, which

> holds that the Deity transcends the temporal order, and therefore that the moral ideal is objective, and objective as an ideal. But at the same time, with its doctrine of the immanent Word or Reason, it enjoins us to hold that the apprehension whereby we discern the Good is the reflection of the Divine knowledge, and that the will whereby we attempt to realise the Good is not unrelated with the will whereby God seeks to realise His own end.[15]

He added,

> I may obey [God] because I hope for heaven or dread hell, but it will not be a moral obedience nor will His commands possess any moral authority. It is thus clear that the only moral judgment which can have intrinsic authority is one that springs from the nature of personality. It was this truth that Kant expressed in the phrase "the autonomy of the practical reason," and which was put more simply but I think more accurately by St. Paul and Butler when they said that "man is a law unto himself."[16]

This is part of what's wrong with a wholly voluntarist ethic; it divorces the content of the moral law from our truest selves: "The effort of the moral life is not thought of as an attempt to destroy our personality and to become someone else. It is conceived as a striving to be oneself, to enter into possession of one's full nature, to give expression to a character which is immanent, latent, waiting to be born, which nevertheless has more right to exist than the actual self of our normal lives."[17]

The objectivity of the moral law likewise makes sense on a theistic hypothesis. If moral ideals can be said to have an objective reality by featuring content distinct from the existing empirical order, we are led to postulate a transcendent teleology, a "purposive Intelligence not identical with the actual world."[18] Yet the paradox is that moral ideals need to remain tethered to this world, for if we remain content with a doctrine of pure transcendence we should cut ourselves off from all hope of giving any satisfactory account of the authority of the moral ideal, the way it speaks to us at the deepest levels of our being.

If the purpose of morality fails to "echo in my soul," said Matthews, "if I can know it only by a revelation which is accredited solely by external evidence, if I can cooperate with it only by conforming to rules which have no ground in my own being, such a purpose can never command my reverence with that authority which we attach to the dictates of the conscience."[19]

The Ethical Method

Finally, Matthews turned to a third moral phenomenon, that of the content of moral consciousness—namely, rational benevolence and rational progress, asking on what hypothesis about the general structure of reality may these two principles be regarded as rational? Henry Sidgwick had argued that the principle of benevolence is self-evident and consequently neither needs nor is capable of any further justification—that it would be as absurd to require any further ground for it as it would be to ask what the reason is for the logical principle of noncontradiction.

Matthews responded, however, that such benevolence is far from something self-evident; there are plenty who understand it without affirming it. His point wasn't designed to cast doubt on the truth of the principle but rather to point out that its truth depends on a metaphysical assumption, some implicit view of the nature of the world.[20] If we continue to affirm both that the good life includes benevolence and that it is rational, it must be because we have some metaphysical grounds for doing so. In other words, there must be some view of the universe, held explicitly or implicitly, in the light of which the principle will appear rational. In short, on the theistic hypothesis the life of goodness is rational, while on any other it is not.[21]

The category of moral progress also raises questions about what sort of world makes sense of such a category. In light of the foibles and finitude of human persons and societies, what realistic hope can there be of a perfected kingdom of man? Precious little. "The theistic hypothesis," Matthews argued, in contrast, "allows us to conceive of a perfected intercourse which is all-embracing, including all persons, and which, at the same time, preserves and perfects their individual being."[22]

Theism, in fact, makes better sense of the very process of individual and collective moral maturation. The sphere of moral effort is not an otiose or irrational addition to an otherwise rational world but is in fact "a necessary element of that world without which the end could not exist." To any mind that is not prepared to overlook the facts of ethics in forming an estimate of reality, all of these considerations, especially cumulatively considered in the aggregate, must have considerable weight. To someone inclined to attribute to these facts a primary importance, the argument, Matthews believed, has overwhelming force.[23]

> Synopsis: As Sell puts it, Matthews found the moral argument (along with the teleological argument) the most persuasive of all the theistic arguments:
>
> He reflects upon the "moral evolution of mankind" and asks what it implies concerning the nature of the universe; he discusses the conscience and asks, "On what grounds can we justify that sense of obligation which is the characteristic property of moral experience?" He ponders the nature of the good, and asks, "What is the place of the Good in the general structure of the universe?" He finds that in each case he is led to the theistic hypothesis.[24]

13

A Dinosaur

C. S. Lewis

There is some irony in the fact that the best-known version of the moral argument, at least in the English-speaking world, is not that of a professional philosopher but of a scholar of English literature who was more famous for his works of popular Christian apologetics and children's stories than he was for his distinguished books in his academic discipline. Indeed, that version of the argument appears in C. S. Lewis's most famous book of Christian apologetics—namely, *Mere Christianity*.

Lewis was born in Belfast, Northern Ireland, on November 29, 1898, to Albert James Lewis and Flora Augusta Hamilton Lewis. His mother died in 1908 when he was only nine years old, one of several experiences that inclined him to a rather pessimistic view of life early on. In the same year, his father sent him and his older brother off to a boarding school in England, the first of several such schools he attended. These were very unhappy years for the youthful Lewis, further instilling his bent toward pessimism. During these same years, he abandoned his childhood Christian faith as well as many of his moral scruples.

In 1916 he won a scholarship to University College, Oxford, but his studies were interrupted by the First World War and he reached the front line on his nineteenth birthday. He was wounded in April 1918, returned to duty in October, and was discharged in December of that year. From January 1919 until June 1924, he resumed his studies at Oxford, where he took degrees in Greek and Latin literature, Greats and English, receiving a "first" (the highest honor classification) in all three. The degree in Greats focused on classic philosophy and ancient history.

Lewis's early ambition was to be a philosopher, and indeed, his first job at Oxford was tutoring philosophy at University College for two terms, from October 1924 through May 1925, to fill in for a faculty member who was on leave studying in the United States. His responsibilities also included lecturing, and for our purposes it is interesting to observe that he chose for his topic "The Good, Its Position among the Values."[1] In 1925, he was elected a fellow of Magdalene College, where he taught for the next twenty-nine years. Although his primary job was to teach English, part of the reason he got the job was because they wanted someone who could also tutor philosophy. Lewis's academic career was eventually focused on English, but he also tutored several students in philosophy during his early years at Magdalene.

Lewis's conversion from atheism was a two-stage process, first to theism and then to Christianity. It was a gradual process over several years in which his views shifted from a belief in naturalism to a belief in supernaturalism before he finally arrived at the conviction that a personal living God had been pursuing him the entire time. In the famous words of his spiritual autobiography, *Surprised by Joy*, he described this encounter as follows: "That which I greatly feared had at last come upon me. In the Trinity Term of 1929, I gave in and admitted that God was God, and knelt and prayed: perhaps, that night, the most dejected and reluctant convert in all England."[2] His good friend J. R. R. Tolkien played an instrumental role in helping him overcome his objections to Christianity, which remained even after his conversion to theism, and he became a Christian the following year.

Lewis had a distinguished career at Oxford, but he was passed over for a professorship more than once. A number of persons believe that a significant factor in all this was that several of his colleagues resented the fact that he wrote popular books defending Christianity in addition to his critically acclaimed works in English literature. And indeed, Lewis produced numerous such books, seemingly with little effort. He wrote and published most of the Christian apologetic works for which he is famous in a rather short period of time, from 1940 to 1947, including *The Problem of Pain, The Screwtape Letters, The Great Divorce, Miracles*, and the 1941 radio talks that were later published as *Mere Christianity*. His classic children's stories, the seven-book set known as *Chronicles of Narnia*, were published in the years from 1950 to 1956.

Although he was denied promotion to the rank of professor at Oxford, that honor came to him in 1954 when he was elected to the chair of medieval and renaissance literature at Cambridge. He was also married late in life to the American writer Joy Davidman, first in a secret civil ceremony in 1956 and then by a priest in 1957 at her hospital bed. Lewis only married her initially to allow her to remain in Britain after her application for continuing residency was denied. She discovered she had cancer shortly after the marriage. During this time, Lewis fell in love with her, leading to his second wedding and her moving into his house. Davidman had a period of recovery, and it even appeared she might be healed, but she died in 1960. Lewis himself died three years later, on November 22, 1963, the same day John F. Kennedy was assassinated and Aldous Huxley died.

Lewis's most famous book of Christian apologetics began as a series of short radio talks he gave on the BBC beginning in 1941. He was initially asked to talk about the Christian faith from the perspective of a layman, but Lewis was convinced that he needed to start at an earlier stage of the discussion before he could engage his audience with specific Christian claims. He proposed talking about the objective nature of right and wrong, which is taken for granted in Christianity but requires defending for many modern people. They finally settled on " 'Right and Wrong': A Clue to the Meaning of the Universe." The four series of talks were originally published as three short books and were later published together as *Mere Christianity* in 1952.

Defending Morality without God

Although Lewis's most famous version of the moral argument is the one he crafted for a popular audience in *Mere Christianity*, right around the same time he was doing those radio talks, he developed a more extended defense of objective moral truth for an academic audience. In February 1943, he gave the Riddell memorial lectures at the University of Durham, which were published the next year as *The Abolition of Man*. What is particularly interesting for our purposes is that Lewis advanced a sophisticated argument for objective right and wrong and moral duty without invoking the existence of God or arguing that morality depends on God or requires God to account for it. Indeed, he explicitly denied that he was arguing anything of the sort.

Lewis approached his subject by examining a secondary-school English textbook in which the authors tell the famous story of Samuel Taylor Coleridge at a waterfall, where he heard two tourists comment on it. One said the waterfall was "sublime" while the other said it was "pretty," and Coleridge mentally endorsed the judgment of the first but strongly rejected the second. The authors of the textbook, however, are critical of Coleridge's assessment, suggesting that nothing much of significance was going on in the judgment of the tourist who pronounced it sublime. Although he appeared to be making a statement about the waterfall, he was actually only making a statement about his own feelings. Indeed, all statements of value, according to the authors of this textbook, are subject to the same critical analysis. While we appear to be saying something important about some other thing or object, in reality we are only commenting on our own feelings.

Lewis saw in this analysis a deeply wrongheaded set of judgments that would have disastrous consequences for the educational enterprise and ultimately destroy any society that adopted this way of thinking. By contrast, classical education was based on an altogether different set of assumptions. "Until quite modern times all teachers and even all men believed the universe to be such that certain emotional reactions on our part could be either congruous or incongruous to it—believed, in fact, that objects did not merely receive, but could *merit*, our approval or disapproval, our reverence or contempt."[3] For classical education, the waterfall merited the response on the part of the viewer that it was sublime, and the tourist who described it as such was not merely registering his personal feelings but was responding appropriately to the waterfall.

This conviction is not distinctive to the Judeo-Christian tradition, Lewis insisted, but rather it is common to Platonic, Aristotelian, Stoic, and oriental traditions as well. What is commonly shared here is something quite important. "It is the doctrine of objective value, the belief that certain attitudes are really true, and others really false, to the kind of thing the universe is and the kind of things we are."[4] This substantial moral agreement that is shared by all these traditions Lewis dubbed "the Tao."

Lewis underscored the educational dilemma for those who rejected the doctrine of objective value by appealing to an instance that had much more existential weight than his earlier example of the waterfall—namely, the traditional judgment that a sacrificial death for others is morally praiseworthy. The Roman soldier, schooled in the ways of Tao, sincerely passed on to his son his own heartfelt conviction "that it was a sweet and seemly thing to die for his country."[5] This example had a particular edge in the time Lewis gave his lectures, for England was engaged in World War II, and young men from Britain, like young men from many other countries, were being called upon to put their lives on the line to defend their country. Lewis pressed home the poignant issue of how young men could be called upon to accept this call to sacrifice by those who rejected the Tao and who considered all value judgments to be mere sentiments that have no rational authority. Indeed, Lewis thought such persons faced a terrible dilemma: "Either they must go the whole way and debunk this sentiment like any other, or they must set themselves to work to produce, from outside, a sentiment which they believe to be of no value to the pupil and which may cost him his life, because it is useful to us (the survivors) that our young men should feel it."[6]

Lewis continued in his second lecture to focus on this example of death for a good cause because he believed it is "the *experimentum crucis* which shows different systems of thought in the clearest light."[7] He was confident, moreover, that his moral innovators who face this dilemma would choose the first horn, and debunk traditional patriotic convictions about the honor of dying for one's country. But he also thought these innovators would remain convinced that there is some other "basic" or "realistic" ground that will rationally sustain this value. The innovator might appeal to utilitarian considerations, but the obvious question this poses is why any given man should forfeit his life for the sake of others. In the same vein, the innovator might try to deduce practical conclusions from factual premises, such as the claim that being willing to die for a good cause will preserve society.

But Lewis insisted, following Hume, that "ought" statements cannot be derived from "is" statements. Unless we know that we ought to preserve society, we will not be moved to sacrifice our life on the grounds that our sacrifice will preserve society. Or we might take another tack and argue that human beings have an instinct to preserve society. Lewis was doubtful that we have any such instinct, but if we do, the question arises of whether these instincts are so strong that we cannot but obey them or whether, alternatively, we actually have a choice in the matter. If the former is the case, why are we urged to do what we inevitably must do? If the latter is true, it looks like we are being told that we ought to obey instinct and that we have an obligation to do so. Once again, unless we already know we have a duty to preserve society, how can we have a duty to freely follow the instinct to do so?

After surveying these sorts of options, and finding them unconvincing, Lewis came to the heart of his case for objective moral truth. As he saw it, there is no alternative to accepting the authority of the Tao. All the principles that the innovator vainly seeks elsewhere to ground morality are to be found there, but nowhere else. "Unless you accept these without question as being to the world of action what axioms are to the world of theory, you can have no practical principles whatever. You cannot reach them as conclusions: they are premises.... If nothing is self-evident, nothing can be proved. Similarly, if nothing is obligatory for its own sake, nothing is obligatory at all."[8] We can argue *from* these fundamental truths, but we cannot argue *to* them. It is the very essence of rationality to recognize the self-evident nature of fundamental moral truth.

Several pages later, Lewis reiterated his essential argument and insisted that he was not engaging in a sleight-of-hand argument for God:

> In order to avoid misunderstanding, I may add that though I am myself a Theist, and indeed a Christian, I am not here attempting any indirect argument for Theism. I am simply arguing that if we are to have values at all we must accept the ultimate platitudes of Practical Reason as having absolute validity: that any attempt, having become skeptical about these to introduce value lower down on some supposedly more "realistic" basis is doomed. Whether this position implies a supernatural origin for the *Tao* is a question I am not here concerned with.[9]

Lewis's core argument, then, is a straightforward modus ponens, in which he assumes his audience will be anxious to affirm the antecedent.

1. If we are to have values at all, we must accept the ultimate platitudes of practical reason as having absolute validity.
2. We (must) have values.
3. Therefore, we must accept the ultimate platitudes of practical reason as having absolute validity.

His critics, of course, would deny the conditional as a whole since they would reject the consequent. The viability of this move depends on whether there is a plausible way to ground moral truth and values without taking basic moral convictions as axiomatic; it also depends on whether one agrees with Lewis that appeals to utilitarian considerations, matters of fact, instinct, and the like cannot provide an alternative basis.

There is another variation on his central argument in his third and final lecture where he discussed the scenario that gives *The Abolition of Man* its title. There he imagined a scenario, far in the future, when the science of eugenics has been perfected, and a generation of conditioners has the power to alter the human race however they choose, including our conscience. These conditioners, having stepped outside the Tao, would not be guided by any objective moral truth but would rely only on their strongest-felt desires. Stripped of traditional moral convictions and the character that flows from that when our emotions and dispositions are properly trained, the result, Lewis contended, would be "the abolition of man." What makes us distinctively human would be abolished, and man would be reduced to a natural artifact.

With this deeply disturbing scenario before us, Lewis made another appeal for the axiomatic authority of the Tao:

> Either we are rational spirit obliged forever to obey the absolute values of the *Tao*, or else we are mere nature to be kneaded and cut into new shapes for the pleasures of masters who must, by hypothesis, have no motive but their own "natural" impulses. Only the *Tao* provides a common human law of action which can over-arch rulers and ruled alike. A dogmatic belief in objective value is necessary to the very idea of a rule which is not tyranny or an obedience which is not slavery.[10]

Once again, the structure of Lewis's argument is straightforward, and once again he was confident that he knew what his audience would choose when faced with these alternatives.

4. Either we are rational spirit obliged forever to obey the absolute values of the Tao, or we are mere nature to be cut into new shapes for the pleasure of masters who have no motives but their natural impulses.
5. We are not mere nature to be cut into new shapes for the pleasure of masters who have no motives but their natural impulses.
6. Therefore, we are rational spirit obliged forever to obey the absolute values of the Tao.

Critics of course will charge Lewis with presenting us with a false dilemma, and they will insist that we have other options besides the two offered here. In any case, it is worth noting that Lewis employed the strong language of obligation.[11] This goes beyond his earlier claims that certain reactions on our part can be congruous to reality or that objective value merits a response of approval or disapproval. The language of obligation to obey has more teeth, as it were.

Notice too that Lewis spoke of obedience to the Tao as a sort of obedience that is not slavery. Why is this so? Is it merely because ruler and ruled alike are under its authority? Is it because there is a fit between the obligations of the Tao and our nature? Or is there more to the story?

Objective Moral Truth Implies God

The question Lewis left aside in *The Abolition of Man* as to whether objective moral truth and obligation implies a supernatural source is one he took up in *Mere Christianity*. Before taking up this issue, however, he first made the case for objective morality. As noted, Lewis recognized that for many modern people of his time objective morality was not taken for granted, and he thought it essential to establish this point before he would have any chance of convincing them that Christianity is true.

In keeping with the popular nature of his talks, he began with the commonsense observation that in everyday life, we repeatedly make judgments that imply that we do in fact believe in objective moral truth. In incidents as commonplace as protesting when someone cuts in line or asking our friend to share his orange with us because we shared ours with him, we are appealing to a standard of fair play, or a law of right and wrong, which we think everyone must acknowledge. That is the first truth he aimed to establish in his first chapter. And even though we often fail to live up to the law of right and wrong, we are not inclined to brush it off. Rather, we make excuses for our failure, which is itself a backhanded recognition of the standard. In the very last lines of the chapter, Lewis summed up the human condition: "They know the Law of Nature; they break it. These two facts are the foundation of all clear thinking about ourselves and the universe we live in."[12]

Earlier in the chapter, Lewis explained that in previous generations the term "law of nature" was used to name the law of right and wrong because it was assumed that everyone knew it by nature. He hastened to distinguish that from what are typically called laws of nature today—namely, the scientifically discerned laws that govern the physical world. While the physical world has no choice but to "obey" the laws of nature, human beings are not determined to obey the (moral) law of nature, as demonstrated by the fact that they frequently fail to uphold the very law they invoke against others.[13] Moreover, Lewis acknowledges that there may be an odd person here and there who does not know this law of right and wrong, just like there are some persons who are color-blind. "But taking the race as a whole, they thought that the human idea of decent behavior was obvious to everyone."[14] Indeed, Lewis went on to insist that "the Nazis at bottom knew as well as we did" that what they were doing was wrong.

Notice that Lewis described the law of human nature as "obvious to everyone." This is noteworthy because in *The Abolition of Man*, he described the Tao as self-evident in the axiomatic sense. The two notions are not the same. It is obvious, but not self-evident that there are dogs. It is self-evident but not obvious modus tollens is valid, whereas affirming the consequent is a fallacy. Self-evident truths often need to be pointed out and illustrated, but they are necessarily true, whereas obvious truths are not.

It is not clear that Lewis meant to distinguish these two, however. In the very first chapter of *Mere Christianity*, he cites the appendix of *The Abolition of Man*, where he listed several examples of moral truth held by different cultures in order to answer the objection that different ages and civilizations have had quite different moralities. He insisted that it is inconceivable that any culture could actually have a moral code that fundamentally goes against the Tao. "You might as well try to imagine a country where two and two make five."[15] This suggests that he was thinking that the moral truth he had in mind was not only obvious to all people, but also necessarily true, and as such it was also self-evidently true. Again, the difference in language may simply suggest that he used the term "obvious" because it would communicate to a popular audience who may not understand the world of axioms and self-evidence.[16]

In any case, what is quite clear is that he wanted to convince his audience that the law of right and wrong is a real thing that requires a satisfactory explanation. Lewis advanced this case by briefly considering various explanations of morality that reduce it to some sort of human construction or as something that depends on us. He briefly considered a number of reductionist and biologically grounded explanations of morality, but he quickly dismissed them as failing to account for the depth and inescapability of our conviction that some things really are right and wrong and that some moral ideas really are better than others. "If your moral ideas can be truer, and those of the Nazis less true, there must be something—some Real Morality—for them to be true about."[17] In the final lines of his chapter on the reality of the moral law, Lewis insisted that it "is really there, not made up by ourselves," and this led him to the following important preliminary conclusion: "It begins to look as we shall have to admit that there is more than one kind of reality; that, in this particular case, there is something above and beyond the ordinary facts of men's behavior, and yet quite definitely real—a real law, which none of us made, but which we find pressing on us."[18]

With this conclusion in hand, Lewis was prepared to advance the critical step of his argument. The question to be answered now is how to account for this reality, a law of right and wrong that we know from immediate experience is "pressing on us." We did not create it, and we would often like to evade it or ignore it, but we find ourselves acknowledging it nearly every day in the judgments we render on our own behavior as well as that of others. Here is Lewis's reasoning, which led him from objective moral truth in the direction of theism. At this stage, he cautioned his readers—or perhaps reassured them—that he "is not yet within a hundred miles of the God of Christian theology." He only knew that something is directing the universe, and from immediate experience it appeared to him as a law urging him to do right, and making him feel guilty when he does not. "I think we have to assume it is more like a mind than it is like anything else we know—because after all the only other thing we know is matter and you can hardly imagine a bit of matter giving instructions. But, of course, it need not be very like a mind, still less like a person."[19]

The argument here is an argument from analogy that goes something like this:

7. We experience whatever it is that is directing the universe as a law that gives us instructions and urges us to do what is right.
8. The only thing we know that can give instructions is a mind.
9. Therefore, whatever it is that is directing the universe is more like a mind than anything else we know.

This is a very minimal claim, particularly insofar as Lewis allowed that what lies behind the law may not be very much like a mind even if it is more like a mind than anything else that we know. Much less did he insist it is like a person.

Still we may wonder how anything could do things like give instructions or urge good behavior if it was anything less than a fully conscious intelligent being—indeed, very much like a mind. In the final chapter of book 1 of *Mere Christianity*, Lewis repeated his minimal claim, but again, talked about this being, or whatever it is, in terms that are hard to understand of anything less than an intelligent personal being. He said that "the Being behind the universe is intensely interested in good conduct," that the Being "detests" our greed, trickery, and exploitation.[20] Then on the last page, he made the provocative claim that Christians "offer an explanation of how God can be this impersonal mind at the back of the Moral Law and yet also be a person."[21]

This intriguing suggestion, which Lewis tossed out with one line, was developed in more detail in his essay "The Poison of Subjectivism." There he claimed that our unconditional allegiance to the moral law must be acknowledged as the duty of man and also that we owe absolute allegiance to God. These two allegiances must actually be the same, moreover, and if this is true we must consider how the relationship between God and the moral law should be represented. This led Lewis to discuss the famous Euthyphro dilemma, and he rejected both horns as unacceptable. He saw a way out, however, by considering the central Christian doctrine of the Trinity. What this doctrine teaches us, Lewis explained, is that a trinity of persons is united in one God. Similarly, he suggested, when we think first of our Father in heaven, and second, about the "self-evident imperatives of the moral law," we cannot help but think of two distinct things. It is possible, however, that our thinking in this regard is not merely an error but instead is a real "perception of things that would necessarily be two in any mode of being which enters our experience, but which are not so divided in the absolute being of the superpersonal God."[22]

Lewis went on to spell this out in more detail several lines later.

> God neither obeys nor creates the moral law. The good is uncreated; it never could have been otherwise; it has no shadow of contingency; it lies, as Plato said, on the other side of existence.... But we, favored beyond the wisest pagans, know what lies beyond existence, what admits no contingency, what lends divinity to all else, what is the ground of existence, is not simply a law but also a begetting love, a love begotten, and the love between these two, is also immanent in all those who are caught up to share the unity of their self-caused life. God is not merely good, but goodness; goodness is not merely divine, but God.[23]

This richly suggestive passage obviously goes way beyond the minimal notion that the Being behind the law is merely more like a mind than anything else we know, all the way to Christian Trinitarian theism.

However, Lewis did not develop the argument in book 1 of *Mere Christianity* to full-blooded theism, let alone the Trinity. Indeed, he concluded book 1 by returning to the central points of the first chapter and reiterating that Christianity won't make sense until we fully come to terms with the moral reality for which he has been arguing. "It is after you have realized that there is a real Moral Law, and a Power behind the law, and that you have broken that law, and put yourself wrong with that Power—it is after all this, and not a moment sooner, that Christianity begins to talk."[24] While Lewis went on briefly to tell us that according to the Christian story, "God Himself becomes a man to save man from the disapproval of God," he did not spell out the good news or explain it. Rather, he concluded book 2 by driving home the bad news of the human predicament that results from the moral truths he has been defending.

Book 2 of *Mere Christianity* is where Lewis expounded the Christian solution to our moral predicament. He proceeded to defend full-blooded theism not so much by arguing for it as by contrasting it with other views of God. Significantly, moral concerns continue to drive the case he was building. Over against the pantheistic view that God is beyond good and evil, Christianity is a "fighting religion" that teaches that God takes sides for the good and against evil. Dualism is to be rejected because the very idea that there are two powers, one of whom is good and the other evil, assumes an objective moral standard of goodness according to which the good Power is really God. Even his climactic, and often quoted, argument for the divinity of Jesus relied on his foundational moral convictions. We know from obvious or self-evident truth what a great moral teacher looks like, and why a liar does not qualify. "A man who was merely a man and said the sort of things Jesus said would not be a great moral teacher. He would be either a lunatic—on a level with a man who says he is a poached egg—or else he would be the Devil of Hell. You must make your choice. Either this man was, and is, the Son of God: or else a madman or something worse. You can shut Him up for a fool, you can spit at him and call him a demon; or you can fall at His feet and call Him Lord and God."[25]

While this is the most famous passage in the book, and indeed one of the best known in all of Christian literature, the next chapter on the atonement is where Lewis finally explained the Christian solution to our moral dilemma. There we learn that the very reason the Son of God became incarnate was to offer us not only forgiveness but also the power to enable us truly to repent and undergo thorough moral transformation. Here we come to understand that we can be made right not merely with some impersonal Power behind the law. Rather, we can be restored to a loving relationship with a "superpersonal God," the God who is "begetting love" as well as "love begotten," and we may have the supreme joy of being "caught up to share the unity of their self-caused life."[26]

Rationality, Morality, and the Problem of Evil

While Lewis clearly placed a good deal of stock in the moral argument, it is worth noting that he gave scant attention to other classic theistic proofs, such as the cosmological and teleological arguments. These arguments were in retreat when Lewis wrote, so his indifference to them is hardly surprising. However, Lewis advanced another potent theistic argument for which he can claim some originality—namely, his argument from reason. This argument, which appears in chapter 3 of his book *Miracles*, is perhaps the most philosophically sophisticated thing he wrote. The argument was subjected to sharp criticism by Elizabeth Anscombe in 1948 at the Oxford Socratic Club, a debate society that focused on issues related to Christianity and of which Lewis was the president. Lewis believed the essential point of the argument was still defensible, and he published a refurbished version of it in a new edition of *Miracles* in 1960.

The heart of the argument is that reason cannot be adequately explained in naturalistic terms. Naturalism explains everything ultimately in terms of physical reality and the relations between particles of matter. One brain state causes another brain state in accordance with natural laws. The sort of causality in the realm of reason, however, seems to be altogether different. One thought is caused by other thoughts when we see the rational connection between them. As Lewis put it, "The one indicates a dynamic connection between events or 'states of affairs'; the other, a logical relation between beliefs or assertions."[27]

It would take us too far afield to explore this in detail, but here is the upshot. Whereas naturalism struggles to explain how matter gave rise to consciousness and rational thought, theists face no such difficulty since for them consciousness and rationality are fundamental to reality.

> [The theist] is not committed to the view that reason is a comparatively recent development moulded by a process of selection which can select only the biologically useful. For him, reason—the reason of God—is older than Nature, and from it the orderliness of Nature, which alone allows us to know her, is derived. For him, the human mind in the act of knowing is illuminated by the Divine reason. It is set free, in the measure required, from the huge nexus of non-rational causation; free from this to be determined by the truth known.[28]

Lewis combined a variation of this argument with his moral argument in a fascinating paper titled "De Futilitate," which he gave as an address at Magdalen College Oxford at the invitation of the president of the college sometime during the Second World War. His aim in this lecture was to challenge the notion of cosmic futility that was commonly held among intellectuals, and perhaps understandably so, with memories of the First World War still fresh and another war in full swing. This reminds us that ethics is about far more than the relatively formal question of what is right and wrong. Close to the heart of ethics is the question of what makes for a meaningful life, a life that is not ultimately futile but rather deeply satisfying and worthwhile.

Lewis's first major argument proceeded from the observation that at least some human thought and reason must be true, and reliably convey the truth about our universe. The claim that no thoughts are true is itself either true or false, and either way it follows that some thoughts must be true. As in *Miracles,* Lewis believes the phenomenon of reason points to the conclusion that mind is not a foreign latecomer in a universe that is fundamentally materialistic but, rather, that mind is the more fundamental reality. "Unless all that we take to be knowledge is an illusion, we must hold that in thinking we are not reading rationality into an irrational universe but responding to a rationality with which the universe has always been saturated."[29]

But the inescapable reality of logic is not enough to fend off the threat of cosmic futility. As Lewis recognizes, the universe as a whole does not appear to be good, despite the fact that it tosses up good things like strawberries and songbirds. So even if ultimate reality is logical, it may have no regard for the values we recognize; we may therefore still charge it with futility. At this point Lewis sees a problem. Our very act of accusing the universe assumes some standard of value by which we render that judgment.

> You must trust the universe in one respect even in order to condemn it in every other. What happens to our sense of values is, in fact, exactly what happens to our logic.... Our sense that the universe is futile and our sense of a duty to make those parts of it we can reach less futile, both really imply a belief that it is not in fact futile at all: a belief that values are rooted in reality, outside ourselves, that the Reason in which the universe is saturated is also moral.[30]

But the challenge to the notion "that the Reason in which the universe is saturated is also moral" runs deeper than the fact that the universe as a whole is not positively good. The "glaringly obvious" reality we must face is the wasteful cruelty and indifference to life that characterizes our world. Again, however, Lewis contends that we are in no position to level this charge with any sort of moral force if we deny the ultimate reality of morality. "Unless we judge this waste and cruelty to be real evils we cannot of course condemn the universe for exhibiting them."[31]

Ironically then, the atheist who passionately protests against the evil in this world may actually be acknowledging and honoring God, even if that is not his intention.

> The defiance of the good atheist hurled at an apparently ruthless and idiotic cosmos is really an unconscious homage to something in or behind the cosmos which he recognizes as infinitely valuable and authoritative.... The fact that he arraigns heaven itself for disregarding [mercy and justice] means that at some level of his mind he knows they are enthroned in a higher heaven still.[32]

Lewis's argument here as represented in these passages can be put as follows:

10. If our moral condemnation of the cruelty and indifference in our world is a true judgment, then the ultimate Reason behind our universe is moral.
11. Our moral condemnation of the cruelty and indifference in our world is a true judgment.
12. Therefore, the ultimate Reason behind our universe is moral.

Now Lewis realizes that embracing this conclusion leaves one with an enormous problem—namely, one is now faced with the classic problem of evil. "Having grasped the truth that our very condemnation of reality carries in its heart an unconscious act of allegiance to that same reality as the source of our moral standards, we then of course have to ask how this ultimate morality in the universe can be reconciled with the actual course of events."[33]

In other words, it is precisely the conviction that ultimate reality is moral, that God is good, that generates the challenge of theodicy. Consider David Hume's classic argument from evil and how it hinges on the conviction God is good in the sense that we normally use that term. This claim is rejected of course by Philo, the character in Hume's *Dialogues Concerning Natural Religion* who argues that the most reasonable conclusion we can draw from the empirical facts about our world is that the creator is amoral. Notice, the notion that the creator is amoral dissolves the problem of evil in an important sense. If the creator is morally indifferent, and has no interest one way or another in our happiness and flourishing, the misery of our world is hardly surprising and perhaps is even to be expected. So evil is not a "problem" in the classic sense that poses the thorny challenge of theodicy, which is to explain how the goodness of God "can be reconciled with the actual course of events."

So there is a sort of paradox here. While the belief that ultimate reality is moral intensifies the problem of evil, it is also the source of our hope that evil is not the norm, that evil will be defeated, and that good will ultimately triumph. The conviction that elevates the problem is the same conviction that grounds our hope against the specter of cosmic futility.[34] In short, the reality of evil provides us with another way to advance the moral argument.

The Tao Is Not Enough

One way to assess Lewis's moral arguments is to note where his case for objective morality without God is unconvincing and vulnerable to objection. To begin, notice that his argument for objective morality is cast in epistemic terms. His appeal is to the axiomatic nature of the Tao, to its self-evidence, to the claim that we must have a dogmatic belief in the platitudes of practical reason, if we are to have morality at all. Critics may be skeptical both that the Tao enjoys such axiomatic certainty and that our only alternative to giving up morality altogether is to affirm a dogmatic belief in these allegedly self-evident moral truths. Decades before Lewis wrote, the self-evident nature of traditional morality came under fire from Nietzsche, whose antirealist views were still a long way from gaining popular currency.

Indeed, the following passage from Nietzsche almost sounds like it could have been written as a response to Lewis:

> When one gives up Christian belief one thereby deprives oneself of the right to Christian morality. For the latter is absolutely not self-evident: one must make this point again and again in spite of English shallowpates.

Christianity is a system, a consistently thought out and complete view of things. If one breaks out of it a fundamental idea, the belief in God, one thereby breaks the whole thing to pieces: one has nothing of any consequence left in one's hands . . . the origin of English morality has been forgotten, so that the highly conditional nature of its right to exist is no longer felt. For the Englishman morality is not yet a problem.[35]

It is worth remembering that many of Lewis's contemporaries were skeptical of the idea of objective morality and would likely resonate with Nietzsche's claims here. At the very least, his line of attack represents a challenge to Lewis's appeal to the axiomatic nature of basic morality and of its power to command our assent on the basis of its alleged self-evidence.

The fundamental point here is that epistemic claims about the clarity or certainty of moral truth are distinct from ontological or metaphysical claims about the nature of morality and why we are obligated to follow it. Even if we grant that fundamental moral truth is self-evident, the question remains why we are accountable to it or even rationally required to follow it. Do we owe obedience to moral truth, even necessary moral truth, merely by virtue of its rational necessity?[36]

Here we should recall Kant's effort to ground morality in rational principles that he took to be binding on all rational agents. Despite his best efforts, he could not make full rational sense of moral obligation without postulating God and immortality. The necessary postulates of practical reason are not only freedom but also an afterlife and a God who will guarantee that happiness is proportional to virtue.

Lewis's confidence that he could rationally ground morality without God and immortality particularly seems especially unwarranted when we consider his own favored *experimentum crucis*—namely, the person who gives his life for a good cause. If there is no God and no afterlife, it is far from clear how anyone can be morally required to give up his life so that others may enjoy the very sort of life he sacrificed for them. This is not to deny that such a sacrifice may be a beautiful thing we instinctively admire. But if this world is all there is, if the only goods to be had are those of this life, it is hardly self-evident that anyone can be rationally required or duty-bound to sacrifice his own chance at these goods so that others may enjoy them.[37]

Lewis's moral argument in *Mere Christianity* recognizes that the law points to something behind it, and it this, not merely the law, that we ultimately encounter when we feel it pressing on us. As he describes it here, we are not merely recognizing self-evident truth, but rather, we are being given instructions about how we ought to live. These instructions seem to be communicated by something like a mind, a mind that seems to be "intensely interested in right conduct" and to "detest" our selfish behavior. Although he allows that whatever it is behind the law may not be like a person, it is only when he introduces personality into his argument that we have a fully satisfying account of how and why we are obligated to follow the moral law. Again, he does not so much argue for the personality of God as explain how Christianity provides the resources to make sense of how the moral law is one with a Father in heaven.

The profound implication of this idea is that we are obligated not merely to a law or a moral principle but to a perfectly loving person. Moral failure is not merely a lapse in doing our duty; it is a failure of love for a person who deserves our deepest loyalty and devotion. This is the powerful idea that comes fully to the fore in Christian revelation. As Glenn Tinder comments on the explosive implications, "Once personality has come to light it is seen, under the authority of irresistible intuition, as morally prior to everything impersonal. Having become cognizant of the personal, the only realities we can think of as valuable beyond measure and therefore as intrinsically ends in themselves, are those we can love and trust, listen to and address."[38]

The conviction that a personal God whose very nature is love is the One addressing us in morality also grounds our conviction that he also listens to us and cares for us. And this gives us reason to trust him and to live with confidence that our own ultimate well-being can never be at odds with doing his will and following his commands.

The same fundamental reason we have grounds for trust with regard to our individual lives also gives us reason firmly to believe that evil is real, that it is a problem in the deep sense that the world is not the way it ought to be, and that evil will finally be defeated. The moral argument, as we have noted before, is uniquely poised to neutralize the problem of evil. Many other classic theistic arguments leave God's moral nature out of the equation. Hume was happy to concede centuries ago in the *Dialogues* that something like a mind best explains our universe, but the problem of evil was left untouched in his view, since there is no reason to believe that God is good in anything like our normal understanding of the term. But if God is perfectly good as well as all powerful and knowing, then we have every reason to believe the problem of evil has a solution, even if we do not fully see it at this time.

The belief that such a God is "behind" the law ultimately relativizes morality in one sense and points up that the meaning of our lives is far richer and more significant than morality can capture. Lewis made this point in a little essay in which he addressed the question of whether we can live a good life without believing in Christianity. Summing up his answer, he noted that according to Christianity, we cannot be good on our own, but even if we could, we would not have achieved the purpose for which we were created.

> Mere morality is not the end of life. You were made for something quite different from that. . . . The people who keep on asking if they can't lead a decent life without Christ don't know what life is all about; if they did they would know that "a decent life" is mere machinery compared with the thing we men are really made for. Morality is indispensable; but the Divine Life, which gives itself to us and which calls us to be gods, intends for us something in which morality will be swallowed up. We are to be remade . . . a real Man, an ageless god, a son of God, strong, radiant, wise, beautiful, and drenched in joy.[39]

Here is the ultimate ground for the "very idea of a rule which is not tyranny or an obedience which is not slavery." To be ruled by such a God is to be made fit for a kind of happiness that mere morality cannot conceive, let alone produce.

> Synopsis: Probably the most famous moral argument in Western philosophy is the popular version C. S. Lewis developed at the beginning of his enormously influential book *Mere Christianity*. Lewis starts with the common-sense observation that we make moral judgments about right and wrong that we take to be objectively true. This suggests a reality beyond and behind the moral law that Lewis goes on to argue is like a mind, which points ultimately to a theistic explanation. Around the same time Lewis articulated this argument, he spelled out another version for a more academic audience based on the claim that if we are to have morality at all, we must take our basic moral judgments as self-evidently true. Lewis also developed other variations of the moral argument in his essays "The Poison of Subjectivism" and "De Futilitate," the latter of which argues that our condemnation of cruelty and indifference gives us the substance for a moral argument.

14

A Reverend Don

H. P. Owen

Born in the twilight of 1926, educated in the "Greats" and theology at Jesus College, Oxford, the Welsh theologian, writer, and academic Huw Parri Owen was ordained as a minister in the Presbyterian Church of Wales in 1949. He served as professor of New Testament at the United Theological College Aberystwyth from 1940 to 1953 before moving to Bangor as lecturer in New Testament studies at the University College of North Wales. Later he was appointed as a lecturer in the philosophy of religion at King's College, London, becoming reader in 1963. Theological issues were his passion that persisted throughout his life and writings, especially a concern for traditional theistic and distinctively Christian belief. In 1971 Owen was appointed professor of Christian doctrine at King's College, a post he held until 1983. Two months shy of his three score and ten, he died in Cardiff—the capital and largest city in Wales—in October 1996.

Studying the Greats at Oxford involves a focus on classics (ancient Greece and Rome, Latin, ancient Greek, and philosophy), the "more human literature" distinguished from *res divinae*: theology. Owen's eclectic study encompassed both. Such a rich background combined with his fertile mind and able pen allowed him to leave behind as part of his legacy *Revelation and Existence* (1957), *The Moral Argument for Christian Theism* (1965), *The Christian Knowledge of God* (1969), *Concepts of Deity* (1971), and *Christian Theism: A Study in Its Basic Principles* (1984). Owen's prose is admirably clear, rife with philosophical sophistication, and a joy to read. The main source material used for this chapter will be his *Moral Argument for Christian Theism* and a gem of an article he published nineteen years later in the journal *Religious Studies*, called "Morality and Christian Theism."[1] It should already be obvious that Owen's moral argument won't point merely to theism generally but also to Christian theism particularly.

A Few Preliminaries

Owen identified Kant as the first philosopher to formulate the moral argument. As we have confirmed in this book, most every subsequent moral apologist, including Owen, spent significant time and energy situating their own favored analyses of the argument relative to those of Kant—noting points of resonance, discord, or both with the German sage. Among later distinguished thinkers who followed in Kant's footsteps that Owen notes are Newman, Rashdall, Webb, and Taylor, and of these he admits that he owed a special debt to Newman and Taylor. "The former's *Grammar of Assent* and the latter's *The Faith of a Moralist* deserve to be placed among the classics of philosophy."[2]

Owen hoped to show in his book that morality provides firm grounds for believing not just in a transcendent, personal, and holy God but in the God of Christianity more specifically, which gives his argument a distinctive flavor beyond an inference to generic theism. He offered two reasons why he chose to write on the moral argument rather than the ontological, cosmological, or teleological. First, he didn't think the argument had recently been given the prominence it intrinsically deserves. Second, he thought that a fresh presentation of it might help to make Christian theism more intelligible and meaningful to believers and unbelievers alike, for "every reflecting person must be concerned to discover the metaphysical foundations of his moral life."[3]

Owen's *Moral Argument for Christian Theism* is an essay in natural theology. Its purpose was to show that it's possible to infer the existence of a self-existent, personal, and creative God from the objective order of morality that is apprehended by the natural intellect. Two theses must be held together. On the one hand, moral claims and values can be nonreligiously perceived. On the other hand, their status can't be explained unless they are grounded in the holiness of God. The argument from morality to religion is examined through the concepts of duty, goodness, and beatitude. The last section described the ways in which the argument is both clarified and fulfilled by Christian revelation. In what follows we will accentuate several of the most distinctive features of Owen's approach.

The Nature of Morality

Owen's book was published in the mid-1960s, when logical positivism was in decline but was still a fairly influential force in philosophy, and many still thought of metaethics as almost exclusively concerned with semantic investigations. Perhaps it's not surprising, then, that he started his book by broaching this topic of what various moral locutions like "good" and "right" *mean*.

Owen thought that close examination of the language of philosophy was a useful starting point to understand morality itself. Inquiring into the status of such moral locutions as "right" and "wrong," "good" and "bad"—as applied to dispositions, motives, intentions, actions, and consequences—was Owen's goal to begin his book. His thesis was that these moral terms are (and thus morality *is*), first, irreducible and unique and, second, capable of being given a fully objective reference. "Unless these two theses can be maintained it is impossible to take morality as a ground for belief in God—or indeed to believe in God at all."[4] So this portion of his argument was his effort to identify the relevant moral facts in need of explanation.

After distinguishing between ethical hedonism and psychological hedonism, Owen made clear he was quite open to the possibility of a synthetic connection between goodness and pleasure. This insight is at the heart of one of the important variants of the moral argument that has arisen several times in the history of moral apologetics. The pleasure or joy perfectly corresponding with goodness may not be completely attainable until the life to come.

Moral terms are not only irreducible—indeed, unique and sui generis—they are also "objective." Owen distinguished between three ethical meanings for objectivity. First, we can mean that values exist in an absolute form outside the world of sense-experience.[5] Second, sometimes we use the word "objective" in the sense of "universal." By this criterion, an objective standard, ideal, or norm is one that holds for everyone.[6] Third, when we apply a moral attribute objectively we may mean that the attribute inheres objectively in the person, act, or state of affairs to which it is applied. This would imply that moral judgments are descriptive, capable of being true or false, and, Owen thought, must ultimately rest on "intuition."[7] To round out his discussion of the nature of morality, Owen tried showing that both "goodness" and "rightness" are objective in the second and third senses stipulated above, and that a further consideration of rightness reveals that moral claims are objective in the first sense as well.[8]

Owen delimited the main application of "goodness" to persons. On this score he resonated with the words of William Sorley. Most importantly, "the moral consciousness testifies to standards, principles, or norms in the light of which we judge a person good or evil."[9] Owen's position was that we glean moral knowledge through acts of moral reasoning that resemble sense perception more than formal reasoning. Certainty is beyond the reach for inferences about the existence of either material objects, other human selves, or morality, but hankering after certainty is usually an epistemic pipe dream. Owen was content with the evidence of moral experience to convince him that he was rational to infer real objective truth, and he didn't let lack of apodictic certainty dissuade or discourage him.

Finally Owen turned to the issue of moral rightness, the topic of moral obligation. Affirming a duty, say, to keep a promise is to say that it's right for every rational person to do so irrespective of his feelings and desire. There's no way to *prove* a standard's objective rightness, but those who would deny it face the same problems brought against those who deny the objectivity of "good." A claim is something that confronts us, but it can only do so if it has real existence. The moral law comprises the principles or norms that make an action right or wrong. Yet it's also a command—a "categorical imperative" requiring unconditional obedience. But how can the law command unless it exists either in itself or in the will of a divine lawgiver?[10] "In moments of temptation we are aware of two orders competing for our assent: the order of our desires with their insistent clamour, and the order of claims with their unconditional demands."[11]

Still, Owen admitted two criticisms of belief in the objectivity of moral duties. First, the belief is sometimes thought to be inconsistent with differences between moral codes. To which Owen's answer was threefold: First, the variations between moral codes can be, and often are, exaggerated. "Today a humanist, a Hindu, and a Christian could all agree that truthfulness, courage, and compassion are among the principal virtues that they are obliged to cultivate."[12] Second, we should distinguish between the form and the content of moral obligation. "Duties may vary; but duty itself remain the same. At some time and in some mode people of every race have glimpsed a moral order that transcends their finite selves and enforces unconditional claims."[13] And third, even if we admit a wide variety between moral codes, and even if there are people who do not acknowledge any absolute moral law, we could still maintain that such a law exists.

The second criticism of belief in the objectivity of moral duties is based on competing claims. W. D. Ross spoke of duties with only prima facie force. We may have a prima facie duty not to lie, but on occasion we may be obliged to lie. How can we reconcile this conflict between claims with their objectivity? Again, Owen's response was threefold: (1) Whenever a claim is practicable it is unconditional. Many if not most moral choices are simple. (2) When two claims can't be enacted simultaneously we recognize that the moral order can be only partially fulfilled for the time being. Gaps exist between value and existence in this world.[14] (3) There is always one, invariably unconditional demand to discharge duties as faithfully as one can.

Owen thus defended moral objectivity on purely rational grounds, for unless it is granted the moral argument can't get off the ground.

Morality and Religion

Next Owen devoted attention to stating the basic principles that must govern any argument from morality to religion, and to Christianity more specifically. The first principle is this: the theist must admit that moral terms can have a self-evident meaning and validity outside the context of religious faith. This means that unbelievers can assent to moral objectivity, recognizing the existence of moral norms and discerning their objective embodiment in a person's character and will. This comports with St. Paul's assertion that Gentiles "show that what the law requires is written on their hearts," as well as with the fact that discourse about a good God in the first place necessitates a grasp of moral meanings. Indeed, it's mainly on moral grounds that we distinguish between degrees of revelation. "It is by an appeal to independent moral norms that we find a clearer view of God in the Sermon on the Mount than in the imprecatory Psalms."[15]

The second principle distinguishes such self-evidence from self-sufficiency. When morality is true to itself, Owen argued, it will raise "questions to which the Christian concept of God is the only answer."[16] Two points here can help understand the insight: the distinction between the order of being (the *ordo essendi*) and the order of knowing (*ordo cognoscendi*), and the "relative independence" or "derived autonomy" of the created order.[17] In the order of being, the Creator can be supreme, the source of all that exists, while in the order of knowing the Creator doesn't come first. Discerning or discovering God in and beyond creatures and creaturely activities as their ground requires an additional step. So, for example, we are immediately aware of moral claims and values as facts existing in their own right. Then, the "task of the philosopher is to prompt this perception by pointing to those aspects of morality that demand a religious explanation. His aim is to show that what is first in the order of knowing is second in the order of being."[18]

The third principle is that moral arguments must do justice to both the right and the good, which represent two different attitudes to the moral life. Owen chalked the first up to Israel, typified by the Mosaic law. The second, he claimed, derived from Greece and is typified by Aristotle's *Nicomachean Ethics*. Without wading into the vast literature on this, Owen registered his view that it's impossible to reduce "right" to "good" or "good" to "right" in a moral setting. Each needs the other, and each must be weighed separately.

The fourth principle is that the theistic inference must lead to a moral—not to a supramoral or, even less, submoral—God. God can be the foundation of morality only if he possesses supreme moral worth.[19] God "must be wholly good. He must perfectly exemplify all the qualities which we know to be binding on us in our human life. Otherwise he cannot be the source of moral obligation."[20] The God of the Bible, Owen declared, satisfies this requirement. God taught and instructed Israel with the law, which didn't merely enact God's will but reflected his nature. Its culminating formula is "You shall be holy, for I am holy." The "end" of "the good life" is to imitate divine perfection.[21] The picture was incomplete until God gave us a direct image of himself by assuming our nature in Christ.

In both a deontological and teleological sense goodness is to be strived for, but our goodness is distinct from our existence in two ways. First, our existence is contingent, and, second, no human person can say that his existence corresponds completely in his essence. By contrast, God's essence and existence are identical, which we forget to our peril when we say an action is right simply and solely because God commands it and it merits our obedience apart from its congruence with our moral insight.

So far, then, Owen's point has been that morality is autonomous within the order of knowing, but it depends on religion (likely the God of Christianity) in the order of being. In subsequent sections he will give reasons for thinking this is so.

What sort of validity, then, can the moral argument possess? Owen claimed that if the argument is to have any cogency, it must rest on a frank recognition of important facts. First, it's an exercise of faith seeking understanding. Second, the demonstration is informal, a matter of what the twentieth century Anglican theologian E. L. Mascall called "contuition," viewing God and the world together so that we will see God as Creator of the world and the world as dependent on God. In Owen's words, "Every proof seeks to explicate the 'cosmological idea' that even the simplest mind can grasp pre-philosophically." Third, two truths must be balanced: (1) The evidence genuinely points to God—it's a sign or indication of him. Discursive thought has an essential part to play. (2) At the same time, though, discursive reason can't itself compel assent to the truth of the theistic postulate. When it's done its work, it "must leave the final apprehension to *intellectus*—to the mind's capacity for intuiting God in (or contuiting him with) his effects."[22]

Owen added that the relative adequacy of various theistic accounts differentiates between rival theistic hypotheses. To satisfy the moral consciousness, God must be good. From a religious standpoint, God must be personal, one of Webb's recurring themes. Further, God must be absolutely good, since moral claims are unconditional. And if God is infinite in goodness he must be infinite in existence—free from the limitations that affect our own existence. Here Owen seemed to be identifying the features associated with ontological goodness. Beyond all of that, God must be our Creator to deserve our complete obedience.

In this context, Owen identified the four distinctive merits of the moral argument: first, its data are of immediate concern to everyone; second, if morality is objective, it introduces us immediately to an intelligible world beyond the world of space and time; third, the moral sense is nearer than any other to the "sense of the divine"; and fourth, the last and strongest reason for pursuing the moral argument as far as it will take us is that it was through the law that

> God revealed himself to Israel. If, therefore, we are to "philosophize in faith" we shall look to the moral life as cogent evidence for God. Just as it was through Moses and the prophets that God disclosed the secret of his being to the people of his covenant so it is, as by a reflected light, that he discloses himself to all men through the law that he has written on their hearts.[23]

Duty

Among the created moral signs of God fulfilled in Christian revelation is obligation. Although moral claims constitute an independent order of reality, Owen was convinced that there are good reasons to infer to God as their source or ground. He offered five of them.

First, duties are not self-explanatory. They are enigmatic entities that make us feel pressure and constraint, but it's hard to give a further account of their existence by appealing to the resources of morality alone. Part of their mystery is that they apply to persons. As W. D. Ross once put it, "the 'claim' [duty] seems inevitably to suggest two persons, one of whom might make a claim on the other."[24] This becomes especially clear in "law" when this is taken to signify "command," as Webb argued. Owen wrote, "It is impossible to think of a command without also thinking of a commander."[25]

Owen thus thought that we're faced with a choice between taking moral claims or duties as self-explanatory aspects of impersonal existence, on the one hand, or explaining them in terms of a personal God, on the other. He admitted that the first option can't be disproven, but he thought it implausible, because it would mean that the ontological status of moral duties in themselves would be entirely different from their ontological status when empirically embodied. Such unintelligibility renders it difficult for reflective persons to continue believing in them.[26]

Owen recognized that there are challenges to his theistic account, admitting that to some people "ultimate explanations" will always seem gratuitous. There is of course no magical formula for dealing with an antimetaphysical attitude, only the hope of dispelling it by showing the contradictions or at least tensions it involves. Owen also conceded that theism is likely to seem chimerical if it's severed from its experiential roots. Moral duties, or even human rights, are painless to trivialize and excise in a philosophy seminar room but not in a concentration camp.

A second reason to infer to God as the ground of moral duties is the *obedience* that those duties require. Owen discerned a paradox: while moral claims transcend every human person and every personal embodiment, still we value the personal more highly than the impersonal. Thus it's contradictory or at least involves a tension to assert that impersonal claims are "entitled to the allegiance of our wills." The solution to the paradox, Owen argued, "is to suppose that the order of claims, while it appears as impersonal from a purely moral point of view, is in fact rooted in the personality of God."[27]

Claims are apt to be most stringent when they are personally mediated. We feel especially guilty when our wrongdoing betrays another person's confidence. And from the Christian standpoint all wrongdoing takes this form; for it is, directly or indirectly, a betrayal of God's love. Moreover, when moral conflicts arise, we tend to give priority to the claim possessing the greater personal stringency. This is why most people, even among those who have a high regard for truth, would be prepared to lie to the German soldier during World War II about the whereabouts of a concealed Jew.

A third reason to think of God as the source of moral duties is that persons are able to exert claims in their own right. Even most secularists concur with Kant's dictum that each person must be treated as an end and never simply as a means. This makes the subordination of the individual to the state condemnable. People have intrinsic worth, deserve unlimited respect solely because they are human beings, and are entitled to be accorded dignity and value as a result. Cambridge professor Basil Willey wrote that Christianity teaches just this: that humanity inevitably becomes subhuman when cut off from the superhuman; that, as Chesterton expressed it, nature becomes unnatural unless redeemed by the supernatural.[28] Unbelievers can surely treat others with dignity, but such practice finds for an underlying theory more support in theism than atheism.

A fourth reason for a theistic account of duties comes from an analysis of three major terms: *reverence, responsibility*, and *guilt*. It has been the impression of many, including Owen, that reverence and devotion to the moral law, which seems to be a fitting attitude, makes sense, or at least makes *best* sense, only if it's something personal. Similarly, to be responsible involves the idea of a person or persons to whom responsibility is due. Even when no human person is in sight, we can still speak of responsibility—for example, responsibility to use one's gifts properly. To whom, Owen asked, is one responsible if not to God who bestows all gifts on trust? Explaining it instead by talk of responsibility to oneself or to an abstract order of claims seems, in the first instance, to neglect the other-regarding nature of responsibility, and, in the second, to strain credulity.

What about guilt? Newman, Taylor, and others in the history of the moral argument have fixed their attention on this intractable feature of the moral landscape. If the cause of conscience and the one before whom we're morally guilty for wrongdoing doesn't belong to the visible world, it must, Newman argued, be supernatural and divine—a Supreme Governor, a Judge, holy, just, powerful, all-seeing, retributive, the creative principle of religion.

Owen resonated with Newman's "persuasive," not "demonstrative" argument, thinking it eminently reasonable to conclude that our shame at having violated the moral law is due to the fact that we are in the presence of a holy lawgiver.

Finally, fifth, the law requires our obedience, yet we are unable to give it. And yet *ought* implies *can*. Nobody can honestly say he's able to perform the "more exacting claims" of morality "continually with the purity of motive that the moral law requires." Our natures are defective and in need of healing, and where can we realistically look for this except in supernatural aid? "That such aid (or grace) is given through Christ is the gospel ('the good news') that the New Testament proclaims."[29]

Owen thought that morality doesn't give us direct awareness of God but does give us grounds for making a legitimate inference about a dependence relation. God is both transcendent and immanent, which accounts for the double character of the pressure that the moral law exerts—both from the outside and the inside. God's moral authority is not mere power. "We must not think that God's love is separate from his holiness; for his will reflects his character. His holiness is love. He made us out of love in order that we might share in the love that is his very being. Just as his will of love is the imperative of the moral law so also his character of love is the exemplar of the moral life."[30]

This results in a beautiful picture of obligations, a far cry from "might makes right," rigid legalism, or arbitrary divine fiat. "Morality . . . is fulfilled in the belief that the whole life of duty is a debt of gratitude to God for his great love in creating us to share in his perfection."[31] By principled faith we identify the form and content of the moral law with God's will and character. "God wills us to be truthful and compassionate because he possesses these qualities to an infinite degree. Out of love he created us to share his holiness; and our duty to fulfill the moral law is our answer to his love."[32]

Goodness

Owen argued that moral goodness points to God in three different respects: its origin, its status as an ideal, and its relation to empirical fact. To start with, then, how did man first become aware of moral norms? Confident that naturalism is a failed hypothesis, Owen thought that moral consciousness can't be reduced to or explained by the nonmoral state from which it arose, nor moral feelings explained by nonmoral criteria and feeling-states, without committing the naturalistic fallacy. He thought this inexplicable unless we assume the moral order exists as a higher environment to which man *can* and, if he is to fulfill his essence, *must* adapt himself; and the capacity for moral adaptation was instilled and actualized by a designing Power. To harmonize these two assumptions we must infer that this Power is the source of the moral order.

His second argument concerned the status of goodness as an ideal, in which he extended his earlier analysis to suggest that values must possess an independent existence. Is there justification to infer that moral values exist in a spiritual realm inaccessible to sense-experience? Owen thought there are four reasons that can be given for this, but he thought only the fourth was valid. The first three are Aquinas's fourth way, an Augustinian argument in Descartes's *Third Meditation*, and religious experience. After rejecting those efforts, Owen instead pointed to the way moral values affect us in two distinct ways: attraction and obligation. That is, first they attract us as "ideals" to aspire to, and second, values can be viewed in terms of obligation.

We feel obliged to enact values. The moral consciousness, Owen thought, requires that we combine the Platonic with the Kantian attitude by viewing values not simply as ideals that attract a natural desire but also as facts that impose an unconditional obligation.[33] Once we show the existence of a value, we have reason to think that it's goodness itself that attracts us, "as a magnet attracts iron filings from afar."[34]

Is such goodness personal or impersonal? Are we to equate it with Plato's idea of the Good or with the personal God of Christianity? Rightly or wrongly, Owen seemed convinced these were the two best alternatives. Owen clearly gravitated toward the latter; how could we, as persons, participate in a goodness that is impersonal, for example? "Platonic Forms could, perhaps, attract. But how could they impose an obligation? How could we be indebted to them? Why should the failure to enact them engender guilt?" Personal theism offers the explanation by affirming that value-claims inhere in the character and will of God. "In rejecting them we do not merely reject an abstract good; we do not merely reject our own 'good' (in the sense of our 'well-being'); we reject the love which God is in his tri-une being."[35]

What was Owen's third reason for ascribing a theistic basis to morality? On the one hand we are obliged to obey the moral order unconditionally. On the other hand our achievement of the good is thwarted by the evil powers of sin and death. "Our moral natures cannot be fulfilled unless we are destined for another world in which the realm of values can be perfectly expressed."[36] Here he considered H. J. Paton's *The Good Will*, in which Paton, to put it briefly, argued it's not less moral, but arguably more moral, to fight for a victory whose issue is in doubt and whose attainment may be forgotten, rather than fighting in order to win any external reward.

Owen argued Paton underestimated the long-term deleterious impact on robust moral conviction that atheism will have as an undercutting or perhaps even rebutting defeater. He also thought that Paton grossly misgauged both the truth claims and the transforming power of religion. "While the attitude he depicts is perhaps tenable by a Stoic sage can we realistically expect it to be held by a person of average character?"[37] He noted, too, how Paton's words conveyed a dark mood of stark resignation while excluding the joy that is a mark of Christian sanctity.

One last remark is in order before moving on. As was his wont, whenever Owen talked about "rewards and punishments," his focus was, to a fault, always on their *intrinsic* features, never something externally imposed. Joy and a life of virtue were, for him, never to be separated; and there's nothing arbitrary about God's commands; they are all supremely strategic. It's about learning the Trinitarian dance steps of eternal joy. When the moral life is viewed in more than a provisional and partial way, Owen saw it as inextricably linked to a joyous relationship with a good God. "It is God's goodness—the love which he is in his inmost being—that constrains us. And (according to the 'moral eschatology' of Christian theism) it is for the vision of his goodness 'face to face' that he is preparing us in every claim that he imposes . . . in our earthly pilgrimage."[38]

Beatitude

Next Owen extended his moral case for God and an afterlife through the concept of happiness, or beatitude, recognizing that the best-known form of this argument was Kantian: Since in this life goodness is not always accompanied by happiness, yet it ought to be, we must postulate another life in which the defect is remedied. We must also postulate God because only he has the power and goodness to make it possible.

Owen recognized three flaws in Kant's argument. First, Kant was entitled only to the hypothetical proposition that if God existed he would ensure that the virtuous are the happy, not the categorical conclusion that such a being exists. Second, the relation that Kant posited between God and man, being external, can't satisfy religious needs. Owen remained firm that the deepest joy is to know God himself. Third, one would have expected Kant to spurn the very idea of a reward in the form of an externally conditioned happiness.

Acknowledging the limitations of Kant's version of the argument led Owen to give this variant last, after he made the case for inferring God from the moral evidence that is fully within our present grasp. What the second and third criticisms show, Owen thought, is that we must start with a concept of happiness that is much more profound than the one that Kant used. What's needed, again, is an integration of Kantian deontology with the tradition of teleological ethics we inherit from Plato and Aristotle, Augustine and Aquinas.

The teleological view of ethics rests on three concepts: "end," "good," and "happiness." Regarding "ends," every being moves toward an end or goal that is appropriate to its nature. With respect to "good," this can signify the fulfillment of a goal or end. It is that at which any form of being aims. Owen's main theme was "happiness," which can have the following senses: (1) happiness may mean the well-being of the soul; (2) it can indicate the activity or object that constitutes well-being, and thereby also the good or end of human nature; and (3) happiness can indicate the feelings or emotions that are summed up in the words "pleasure," "satisfaction," or "delight."

This account of happiness raises several questions, the most frequent of which is that once we take happiness as an end we can no longer act for the sake of duty. Owen offered four replies to this objection:

(1) If the final end of man is defined in terms of the moral order there can't be a conflict between happiness and duty. Stoics, Epicureans, and Christians should all agree on that, for different reasons.
(2) It's important to give a psychologically accurate account of the relation between happiness and duty. To say we are morally good because we desire happiness misrepresents morality; saying our happiness is a

wholly unintended consequence of moral goodness misrepresents our desire for happiness.[39]

(3) One must distinguish between long-term and short-term choices. The moral path doesn't require that every choice have one's own ultimate beatitude in mind. To the contrary, it would often be inappropriate, such as on occasions when nothing but, say, compassion for another should be one's motivation. But that doesn't entail a vitiation of the legitimate desire for ultimate happiness.

(4) If morality is our final end it will determine our lesser ends.[40]

On that foundation Owen took what he described as an indirect route from happiness to God. The order he took, one imposed not by revelation but by natural theology, starts with the postulation of immortality. If the final end of man is morality, it's not hard to see how at two crucial points the end can't be achieved within the limits of this present life. Nothing less than perfection is our final end. Yet the fact of moral failure is as universally verifiable as any spiritual fact can be. No one insisted on this more strongly than Kant. If then we are to achieve our end, there must be another life to which the achievement will be somehow possible.

The demand for immortality becomes still more urgent when we reflect on the social nature of the moral life. While some duties don't involve any reference to other people, most of them directly or indirectly do so. The chief command at the human level is to love one's neighbor as oneself. If our final end consists in the personal relationships that we form through love, however, it can't be reached in this present life; think of lost loved ones we loved imperfectly.

However, even if these moral arguments for immortality are sound, we must still justify the further inference to God. Christian theism affirms that man's last end (moral goodness) is a participation in the absolute goodness (the holiness) of God. A case to God can be made in a few different ways. First, it is well known that Kant argued from holiness to immortality, but his argument also required the postulation of an infinitely personal God. God can and will impart to our perfected natures a living likeness of his immutability.

The argument from happiness is ancillary to Owen's main moral argument, but he thought that if it only inclined the intellect to faith, it will have done its job. If the theistic argument from happiness merely awakens a dormant sense of "belonging" to "another" world, it will have served as a prelude to the gospel, to which we now turn.

Christian Revelation

Owen was convinced that any knowledge we have of God by arguments is only an obscure reflection of the light conveyed by Christian revelation. So, using his dual training in philosophy and theology, Owen tried to show how the content of biblical revelation fulfills the evidence for faith that is obtainable from moral premises.

The only full and final revelation is given in Christ who is God manifest in human form. In Christ we see that God *is* love—the love that died and rose again on our behalf. It's impossible to understand the ultimate and distinctive meaning of biblical ethics outside this context of revelation. The New Testament (NT) fulfills the Old Testament (OT). Just as the OT derives morality from the revelation of God in the law, so the NT derives it from his final, complete revelation in Christ. Two passages serve as illustrations: Jesus's command to love one's enemies—because such love is shown by God who freely bestows his gifts on all. The dependence of ethics on religion is equally evident in the epistles. Both the content and the inspiration of the moral life are provided by the saving ministry of Christ. The epistles deduce *didache* from *kerygma* (imperatives from indicatives). A good example is Romans 12, though it's a pattern that recurs. Chapters 1–11 of Romans deal with theology, and 12–15 with ethics.

While Christian morality gains its ultimate and distinctive meaning through its dependence on Christian revelation, it always has *some* meaning on a nonreligious plane. Agnostics frequently show a tenderness, generosity, and self-sacrifice that are lacking in many orthodox believers. The Christian ought never to deny or disparage the love exhibited by unbelievers. Rather he ought to show how it is deepened and strengthened by the revelation of God in Christ.

The NT itself features moral teachings that can both positively and negatively lead the mind to belief in God:

> *Goodness.* Be holy as God is holy; be perfect as your heavenly Father is perfect. (1 Pet. 1:14–16; Matt. 5:48). Divine goodness is no longer a

transcendent and barely accessible ideal; it has become "man in Jesus," so that both its obligatory and its attractive aspects are identical with his influence. As one who was both God and man, Jesus offered an example of supernatural perfection. To follow him is to imitate the qualities of his divine humanity—the qualities of obedience, gentleness, love, endurance, humility. He became what we are so that we might become what he is.

Duty. God's sacrificial love imposes on its recipients an obligation to show such love toward each other. Forgiveness is not a natural virtue, the overflow of a kindly disposition. Like love it is required by the supernatural example of Christ. Like love, too, it takes the form of a response. Christians are morally obliged to forgive each other in return for the forgiveness that has been granted to them by God. The word that best describes this union of imitation and response is *gratitude*. Yet it can't be done in our own strength alone.

Beatitude. Revelation fulfills the concept of "beatitude." Reason can suggest that our highest end or goal is to achieve perfection in an everlasting life with God, but it's doubtful whether reason alone can convince us that the goal exists. God promises believers that, through the Spirit, they can share in the beatitude won for them by Christ who is "the first-born among many brethren," the inclusive head of a "new creation." Christians can't share the glory of their Lord unless they share his death—unless they are crucified with him to their lower selves and to the vanity of this fleeting world. The way of sacrifice is more than the condition of an immortality that is yet to come. It is itself the beginning of eternal life. The Christian's task is to embody the life of the new age within the context of the old, filled with eschatological hope.

Owen's work in this culminating chapter represents, to our thinking, a topic of cutting-edge importance today: the effort to extend the moral argument beyond generic theism to more specific and fine-grained theologies. Delineating resonances between general and special revelation is also a vital research agenda among prospective moral apologists.

Synopsis: H. P. Owen was a wonderfully systematic thinker, and his work is a joy to read. He was also a student of history; his moral argument is couched in what to this day remains one of the better cursory sketches of the history of the moral argument. On the shoulders of Newman, Sorley, Taylor, and others,

Owen constructed an intelligent moral argument. Distinguishing between self-evidence and self-explanation, he argued that various moral phenomena, though they fall into the former category, don't fall into the latter. In discussing the deliverances of morality and delineating their salient features, he patiently demonstrated their theistic implications, without pretending to have offered anything in the vicinity of a logical proof or demonstration. Significantly, he extended his case not just to theism generally, but to Christianity particularly.

15

Contemporary Moral Apologists

Several top-drawer philosophers labored on the moral argument throughout the twentieth century. They were all major scholars with long track records of achievements, but here we will quickly make mention only of their material most germane to this particular narrative.

A. C. Ewing lived from 1899 to 1973. Having studied at Oxford, he started teaching at Cambridge in 1931. He authored numerous books including *Value and Reality,* which is the book most relevant for our concerns. Ewing did quite a bit of work on the topic of moral goodness, and he canvased an array of moral arguments in chapter 8 of *Value and Reality*. Much of what he said there was by way of reiterating the arguments of others, conjoined with incisive analysis, but one particular point of note: although he thought the argument(s) have tremendous potential, he also thought the lack of "rigorous conclusiveness" in the moral argument to have certain advantages.

"It is a danger in moral arguments for God that somebody who found God's existence incredible might think he must then reverse the argument and repudiate any objective ethics. There is in my view nothing to justify this." He added, "That the moral law has being in God and that the moral law is bound up with the basic principle on which the whole of reality depends are not certain entailments of ethical propositions but hypotheses supported by the objectivity and authority of the moral law and intended to help towards solving the problem of its connection with existent reality." The result, he concluded, was a "weighty argument for God," but nothing like certainty, and on this point he echoed the refrain from several other luminaries from the history of the moral argument.[1]

David Elton Trueblood (1900–1994) was born a year after Ewing and was a noted twentieth-century American Quaker, prolific author, and well-known theologian, who served as chaplain at both Harvard and Stanford. In his *Philosophy of Religion*, he reasoned that any subjectivity applied to morality is nonsensical and precludes serious discussion of moral judgments. He pointed out that humans are poignantly aware of their moral failures, both individually and collectively. Loyalty and truth are things for which humans will die, but if loyalty is not to a *person*, and if truth is not about a *person*, then such sacrificial deaths are nonsensical.

On Trueblood's favored account of the moral argument, he thought it crucial to distinguish between theistic *sanction* of the moral law and a theistic *explanation* of the moral law (echoing Owen's distinction in different words). "The problem is not that of what will give the moral law power in men's lives, but that of a conception of the universe which will make the very existence of a moral law understandable. It is often supposed that the theistic emphasis on objectivity refers to sanction when, in fact it refers to understanding." He also emphasized that the moral argument is most effective when it's part of a larger cumulative case, and he noted the distinctive power of the moral argument to reveal more of God's character than does, say, an argument from nature. Like Taylor, he felt that within our own moral life we see God with the mask "half fallen off."[2]

Austin Farrer, another Oxford man, lived from 1904 to 1968, and is the subject of a biography by Philip Curtis.[3] His academic colleague, Basil Mitchell, said of Farrer that he was, by common consent, one of the most remarkable men of his generation, possessing the qualities of originality, independence, imagination, and intellectual force to a degree amounting to genius. Farrer was the Anglican whom C. S. Lewis asked to review a portion of *Mere Christianity*. Lewis and Farrer were close friends—Lewis saying Farrer was on the front lines of apologists—and many thought that Farrer would be the natural successor to Lewis's status as public Christian apologist.[4] Unfortunately, Farrer's complete potential wasn't realized, as he died a mere five years after Lewis did. Still, his contribution to Christian thought was notable, with Rowan Williams dubbing him "possibly the greatest Anglican mind of the twentieth century."[5]

Gordon Phillips at the end of his second Gresham lecture said this of Farrer:

> I regard him as one of the most remarkable men I have ever known. He combined so many excellences. He was a scholar, a wit, a saint, a philosopher, and a man of prayer. Few men have given more freely of their talents to the service of a Church. Yet in the life of his friends and of his pupils his influence will continue and others will perhaps turn to his books in times when the theological and intellectual climate will once again pay more attention to learning, spirituality, and style than it does at the moment. When we read his letters we shall also find that there too is one in whom the lost

art still survived. He was a hawk among sparrows and it was an honour and grace to have known him.⁶

Farrer put forth a moral argument of his own, which can be found in his book *Reflective Faith*. For a taste of its flavor, consider the way we normatively ought to think about other people. It is of great importance, he argues, that we value them rightly, that we think about others in such a way as to regard them properly. The only limitations that such deep regard for others should encounter are those that cannot be avoided—those set by the conditions of our life, as he put it. Such regard should be at once so pure and so entire that it leads to a sort of frustration deriving from the incompleteness of our definition of those we so regard. Thinking of our neighbors in too garden-variety a way can't sustain the esteem we intuitively think they deserve. The conclusion to which Farrer felt compelled is that what deserves our regard is not simply our neighbor, but God in our neighbor and our neighbor in God.⁷

Across the pond, meanwhile, George Mavrodes (born in 1923) wrote an article, "Religion and the Queerness of Morality," that has proven seminal.⁸ A graduate of Calvin College and a long-time philosophy professor at the University of Michigan, Mavrodes, echoing J. L. Mackie, argued that moral obligations are an odd fit in a Russellian (naturalistic) world. They seem to possess a sort of authority to which a naturalist account of moral obligations fails to do justice. On a theist picture of reality, in contrast, moral obligations make excellent sense.

Incidentally, in his contribution to Tom Morris's *God and the Philosophers*—a collection of "spiritual-intellectual autobiographies" of contemporary Christian philosophers—Mavrodes recounts an anecdote involving Lewis's *Mere Christianity*. This episode, in fact, initiated what became one of the central concerns of his philosophical work: the intersection of reason and faith. At dinner with a fellow Christian and his atheist friend, Mavrodes was anxious to make a convert through rational argument. He tried out Lewis's moral apologetic because he had found it so convincing himself. As the evening and conversation wound down, he could see that his interlocutor was no closer to belief in God than he was at the start. The whole affair was, for Mavrodes, "the beginning of a long reflection on the role of argument in religious affairs and in human life generally."⁹

Basil George Mitchell (1917–2011) was an English philosopher and, at one time, Nolloth Professor of the Philosophy of the Christian Religion at Oxford. He embarked on an academic career in 1947 as a tutor in philosophy at Keble College, Oxford, then moved to Oriel College at Oxford in 1968 to take up a university chair. In 1955 he was elected president of the Oxford Socratic Club, a position he held until 1972 when the club dissolved. Mitchell delivered the 1974–1976 Gifford lectures at Glasgow, which resulted in his 1980 book *Morality, Religious and Secular*, one among many significant publications.[10] The lectures analyzed the moral confusion of contemporary society, relating rival conceptions of morality with a wide variety of views about the nature and predicament of man. Mitchell argued that many secular thinkers possess a traditional "Christian" conscience that they find hard to defend in terms of an entirely secular worldview.

American philosopher Clement Dore was one of those specifically mentioned by Plantinga in his lecture-notes-turned-paper "Two Dozen (or So) Arguments for God."[11] Born in 1930, Dore offered a moral argument in the fourth chapter of his book *Theism*.[12] He started with the Platonic insight that a person's wrongdoing inexorably harms himself. This is an aspect of morality that no Hobbesian view of ethics can adequately explain. According to Hobbes, ethics functions to adjudicate conflicts arising from self-interest. What kind of harm does wrongdoing entail? Dore argued that this harm must be more than merely being a bad person, because some people are perfectly content to be bad people. In fact, some hedonists relish the prospect, while still seeming to avoid harm in this life. But if morality is overriding, such people will be harmed by their significant wrongdoing. Dore contended that a being with "God-like power" and "God-like knowledge" and who is thereby a *person* provides the best explanation of this.[13] Although Dore's argument hardly proved the existence of the full-fledged God of orthodox theism, he asserted that it did imply that another doctrine, which is normally associated with theism, is true—namely, that human beings survive earthly death.[14]

Born in 1937, the American scholar Robert Adams has done some truly groundbreaking work in theistic ethics, and in the process he constructed a few variations of the moral argument for God's existence.[15] His magnum opus, *Finite and Infinite Goods*, is nothing less than a classic. He's also a prominent scholar on Gottfried Wilhelm Leibniz. In addition to explicating versions of Kant's moral argument, Adams offered one of his own on the basis of his favored theory of moral obligations—namely, divine command theory. According to divine command theory, on Adams's account, when God commands us to perform an action, the action thereby becomes our moral obligation. Adams thought it perfectly legitimate to deploy strong moral convictions about right and wrong as premises in a reasoned argument. After defending at length a divine command theory as the best explanation of the nature of right and wrong, he observed that since such a theory entails God's existence, he took this commitment as evidence for God's reality.[16]

Adams's wife, Marilyn McCord Adams, was also a preeminent philosopher of religion who wrote extensively on the problem of evil, tackling even the most difficult cases of what she called "horrendous evils" that require defeat by nothing less than the goodness of God. She wrote, "My strategy for showing how this can be done is to identify ways that created participation in horrors can be integrated into the participants' relation to God, where God is understood to be the incommensurate Good, and the relation to God is one that is overall incommensurately good *for the participant*."[17]

Linda Zagzebski, born in 1946, writes on epistemology, philosophy of religion, and virtue ethics. A more recent book was based on her Wilde lectures at Oxford in 2010. She has done important work in the arena of theistic ethics, most particularly with her major book *Divine Motivation Theory*. Rather than asking the question "Why be moral?" she asked another, not so easily answered question in the same vicinity: "Should I try to be moral?" Why is this question different and important? Because, in short, it doesn't make sense to attempt something one can't do. If we are relegated to depending on our moral powers and capacities alone, our moral effectiveness seems to be in serious jeopardy, thus rendering the whole enterprise of morality, in an important sense, futile. Since morality presumably isn't futile, we have reason to think we are not relegated to depending on our own moral capacities and powers alone.

She identified three ways in which we need moral confidence, particularly in light of the sometimes costly nature of doing the moral thing: (1) We need confidence that we can have moral knowledge—good reasons that our individual moral judgments, both about obligations and values, are correct. (2) We need confidence in our moral efficacy, both in the sense that we can overcome moral weakness and in the sense that we have the causal power to bring about good in the world. And (3) insofar as many moral goals require cooperation, we need confidence in the moral knowledge and moral efficacy of other people.

As it happens, she also thinks that deep skepticism is warranted in each of these three areas if all we have to go on morally is our own moral intuitions and reasoning and the intuitions and reasoning of others. We all know how flawed we ourselves and others can be! Again, such resulting moral despair, she assumes, cannot be rational, so she concluded that we must be able to rely on more than our own human powers and those of others in attempting to live a moral life.[18]

C. Stephen Evans, born in 1948, a prolific philosophy professor at Baylor University, and educated at Yale, is the author of *God and Moral Obligation*, among others, including a half dozen important works on Søren Kierkegaard. His *Natural Signs and Knowledge of God* won the C. S. Lewis Book Prize in 2012 from the University of St. Thomas, which was awarded to the "best recent book in religious philosophy written for a general audience." Evans has privileged language of "natural signs," which serve as pointers toward God—though nothing like absolute demonstrations. Natural signs, on his view, provide a measure of good evidence for belief in God; they satisfy the Pascalian constraints of both widely accessible and easily resistible. He has identified various moral natural signs, among them human dignity, or worth, and moral duties.

J. P. Moreland, Distinguished Professor of Philosophy at Talbot School of Theology at Biola University, was born the same year as Evans. Moreland's evidential considerations for God's existence from the arena of morality focused on central philosophical insights and the strictures imposed by what constitutes a workable worldview. His book *The Recalcitrant Imago Dei: Human Persons and the Failure of Naturalism* is one place among others where he laid out this type of case.

One of the roles of a worldview, Moreland has emphasized, is to provide an explanation of facts, of reality, the way it *actually is*. Indeed, it is incumbent on a worldview to explain what does and does not exist in ways that follow naturally from the central explanatory commitments of that worldview.[19] In this light, Moreland characterizes a "recalcitrant fact" as one that is obstinately uncooperative in light of attempts to handle it by some theory. Such a fact doggedly resists explanation by a theory. The particular recalcitrant moral facts on naturalism are threefold: (1) objective, intrinsic value and an objective moral law; (2) the reality of human moral action; and (3) intrinsic human value and rights.

John Hare, born in 1949, is the son of the eminent Oxford don and ethical theorist Richard M. Hare. He currently teaches philosophical theology at Yale University and Divinity School. In his book *The Moral Gap*, Hare gave a particular version of the moral argument. It's a "performative" variant of the argument, according to which God is needed to make up for the gap between our moral status and what morality calls us to achieve. He argued that secular theorists tend to either puff up human capacities to close this gap, lower the moral demand, or generate secular substitutes for God's assistance—all of which fail.

This variant of moral apologetics focuses on one aspect of Kantian moral faith. Hare's book actually touched on the other variant as well by arguing that without God we lose reason to believe that the virtuous are ultimately happy and fulfilled. In late 2015 Hare published a new and groundbreaking book to add to his previous ones, *God's Command*, which deserves to be ranked alongside Robert Adams's *Finite and Infinite Good* as the best books on divine command theory in the last quarter century. Hare's encyclopedic work in the history of philosophy has powerfully demonstrated the important role theism played in the work of several philosophical luminaries from the past.[20]

Also born in 1949, William Lane Craig, with his two doctorates and wide-ranging publications, is arguably the greatest living Christian apologist. He has used a version of the moral argument to powerful effect on a plethora of college campuses across America and around the world. He has also been involved in numerous debates on a variety of subjects, but several times on the question of morality and God (including, quite recently, with Erik Wielenberg).[21] The form of moral argument Craig usually advances is deductive and easy to understand. It's valid and straightforward, and it goes like this:

1. If God does not exist, objective moral values and duties do not exist.
2. Objective moral values and duties do exist.
3. So, God exists.

The conclusion obviously follows from the premises, so detractors need to try calling into question at least one of them. Craig has said that, though the moral argument is not his personal favorite, it is the argument that has had the biggest effect on his listeners, focusing as it does on objective moral duties (or obligations) and moral values.[22]

C. Stephen Layman, emeritus professor of philosophy at Seattle Pacific University, was born in 1955, and he has proposed a different formulation of the moral argument; like others, Layman believes that it works best as part of a cumulative case. Layman began his argument with the overriding reason thesis (ORT), which says "the overriding (or strongest) reasons always favor doing what is morally required."[23] He then introduced the conditional thesis (CT), which says that "if there is no God and no life after death, then the

ORT is not true."[24] The intuition behind ORT is this: "If considerations of prudence and morality conflict, and if the prudential considerations are momentous while the results of behaving immorally are relatively minor, then prudence overrides morality."[25]

Now, it might appear that CT casts doubt on ORT, and it undoubtedly does from the atheist's point of view. But Layman added that it is hardly fair simply to assume that atheism is true, when an argument for theism is being offered. Moreover, surely we ought to be reluctant to jettison ORT.[26] Instead he would encourage readers to remain open to the possibility of both ORT and CT being true. If they are both true, what follows is this: either God exists, or there is life after death in which virtue is rewarded. Note that this leaves open the possibility of something like karma instead of a theistic universe, so an atheist could consistently accept both ORT and CT. In light of the incalculable complexity of a system of karma, however, Layman's response to this approach was to argue that "the moral order postulated by nontheistic reincarnation paradoxically provides evidence for the existence of a personal God."[27]

Born the same year as Layman was Jerry L. Walls, who has worked extensively in Christian eschatology, writing a trilogy on heaven, hell, and purgatory. These doctrines, often ignored in recent theology, have played an interesting role in the history of moral apologetics, as we have noted. He has also argued, notably in his final chapter of *Heaven: The Logic of Eternal Joy*, and in various other places, that Christian theology accounts for morality more naturally and fully than does naturalistic evolutionary theory. In *Heaven*, he advanced three connected arguments for this claim. Not only can Christian theology, unlike evolutionary theory, account for altruism in a way that reinforces our instinctive admiration for sacrificial action, it also has a ready explanation for why moral obligation has an objective ground. In a Christian account, he added, morality is not tarnished with the sort of deception and illusion that some prominent naturalistic accounts rely on at certain points. "Moreover, the doctrine of heaven provides moral philosophy the resources to resolve one of the most difficult problems it has been plagued with for the past several generations, namely, the conflict between egoism [by which he primarily means self-interest] and altruism. Each of these arguments has force in its own right, but taken together they provide strong reason to prefer a Christian account of morality to naturalistic ones."[28]

R. Scott Smith (born 1957), a philosophy professor at Biola, studied under Moreland and attributes much of his analytic approach to Moreland's influence. Smith's moral argument against naturalism and in favor of theism is heavily epistemic and ontological. In his *In Search of Moral Knowledge*, Smith offered an epistemic variant of the moral argument.[29] He carefully articulated, in insightful ways, a number of specific ethical theories. In addition to that large task, he attempted to construct a master argument able to critique all naturalistic ethical theories in one fell swoop. We should completely reject naturalism if indeed his argument goes through. He asked readers to consider a paradigm naturalist, Daniel Dennett, one who takes both cognitive science and the implications of naturalism seriously. Although Dennett is not entirely consistent, to the degree he is consistent about what he takes to be the implications of naturalism, Smith argued that he's hoisted by his own proverbial petard, encountering deep difficulties that undermine many of his claims.

Mark Linville (born 1957) has done outstanding work on the moral argument. In his entry on the moral argument in *The Blackwell Companion to Natural Theology*, he offered two independent moral arguments for God's existence.[30] The first was an argument from evolutionary naturalism, which itself has two parts: first, that on evolutionary naturalism our moral beliefs are without warrant. This argument canvased a variety of (meta-ethical) theories to test their adequacy in accounting for moral knowledge. Those predicated on naturalism are found wanting in light of challenges posed by evolutionary moral psychology. The second part of Linville's first argument was that theism is able to avoid such moral skepticism.

Linville's second argument in this landmark article was an argument from personal dignity, in which he tested an array of normative ethical theories to account for the essential moral standing of human persons, aiming to determine their explanatory adequacy. Egoism, utilitarianism, and virtue ethics are all shown to be ill-equipped to accommodate the Kantian principle of humanity prescribing the treatment of people as ends in themselves and not merely as means. Naturalism per se is further implicated for failing to account for the existence of persons themselves, whereas theism, he argued, is well situated and equipped to explain human persons, moral agency, and personal dignity.[31]

Paul Copan (born 1962), a former student of William Lane Craig's (as was Linville), has proven himself a formidable moral apologist, having written one of the most anthologized versions of the moral argument. Copan has also advanced moral apologetics by showing the reconcilability of certain Old Testament conquest narratives with nonnegotiable moral intuitions.[32]

Angus Menuge was born in 1963, and he's offered a compelling epistemic version of the moral argument. After identifying apparent reasons to be skeptical of naturalism explaining objective moral truth, he distinguished between two sorts of evolutionary ethics (EE): strong EE and weak EE. Strong EE dictates that moral facts themselves would be different had evolution played out differently. If, for example, we had been raised to kill our brothers and sisters or children, then such behaviors would have been morally right. Weak EE, in contrast, says it's only moral psychology (our moral beliefs) that would be different if we had been raised like hive bees.

Strong EE holds no realistic hope of sustaining objective moral facts. On the other hand, weak EE, Menuge suggested, gives us no grounds to think our moral beliefs are true. For they would be formed for reasons potentially quite unrelated to their truth. To make his point, he used an example of looking at what turns out to be a broken clock, unknown to you. It reads 7 p.m., and suppose that it is indeed, by sheer coincidence, 7 p.m. No knowledge results, though, since your reason for thinking it is 7 o'clock has nothing to do with its actually being 7 o'clock.[33]

Unfortunately for weak EE, if it is true, then we are in a precisely similar situation regarding our moral beliefs. For on that view, natural history is causally relevant to our moral beliefs but does not account for moral reality. Menuge wrote, "So if we had been raised like hive bees we would think fratricide and infanticide were right even if they were not. And, it could be that we think fratricide and infanticide are wrong (because we were not raised like hive bees) even though they are right. But now suppose that our belief that fratricide and infanticide are wrong happens to be true. Still, it is not knowledge, because what made us believe this has nothing to do with why our belief is true."[34]

Angus Ritchie (born 1974) has offered his own epistemic variant of the moral argument, and an impressive one indeed. Whereas Menuge focused on the way naturalism functions to preclude moral knowledge, Ritchie's focus was more on the way naturalism has an intractably difficult time explaining moral knowledge. His *From Morality to Metaphysics* did an admirable job identifying weaknesses in a broad array of secular meta-ethical theories.[35] He also convincingly advanced the claim that the teleological nature of theistic ethics is needed to overcome the central epistemic problem he identifies. Ritchie didn't deny that secular ethics can justify moral beliefs; rather he pointed out that their weakness is accounting for how our moral faculties can be reliable.

208   THE MORAL ARGUMENT

Of course this overview doesn't exhaust the field. This short history has been more of a promissory note than anything like a comprehensive chronology. Far better histories of the moral argument will be written; we hope this one might help inspire them. There's an abundance of potential research agendas and dissertations hinted at in these pages; it's been our pleasure making readers aware of them.

Others who've gone unmentioned have worked in the area of the moral argument, both pro and con, while yet others have used their talents to popularize the moral argument (Greg Koukl, Ravi Zacharias, Tim Keller, etc.) and introduce it to a fresh generation. Eventually, though, historical narratives must come to a halt somewhere (hopefully not too arbitrarily or abruptly), even as history marches on. The point of this concluding chapter has simply been to show that the moral argument, on the firm foundation of a history far richer and more extensive than many realize, has seen a real resurgence throughout the twentieth and into the early twenty-first century, and it continues to intrigue and incense, gain strength and momentum, and garner adherents and detractors alike.

Once more on this day, back at the Forest Public Library where we started, the majestic mountains are visible in the distance, though today more shrouded with some murky fog, but otherwise they remain the same, as the story continues.

Synopsis: Ewing worked extensively on moral goodness, while Trueblood directed his attention to the conception of the universe that imbues the moral law with understandability. Farrer focused on the intrinsic, intuitively accessible value and dignity of persons, while Mavrodes underscored the ontologically odd nature of binding moral duties in a naturalistic world. Mitchell demonstrated how secular ethics illegitimately borrow from theism, while Dore argued that morality gives us reasons to believe in a being with God-like power and knowledge. Robert Adams did groundbreaking work in theistic ethics and offered innovative variants of the moral argument on that foundation; his wife, Marilyn Adams, demonstrated how God's incommensurable goodness can help defuse the most otherwise intractable versions of the problem of evil. Zagzebski identified three ways we need moral confidence and how theism provides it. Evans defended divine command theory and a natural signs approach to apologetics. Moreland constructed an argument on the basis of recalcitrant moral facts, and Hare did landmark work on Kantian moral arguments. Craig has used the moral argument (including abductive versions) to powerful effect in numerous books and debates. Layman used the overriding reason thesis and conditional thesis in his variant of the argument. Walls has used moral resources to argue for both theism and Christianity—and he and I have offered a fourfold, abductive, cumulative, teleological moral argument of our own. Smith, Linville, Menuge, and Ritchie have offered brilliant epistemic moral arguments, and Copan has used history to augment the moral argument, extend it to Christianity, and defend the character of the God of the Old Testament.

Conclusion

In the summer of 2018 a touching documentary was released about the remarkable life of Mr. (Fred) Rogers, host of the long-running PBS television show *Mister Rogers' Neighborhood*, a show that invariably evokes nostalgia in many of us as we recall his daily cardigans, shoe-changing ritual, and King Friday the Thirteenth. It's easy to forget that the show went national in 1968, the most heart-rending and harrowing year of that whole tumultuous decade, a time of extraordinary political and social turmoil in the United States. Within that cultural maelstrom, Rogers understood it as his job to help children process all of the tragedy and upheaval of which they were certainly aware. His life shows that to be truly kind and gentle, to demonstrate empathy and to respect others, takes great will. Mockery is easier but takes a toll, eroding confidence and trust and wearing away the social fabric, a lesson Fred Rogers himself learned as a bullied child who had a hard time making friends.

His Christian faith is not the primary focus of the documentary, but it was implicit in everything he did. Junlei Li, director of the Fred Rogers Center, reminds us that Rogers's insistence that all people are inherently valuable, all are deserving of love and capable of giving it, is a fundamental tenet of Christianity. Rogers taught his viewers to see with spiritual eyes, to look at all people they encounter as image-bearers of God. No one is ordinary, and everyone is unique. Rogers calls us to be *tikkun olam*, a concept from Judaism that means "repairers of creation." "Love is at the root of everything—all learning, all parenting, all relationships. Love or the lack of it." Rogers did this in his inimitable and singular way, defying odds, bursting categories, shattering expectations, and debunking stereotypes along the way. Most fundamentally, he aimed instead to make goodness *attractive*, to help children become more aware that what is essential in life is invisible to the eye.

What Rogers embodied, interestingly enough, is so much of what this book has been about. Whether emphasizing our duties to others, the intrinsic value and dignity of people, the animating motivation a vivid picture of goodness provides, or apprehending the beauty of the Good, what

Rogers's inspiring life embodied, it seems to us, is just what the content of moral apologetics concerns. As we saw people leaving the theater in tears, it reminded us afresh of the power of transparent goodness and confirmed our conviction that the time is ripe to rediscover the history of the moral argument.[1]

Here in the conclusion of the book we intend to canvas several key motifs that arose in the history of moral apologetics. Recall from the introduction of the book that we invited readers to ponder certain questions as they read the history. Among the topics broached were guiding epistemological assumptions, operative theories of rationality, and the expansive breadth of empirical approaches. We also directed attention to the forms of arguments involved, the relationship between the moral argument and other pieces of natural theology, and ways in which the historical thinkers shed light on contemporary discussions. In addition, it was important to note disparate historical contexts and how they informed discussions, and to be attentive to the range of learning and rigor of approach among the luminaries in the field from Kant up to the present day. To wrap up this extended essay on the history of the moral argument, our concluding chapter will share some of our own reflections on such questions and others.

First, consider some of the eminently commendable traits exhibited by the scholars themselves. They were, with very few exceptions, remarkably respectful in the way in which they dealt with their interlocutors. They were level, judicious, and scholarly, and though they enjoyed the battle of ideas, they didn't tend to attack those who held opposing views. A few could be tendentious on occasion—Newman's polemicism comes to mind—but that was more an exception than the rule. Several of them expressed reservations about being considered "apologists," preferring to be known simply as philosophers. They were more interested in truth than in winning arguments and were loath to project any appearance of divisive partisanship.

They were also bona fide scholars who, as we have put it, *lived with* the moral argument, in many cases for much of their professional careers. They weren't in too big a rush to arrive at sweeping conclusions; they were exceedingly patient in their explorations and circumspect in what inferences they tentatively suggested. Arguments were to be savored and relished; ideas were to marinate and simmer before serving; epistemic humility was a priority. The ideas of which they wrote were also seen as relevant to all of life; none of this was for them an empty intellectual exercise. They grasped that the power of ideas encompassed all of life and that those ideas featured important implications for how they were to conduct their lives, process tragedy, and expend their energies day in and day out.

Several of the protagonists of our story did their most important work on the moral argument in the midst of tragic circumstances. C. S. Lewis's *Broadcast Talks* featuring his moral argument came in the throes of World War II; William Sorley was constructing his Gifford lectures during World War I, and he received news of the death of his son Charles before he was done. There was nothing Pollyannaish about their reflections; what they said had to square with the most brutal and harsh of life's realities. The ability of their words to pass such an exacting test may provide a certain indication of their profundity and perspicacity, and because this life leaves no one unscathed, this real-world applicability seems a vital component of any moral argument worth its salt.

We began this book with an epigraph from Kurt Vonnegut's *Slaughterhouse-Five* that highlights contemporary culture's bent toward the shallow and flimsy, with the main character's mother attempting to cobble together a meaningful life out of gift shop memorabilia. These "gift-shop" answers, of course, are no match for the devastating destruction of the Dresden firebombing that Vonnegut chronicles in the pages of his novel. Something more, Vonnegut acknowledges, is desperately needed to alleviate the suffering of the world and correct its grievous wrongs. The author himself retained his agnosticism, unwilling to embrace Christianity, but his insights about the dignity of people, the damage of moral transgression, and the need for redemption that humanity itself cannot supply all reinforce the need for a moral apologetics that can take on the most pressing of life's existential challenges. And the figures we've covered in this history, as we've seen, can offer just that.[2]

Nearly to a person, those on our list of historical apologists refrained from acting as though they had made their case in such a compelling way that everyone must be convinced on pain of insincerity, irrationality, stupidity, or obstinacy. Nothing like an airtight case was claimed; few assertions of certitude were advanced. They took pains, in fact, to deny such claims. They believed in following evidence, and they were convinced that arguments play their role; but they paid their opponents the respect of allowing them their mental freedom to arrive at their own conclusions. In the case of Matthews, for example, he saw the task of apologetics as one of *commending* religious conviction. Overambitious goals tend needlessly to strain relations, put people on the defensive, impugn the motives of others, and presume to know more than we do. These apologists' provisionality was as winsome as it was refreshing.

One more laudable trait to make mention of here pertains to that issue of friendship we saw emerge in thinkers like Newman, James, or Lewis. Maintaining friendly relationships with dialogue partners with radically different views held primacy in their lives; in fact, it was often the challenges posed by those relationships that provided the vital crucible in which truths could become clearer.

Within this past year as we write, Supreme Court Justice Antonin Scalia died, and Ruth Bader Ginsburg wrote among the most moving of the tributes to him. Ginsburg and Scalia's interpretations of jurisprudence and the Constitution often stood at odds, if not in diametric opposition. Yet, personally, they were the dearest of friends. Part of what she wrote was this: "He was, indeed, a magnificent performer. It was my great good fortune to have known him as working colleague and treasured friend." Or consider these words from William James to his ideological foe Josiah Royce (about whom James had said "my highest flight of ambitious ideality is to become your conqueror, and go down into history as such"): "Different as our minds are, yours has nourished mine, as no other social influence ever has, and in converse with you I have always felt that my life was being lived importantly."[3] In a similar vein, Lewis wrote in *The Four Loves*: "Friendship is unnecessary, like philosophy, like art. . . . It has no survival value; rather it is one of those things which give value to survival."[4] In tediously tendentious and pitiably partisan times, this is a vitally important model for any aspiring apologist to emulate.

Second, in laying out the threefold focus of the moral argument—evidence to be explained, critique of secular ethics, defense of theistic ethics of the moral apologetic enterprise—rigorous attentiveness to the evidence is a prerequisite for doing solid moral apologetics. An example is Taylor's rigorous effort to delineate the features of moral guilt. Recall his list of its features that come from close examination of its phenomenology: condemnation, indelibility, demand for punishment, pollution, and shame. Time and again we saw our careful scholars delve into the meaning and significance of aspects of moral experience to fish out such stubborn features of moral reality in need of adequate explanation—whether it was the features of moral duties, the authority of the moral law, the transcendent nature of various goods, the inherent value of human persons, the radical need for forgiveness and for both individual and social moral transformation, or the need for morality to be a rationally stable enterprise. The history of the moral argument is replete with such careful examination of the logic, language, and phenomenology of moral realities.

Third, on issues of theories of knowledge, note the expansive epistemology, wide empiricism, and broad theories of rationality of so many of the major luminaries considered. Having rigorously argued for the legitimacy of taking moral evidence into account, following Lotze's dictum and rejecting central variants of the fact-value divide, these figures then spent serious time gathering evidence from a wide array of sources. Few were narrow logic choppers or abstemious empiricists; they were open to the deliverances of relations, literature, poetry, emotions, and aesthetics. They didn't confine their attention to a myopic range of thinkers; rather, they read widely with an open mind and heart and heeded what they read. Students of the human condition, steeped in life's travails, aware of its challenges, acquainted with grief and loss, they took seriously not just the premium of avoiding error but also the needed risks occasionally required to apprehend and appreciate the truth.

Fourth, consider moral faith, which has two parts. One dimension of moral faith broaches the question of whether morality is a fully rational enterprise. We saw that theism provides a powerful resolution to the dualism of practical reason—no small matter, because nothing less than the full rational authority of morality is at stake. The other dimension of moral faith involves what realistic hope there can be for moral transformation. On a Christian story, hope for radical moral transformation—indeed transfiguration—will not disappoint. We can't fulfill the moral law on our own, but God's assistance is available for us finally to be what and who we were intended to be, without domesticating morality by lowering or watering down its standards.

In addition to the need to be changed, we also feature a deep need to be forgiven. This is the juncture at which the moral argument predicated on general revelation dovetails with and serves as the perfect prelude for the Christian gospel that comes from special revelation. Jesus is the face of an all-loving God when he takes human form. Without seeing our need for forgiveness, we won't look for a Savior. If there's indeed an authoritative moral law—and we all down deep know there is—and if we invariably fall short of it, what do we do with the resultant guilt? A. E. Taylor, John Henry Newman, William Sorley, and others spilled quite a bit of ink on this topic. Its indelible features, its nagging reality, and its convicting power tempt us to despair. Into the bleakness of our darkness and sin comes a message of hope and love, an offer of forgiveness that is indeed great "good news."

Fifth, as we've seen, moral apologetics may well be useful to argue for more than mere theism, a point inextricably tied to certain political and social implications of the moral argument. Several of our representative thinkers argued that moral resources pave the way best for Christianity itself.[5] Metaphysics scripts history. It's been argued that the cornerstone of international law is the sacred, the sacredness of man as your neighbor. Today there's a growing opinion among Chinese social scientists that the Christian idea of transcendence was the historic basis for the concepts of human rights and equality. The atheist Richard Rorty admits that throughout history societies have come up with various ways to exclude certain groups from the human family by calling them subhuman, and that by contrast Christianity gave rise to the concept of universal rights, derived from the conviction that all human beings are created in the image of God.

The atheist Jürgen Habermas, similarly, has argued that from the Judaic ethic of justice and Christian ethic of love sprang the ideas of freedom and social solidarity, of an autonomous conduct of life and emancipation, of individual morality of conscience, human rights, and democracy. Paul Copan adds texture to the moral argument by adducing such historical roles played by Christ and his devoted followers in leading to societies that are "progress-prone rather than progress-resistant," including such signs of progress as the founding of modern science, poverty-diminishing free markets, equal rights for all before the law, religious liberty, women's suffrage, human rights initiatives, and the abolition of practices such as slavery, widow burning, and foot binding.[6] The evolution in moral thought that enabled us to see the sacred and beautiful qualities in the Down syndrome child, the aged, and the exile was a function of Christian influence.

As David Bentley Hart says, to reject such ones would be what's most natural; to see, rather than a worthless burden, "instead a person worthy of all affection—resplendent with divine glory, ominous with an absolute demand upon our consciences, evoking our love and our reverence—is to be set free . . . from those natural limitations that pre-Christian persons took to be the very definition of reality."[7] Only a myopic view of history fails to see the revolutionary force of Christianity in generating such moral insight. More cutting-edge work is needed to extend the moral argument to Christianity, but the time may well be ripe for it.[8]

Sixth, and last, a (challenging) word about contemporary relevance. Philosophy is hard, and less a sprint than a marathon. In fact, these conversations span generations—indeed, centuries and even millenia. Too much amateur apologetics today—both pro theism and con—tends to be far too rushed, tendentious, and presumptuous: listening just long enough to disagree; treating criticisms as mic-dropping discussion stoppers; going for the exposed jugular at every opportunity; casting opponents as benighted dolts rather than as collaborative partners in search of truth; gravitating toward selective evidence; reducing thorny, complex, and vexed questions worth pondering into sound bites that allow shallowness to masquerade as profundity.

None of this is altogether new, of course, but all of it, obviously with notable exceptions, has reached epidemic levels in certain quarters, exacerbated no doubt by social media. The lamentable result is a sad state of affairs in which we have become far more proficient at burning bridges than building them. Circumspect, deliberate analysis is out; mouthy firebrands are in. This book is thus not at all in the spirit of the moment, intentionally so. Its purpose, to be explicitly clear, has not been to settle any debate but to encourage, in an irenic and constructive manner, thoughtful engagement with the best representatives of a view. We hardly take such eminent thinkers as authorities whose views are sacrosanct; we *do* take them as worth our time and careful attention. Their inclusion in the contemporary dialogue can serve to invigorate the conversation; it's not meant to provide easy or simple answers. What we can't responsibly do is ignore them, eschew their contributions, or characterize them as anything less than the profoundly serious thinkers they were.

Indeed, we have seen very little that is small or petty in the approach of the luminaries represented here. They lived with these ideas and arguments, discoursed respectfully, nobly embodied the best of the intellectual tradition, steeped themselves in the history of philosophy and patristics, literature and disparate languages, allowing their ideas to gestate, develop, and mature in the crucible of their academic careers and lived experience. Then they entered the fray of the public square, recognizing as they did both the privilege to be part of this great conversation in their brief earthly pilgrimage and the responsibility to do it both excellently and in the right spirit. They were but men, but they showed some of the sublime heights of which human beings are capable.

Often today apologetic arguments get reduced to a few pithy premises and a hastily drawn conclusion; in fact, especially in internet conversations, unless an argument is able to be encapsulated in a few sentences, it often gets dismissed as hopelessly unwieldy or impracticable, as if we ought to be allergic to anything requiring sustained effort and more than a modicum of patience. Needless to say, such an operative assumption is hardly an effective way to infuse the philosophical quest for ultimate meaning, truth, and significance with any sense of the sacred, of its gravity and import, its challenge and promise. Hopefully time spent with the serious thinkers of this book and the story it tells can serve as a corrective and antidote to the superficiality, the frenetic rush to judgments, the partisan spirit, the peremptory dismissals of interlocutors, the trivializing ad hominems, and the penchant for talking without listening that are all lamentable features of too much of today's discourse.

This has been the story of the moral argument, or at least a slice of it. We hope that more and better histories will be written in years to come, but making this modest contribution has been our delight and privilege.

Notes

Acknowledgments

1. A written copy of the whole (by turns serious and silly) memorial service for Francesca can be found here: https://www.moralapologetics.com/wordpress/2018/12/30/memorial-for-francesca-josephine-baggett?rq=francesca.

Introduction

1. After Kant, most of the major players discussed here are from England until we get to the contemporary scene. We don't otherwise cover French- and German-speaking contributors to the broader discussion—for example. Plato and Kant never cease to be relevant to the tale. Among the British writers, perhaps not surprisingly, we found the preponderance of them to be Anglican.
2. The whole text is available online: C. S. Lewis, "De Descriptione Temporum: Inaugural Lecture from the Chair of Mediaeval and Renaissance Literature at Cambridge University, 1954," https://archive.org/stream/DeDescriptioneTemporum/DeDescriptioneTemporumByC.S.Lewis_djvu.txt.
3. William Sorley, *Moral Values and the Idea of God* (Cambridge: Cambridge University Press, 1935), 7.
4. Friedrich Nietzsche, *Beyond Good and Evil*, trans. and ed. Marion Faber (Oxford: Oxford University Press, 1998), 8–9.
5. C. S. Lewis, "On the Reading of Old Books," in *God in the Dock* (Grand Rapids, MI: Eerdmans, 2014), 219.
6. Mark Dooley and Roger Scruton, *Conversations with Roger Scruton* (London: Bloomsbury, 2016), 57.
7. In light of the heavy representation of British thinkers in this volume, we usually went ahead and, when spellings diverged from American variants, adhered to the British renderings.

Chapter 1

1. William Lane Craig, *Reasonable Faith: Christian Truth and Apologetics*, 3rd ed. (Wheaton, IL: Crossway, 2008), 104. The irony is that Plato also wrote the early

Socratic dialogue *Euthyphro*, to which many point as definitive evidence against the propriety of locating holiness or justice in the divine realm, owing to the famous "Euthyphro dilemma." The tenth book of Plato's *Laws* has also proven to be important to aspects of moral apologetics discussed in A. E. Taylor, Clement Webb, and others, as we shall see.

2. Elizabeth Anscombe argued that the notion of moral obligations as law-like verdicts on our actions was a result of the Judeo-Christian tradition, which certainly has wielded a formidable influence on ethical thought in the Western world. What Evans points out challenges this view, showing that moral obligations have a longer history, however much Christianity may have accentuated their importance. Perhaps what John Henry Newman cast as the amplifying role of special revelation is what's at play here: special revelation extends and augments the truths that natural religion had already hinted at.

3. "Or to put it another way, we might say that whatever values a Platonic world imposes on a man are values to which the Platonic world itself is committed, through and through." George Mavrodes, "Religion and the Queerness of Morality," in *Ethical Theory: Classical and Contemporary Readings*, 2nd ed., ed. Louis P. Pojman (New York: Wadsworth, 1995), 587.

4. Arguably, in fact, Platonism makes more sense in a theistic world than a nontheistic one. John Rist writes that "Plato's account of the 'Forms' (including the Good) as moral exemplars leaves them in metaphysical limbo. They would exist as essentially intelligible ideas even if there were no mind, human or divine, to recognize them: as objects of thought, not mere constructs or concepts. But, as Augustine learned, and as the Greek Neoplatonists had asserted, the notion of an eternal object of thought (and thus for Plato a cause of thought) without a ceaseless thinking subject is unintelligible. Intelligible Forms, never proposed as mere concepts, cannot be proposed as Plato originally proposed them, as free-floating metaphysical items." John M. Rist, *Real Ethics: Rethinking the Foundations of Morality* (Cambridge: Cambridge University Press, 2002), 40.

5. A difference in this regard is that the God of Christianity also actively pursues us.

6. David Horner, "Too Good Not to Be True: A Call to Moral Apologetics as a Mode of Civil Discourse," Moral Apologetics, https://www.youtube.com/watch?v=sBSK4Hw1XoY.

7. Augustine, "On the Trinity," in *St. Augustine: On the Holy Trinity, Doctrinal Treatises, Moral Treatises*, ed. Philip Schaff, trans. Arthur West Haddan, vol. 3, *A Select Library of the Nicene and Post-Nicene Fathers of the Christian Church*, first series (Buffalo, NY: Christian Literature, 1887), 244.

8. Besides this argument, Augustine also made an argument from the requirements of moral transformation. Augustine wrote, "If you cling to him [God] in love, you will straightway enter into bliss." In book 15 Augustine added, "For this is the will of the best and most wise Creator, that the spirit of a man, when piously subject to God, should have a body happily subject, and that this happiness should last forever." Thanks to Jonathan Pruitt for help here. See ibid., 223.

9. In recent literature, theistic ethicists like John Hare and C. Stephen Evans have argued for a rapprochement of sorts between elements of natural law and divine command theory.
10. Owen would later question this argument at two points: First, even if we grant the necessity of moral norms it does not follow that they are in the strict sense absolute. They might be no more than very high ideals. Is there an absolute height, for example? Is there a principled reason to think values are exceptional in this regard? Second, even if we were forced to posit an absolute norm of goodness, we need not affirm that it exists. It might be no more than a regulative ideal or limiting concept. The only way to make such a case, Owen argues, is by the ontological argument. H. P. Owen, *The Moral Argument for Christian Theism* (London: George Allen and Unwin, 1965), 74–75.
11. Aquinas writes, "Whatever man desires, he desires it under the aspect of good. And if he desire it, not as his perfect good, which is the last end, he must, of necessity, desire it as tending to the perfect good, because the beginning of anything is always ordained to its completion; as is clearly the case in effects both of nature and of art. Wherefore every beginning of perfection is ordained to complete perfection which is achieved through the last end." Thomas Aquinas, *Summa Theologica*, tr. Fathers of the English Dominican Province (Westminster, MD: Christian Classics, 1981).
12. Thanks to David Horner for useful insight on this score; see Horner, "Too Good Not to Be True."
13. One might wonder, if this is so, why Aquinas isn't listed before Kant as the first major moral apologist. Perhaps the biggest reason is that much of what Aquinas does when it comes to God and morality is explicate his variant of theistic ethics, which is different from offering an explicit moral apologetic. They're closely related, and easily confused, but remain conceptually distinct. Perhaps a better way of putting it is that explication of theistic ethics is a necessary but not sufficient condition for doing moral apologetics. Even if Aquinas did less moral apologetics than explication of theistic ethics, much of what he wrote remains relevant to the former.
14. Allan Bloom, *The Closing of the American Mind: How Higher Education Has Failed Democracy and Impoverished the Souls of Today's Students* (New York: Simon & Schuster, 2012), 52.
15. René Descartes, "Dedicatory Letter to the Sorbonne," in *Meditations on First Philosophy: With Selections from the Objections and Replies*, tr. and ed. John Cottingham (Cambridge: Cambridge University Press, 1996), 3.
16. Letter from Descartes to Mersenne, April 15, 1630. In *Descartes: Philosophical Letters*, tr. and ed. by Anthony Kenny (Oxford: Clarendon Press, 1970), 11.
17. Quoted in Alvin Plantinga, *Does God Have a Nature?* (Milwaukee: Marquette University Press, 1980), 101.
18. Augustine's "divine ideas" tradition, Gottfried Wilhelm Leibniz's effort to root mathematical truth in God's noetic activity, Aquinas's insistence that anything that in any way is, is from God, Descartes' view of constant creation, and even Jonathan Edwards's likely misguided attempt at temporal parts theory were all motivated by

the guiding conviction that God is at the root of all that is. The theological rationale behind such efforts, if not always their specific formulations, occasionally can be seen to receive at least a large measure of vindication. Consider Berkeley's motivating theological concern behind his idealism: that affirming the independent existence of matter will inevitably lead to its worship. When in current discussions, to avoid the force of cosmological or teleological arguments, naturalists resort to attributing qualities to the physical universe traditionally reserved for God, perhaps we can see Berkeley's prescience.

19. E. T. Bell, *Men of Mathematics* (New York: Simon & Schuster, 1965), 73.
20. Blaise Pascal, *Pensées*, tr. Honor Levi (Oxford: Oxford University Press, 1995), 143.
21. As it happens, though, it was a discussion of ethics and revealed religion that had originally served as the impetus for his *Essay*.
22. Later we will hear Rashdall's reservations about language of "rewards and punishments."
23. John Locke, *The Reasonableness of Christianity*, ed. I. T. Ramsey (Stanford, CA: Stanford University Press, 1958), 70.
24. Ibid.
25. Thomas Reid, *Essays on the Active Powers of the Human Mind*, intr. by B. Brody (Cambridge, MA: MIT Press, 1969 [1788]), 256.
26. Terence Cuneo, "Duty, Goodness, and God in Reid's Moral Philosophy," in *Reid on Ethics*, ed. Sabine Roeser (New York: Palgrave Macmillan, 2010), 256.
27. Ibid.
28. Thomas Reid, *Practical Ethics, Being Lectures and Papers on Natural Religion, Self-Government, Natural Jurisprudence, and the Law of Nations*, ed. K. Haakonnssen (Princeton, NJ: Princeton University Press, 1990), 120.
29. Obviously a whole book could have been devoted to the topic of this chapter, and perhaps in time we'll try our hand at it. All four of this chapter's categories—canvassing a smattering of Greeks, medievals, Renaissance thinkers, and Enlightenment scholars—could have been fleshed out considerably. More could have been said of Berkeley and Kierkegaard, of Anselm and Scotus, of Leibniz and Butler, and others besides. For present purposes, however, this rather cursory, far from comprehensive but still suggestive sketch suffices.

Chapter 2

1. Immanuel Kant, *Critique of Practical Reason and Other Writings in Moral Philosophy*, trans., ed., and intr. by Lewis White Beck (Chicago: University of Chicago Press, 1949 [1788]), 258.
2. We follow John Hare's wording here.
3. The final sentence of his 1763 piece on a possible basis for a demonstration of the existence of God maintained that, though we must be convinced of God's existence, logically demonstrating it isn't necessary. His 1763 piece, *An Inquiry into the Distinctness of the Principles of Natural Theology and Morals*, while still expressing

doubts that any metaphysical system of knowledge had yet been achieved, nevertheless maintained confidence that rational argument can lead to metaphysical knowledge, including that of God, as the absolutely necessary Being.
4. David Appelbaum, *The Vision of Kant* (Rockport, MA, 1995), 5.
5. From Beck's introduction in Immanuel Kant, *Critique of Practical Reason and Other Writings in Moral Philosophy*, 7–8.
6. Cited by Roger Scruton, *Kant: A Very Short Introduction* (Oxford: Oxford University Press, 2001), 5. On a more personal note, Kant was known for his punctilious habits and a studious life. The strictness of his daily routine is legend. He could also be a bit of a hypochondriac, and he was notorious for such charming idiosyncrasies as not talking while walking (for health reasons). Apt descriptions of him include the following: disciplined, dutiful, unassuming, consistent, hard-working, and remarkably brilliant most of all. He never married, harboring a bit of a cynical view as to the institution's purpose; but he wasn't antisocial, though he could remain in solitude and bury himself in his work for long periods. He often invited friends to dine with him, however, and was an entertaining host.
7. In a longer treatment more of the interconnections between these various works would be explicated.
8. His *Critique of Judgment* came in 1790. This work investigated the idea of finality and provided an analysis of aesthetic judgment as well as the concept of teleology in the sciences.
9. John Hare sums up Kant's conclusion this way: "If we are sure that we are under the moral law, then we are entitled to believe in the existence of a ruler of the world who makes the evil in the world (which we cannot deny) subordinate to the good." John E. Hare, *God's Command* (Oxford: Oxford University Press, 2015), 11. Interesting that Kant saw the task of moral apologetics standing in diametric opposition to the problem of evil and engaged in a zero-sum game that Kant thinks the problem of evil loses.
10. That book can fruitfully be envisioned as an elaborate thought experiment to see how much of religious revelation is discoverable by reason alone.
11. See http://philosophyfaculty.ucsd.edu/faculty/rarneson/Courses/ADAMS1phil1 reading.pdf.
12. In *Value and Reality*, A. C. Ewing famously called this sort of "ought implies can" argument into question by insisting we can't claim we ought to follow the moral law unless it's first shown we can. One could reply to Ewing that the driving insight is that we must accept as valid the estimate of our powers that the moral law sets forth in the projection of the highest good. See, for example, John R. Silber, "Kant's Conception of the Highest Good as Immanent and Transcendent," *Philosophical Review* 68 (October 1959): 482.
13. This seems to be a needless departure in Kant from Christian theology, which teaches immortality but not on the basis of the never-ending quest for a holy will. The process of sanctification comes to culmination when we are entirely conformed to the image of Christ at glorification. Eternity is then lived as it was meant to be lived, not

in an eternally insatiable quest for what's beyond our reach. A. E. Taylor spends time talking about the quality of life possible after achievement of such an end.

14. Again, much credit goes to John Hare for providing resources and language to formulate Kant's argument so concisely. See his *Moral Gap: Kantian Ethics, Human Limits, and God's Assistance* (Oxford: Clarendon Press, 1997).
15. This is "Spener's problem" (named after a Lutheran theologian): The challenge of becoming not just *better* people but *new* people.
16. An interesting alternative reading of the import of Kant's references to self-conceit, the dear self, and the radical propensity to evil comes from reading Kant not through the filter of Luther but rather through that of Rousseau. On this reading, such a propensity develops only in the social condition. What's corrupting, then, is not our natural condition but rather our interaction with others. Although we won't make the argument here, we instead tend to read Kant as affirming something more like a corrupt moral condition that, when situations of sociality arise, finds manifestation in practice.
17. Kant was inconsistent on this score. What we will be focusing on is what he said about our inability to live morally on our own, but elsewhere he suggested that we have to be able to do it on our own (the "Stoic maxim"). Our point isn't that Kant was entirely right in every place, but that there's value in gleaning what resources he offered to construct moral arguments.
18. Hegel would later criticize Kant for being overly individualist in his ethics, largely because our normative bonds do not follow from imposing an a priori principle upon a recalcitrant or wayward social domain. Rather, we are born into a world that already makes rational claims upon us through the traditions and practices that articulate the meaningful ends of human life, as particularized within this community. There's something right about this criticism, but for now our focus instead is on the social dimensions of Kantian thought, particularly as these may bear on moral apologetics.
19. Jürgen Habermas, *Time of Transitions*, ed. and trans. Ciaran Cronin and Max Pensky (Cambridge: Polity, 2006), 150–151.
20. Two interpretations of the (conjunctive) highest good are possible: (1) the less ambitious is a world in which virtue results in happiness; and (2) the more ambitious is a world in which everyone is happy and virtuous. Arguably rational stability, the full rational authority for morality, requires the actuality of the first and the possibility of the second. Thanks to Hare for this insight.
21. Kyla Ebels-Duggan, "The Right, the Good, and the Threat of Despair: (Kantian) Ethics and the Need for Hope in God," http://www.academia.edu/9803513/The_Right_the_Good_and_the_Threat_of_Despair_Kantian_Ethics_and_the_Need_for_Hope_in_God.
22. Marilyn McCord Adams, *Horrendous Evils and the Goodness of God* (Ithaca, NY: Cornell University Press, 1999), 82–82.
23. Richard E. Creel, *Divine Impassibility: An Essay in Philosophical Theology* (Cambridge: Cambridge University Press, 1986), 149–150.
24. Ebels-Duggan, "The Right, the Good, and the Threat of Despair."

Chapter 3

1. A few months later my wife and I attended his fun *Magic and Skepticism* show in Washington, DC, and had a short enjoyable exchange with him afterward.
2. At this point in the chronology of the moral argument we also find James Martineau and Campbell Fraser, mentioned briefly in this book, but we decided not to cover them in great detail. A fuller and more definitive history would and should canvas their contributions. But a bit more will be said about Martineau in the upcoming chapter 9, on Clement Webb.
3. Frank M. Turner's *John Henry Newman: The Challenge to Evangelical Religion* (New Haven, CT: Yale University Press, 2002) critically describes some of the many facets of Newman's life and character, including the more acerbic ones. Turner's main focus is on Newman's tracts.
4. A trait he shared with, among others, Bishop Joseph Butler (1692–1752).
5. C. S. Dessain and Thomas Gornall, eds., *Letters and Diaries of John Henry Newman* (henceforth L&D), vol. 25 (Oxford: Clarendon Press, 1973), 106.
6. Ibid., 97.
7. John Henry Newman, *An Essay in Aid of a Grammar of Assent* (Notre Dame, IN: University of Notre Dame Press, 1979 [1870]), 13.
8. It might be thought that this answers contemporary epistemologist Duncan Pritchard's challenge for ordinary theistic belief (belief on the part of the man in the street) to garner evidence that amounts to rational support, but a response could be that such belief could be evidence-based in the way Newman suggests without amounting to rational support that one can appropriately "*cite, aloud, in conversation,* in defense of a *claim* (or an implied claim) to have rational support for believing that God exists," as Kegan Shaw puts it. "The difference here is between having rational support R for *p*, and being in a position to appropriately *cite* that rational support in defense of a *claim* (or an implied claim) to have rational support for *p*" (personal correspondence, December 7, 2018). Thanks to Kegan for this distinction, which arguably shows that Newman's epistemological insights here aren't *directly* relevant to Pritchard's challenge. However, the notion that evidence that is explicitly articulable (and appropriately citable in response to a challenge) is necessarily better and stronger than evidence that isn't thus articulable is one with which Newman would have likely demurred. Recall his earlier point about "paper evidence," the legitimacy of real assent, and the fact that Newman wrote that the object of the *Essay* "would be to show that a given individual, high or low, has as much right (has as real rational grounds) to be certain, as a learned theologian who knows the scientific evidence." L&D 19, 294.
9. See William J. Wainwright, *Reason and the Heart: A Prolegomenon to a Critique of Passional Reason*, Cornell Studies in the Philosophy of Religion, rev. ed. (Ithaca, NY: Cornell University Press, 2006). Wainwright argues for middle ground between the opposing claims of reason and religious subjectivity. There is evidence that reason functions properly only when informed by a rightly disposed heart. Wainwright pursues the idea of passional reason through the writings of Jonathan Edwards, John

Henry Newman, and William James. Consonant with these thinkers, he offers an eloquent and powerful defense of the claim that reason functions best when influenced by the appropriate emotions and intuitions.
10. As broadly empiricist as Newman was, he was a radically different sort of empiricist. The *Essay* can be seen as Newman's argument against the dry, even myopic empiricism of his day that had its antecedents in the thought of, for example, David Hume that dismissed the possibility of miracles or supernatural reality. In this regard James would later echo Newman's expansive empiricism. Newman also departed from a narrow impoverished rationalism that is also too closed to what evidence is available (another feature James would emulate). Newman was wont to say it's not reason that is against us, but an emaciated imagination.
11. In Newman, *Essay*, 10.
12. Newman, *Essay*, 217.
13. L&D, 26, 41.
14. Ibid., 21, 146.
15. Ibid., 19, 460.
16. Newman, *Essay*, 253.
17. Ibid., 253–254.
18. Ibid., 94.
19. Ibid., 95.
20. Ibid., 97.
21. Ibid., 98.
22. Ibid.
23. "Conscience is ever forcing on us by threats and by promises that we must follow the right and avoid the wrong," he wrote. Its resemblance to taste is conspicuous, but a few differences obtain, such as this one: conscience does not repose on itself, but "vaguely reaches forward to something beyond self, and dimly discerns a sanction higher than self for its decisions." This inclines us to speak of conscience as a "voice," a term that we don't think of applying to the sense of the beautiful, and a voice that's imperative and constraining, "like no other dictate in the whole of our experience." Ibid., 99.
24. Ibid., 100.
25. Ibid., 101.
26. Ibid.
27. Ibid.
28. In this volume we are not, for the most part, pushing criticisms that could be raised against the various arguments presented, but an interesting one here would be the phenomenon of psychopathy. One of us has written an essay addressing issues of psychopathy in Adam Johnson, *God and Morality: What Is the Best Account of Objective Moral Values and Duties? A Debate between William Lane Craig and Erik Wielenberg* (New York: Routledge, 2020, forthcoming).
29. To disambiguate, by "certitude" Newman was *not* speaking of *Cartesian apodictic certainty*. Delineating the distinction took Newman time, however. Before he did so, he was liable to struggle with the challenge of "false certitude." On reflection Newman

admitted that we can never be wholly *certain* of anything; he agreed that hankering after Cartesian certainty was a futile and misguided endeavor.
30. Andrew M. Greenwell, "Converging and Convincing Proof of God: Cardinal Newman and the Illative Sense," November 2, 2012, https://www.catholic.org/homily/yearoffaith/story.php?id=48296.
31. This approach is instructive for us all and could serve to conduce to more civil discourse generally. We also recognize the irony of this coming from an occasionally acerbic polemicist. That he may not have always lived up to his better insights doesn't vitiate their legitimacy.
32. See "Spotlight: Socrates and Paul in Athens," in David and Marybeth Baggett, *The Morals of the Story: Good News about a Good God* (Downers Grove, IL: InterVarsity, 2018), for conspicuous parallels between Socrates and the apostle Paul at Mars Hill, especially this issue of a reckoning to come.
33. Newman, *Essay*, 303.
34. Ibid., 304.
35. Ibid., 304–305.
36. Ibid., 309–310.
37. Ibid., 311.
38. Rudolf Otto, *The Idea of the Holy*, 2nd ed. (Oxford: Oxford University Press, 1958).

Chapter 4

1. *Henry Sidgwick, A Memoir*, eds. E. M. Sidgwick and A. Sidgwick (Macmillan: London, 1906), 38.
2. See the section on "Religion and Parapsychology" in the article on Sidgwick in *The Stanford Encyclopedia of Philosophy*, https://plato.stanford.edu/entries/sidgwick/.
3. Lewis compiled this list in response to a question from the *Christian Century*: "What books did the most to shape your vocational attitude and your philosophy of life?" See Colin Duriez, *The C. S. Lewis Encyclopedia* (Wheaton, IL: Crossway Books, 2000), 175.
4. Henry Sidgwick, *A Memoir*, 466–467.
5. Charles Taylor, *A Secular Age* (Cambridge, MA: Harvard University Press, 2007), 242.
6. Ibid., 244.
7. Ibid., 245.
8. Ibid., 256.
9. Alasdair MacIntyre, *A Short History of Ethics* (London: Routledge Classics, 2002), 235.
10. Henry Sidgwick, *The Methods of Ethics*, 7th ed. (Indianapolis: Hackett, 1981 [1874]), 404.
11. Ibid.
12. Ibid., 404n1.
13. Ibid., xvii.
14. Ibid., 420–421.

15. Ibid., 498.
16. Ibid., 498–499; see also 462–475.
17. Ibid., 500.
18. Ibid., 501–502.
19. Ibid., 503.
20. Ibid., 506.
21. Ibid., 507.
22. Ibid., 507–508.
23. It is worth noting that Sidgwick acknowledged that on the traditional view that God exists and is the moral governor of the world who will hold us accountable for our behavior in the life to come, then freedom is of fundamental moral significance. See *The Methods of Ethics*, 69.
24. Ibid., 508.
25. Alasdair MacIntyre, *After Virtue*, 2nd ed (Notre Dame: University of Notre Dame Press, 1985), 65ff.
26. See *The Methods of Ethics*, 4, 80–81, 212 (including n2), 475–476.
27. See Thomas Nagel, *Mind and Cosmos: Why the Materialist Neo-Darwinian Conception of Nature Is Almost Certainly False* (New York: Oxford University Press, 2012), 105–111.
28. For argument that theism better explains moral knowledge than naturalism, see David Baggett and Jerry L. Walls, *Mind and Cosmos: Moral Truth and Human Meaning* (New York: Oxford University Press, 2016), 179–212.

Chapter 5

1. Cited in Linda Simon, ed., *William James Remembered* (Lincoln: University of Nebraska Press, 1996), 47.
2. As an instance of the former, an alpine climber must believe in her ability to execute a death-defying leap in order to be able to make it, and she must believe before she has evidence that she can do it. Social coordination cases involve a precursive faith that other members of the social organism of which one is a part will discharge their duties as one discharges one's own. Arguably, though, one could object to James that we don't exert direct volitional control over our beliefs, and only some amount of indirect volitional control, even in these circumstances. Perhaps what's involved in these cases is less the manufacture of new beliefs as a certain increase in confidence to act in a certain way. However, success may still depend on the willingness to act with such confidence, success not otherwise attainable. On some dispositional analyses of belief, too, the distinction between such confidence and full-fledged belief may prove negligible.
3. William James, *The Will to Believe and Other Essays in Popular Philosophy* (Cambridge, MA: Harvard University Press, 1979 (1897)), 31.
4. Ralph Barton Perry, *The Thought and Character of William James* (Cambridge, MA: Harvard University Press, 1948), 389.

5. Daniel W. Bjork, *William James: The Center of His Vision* (New York: Columbia University Press, 1988), 266.
6. David C. Lamberth, "Interpreting the Universe after a Social Analogy: Intimacy, Panpsychism, and a Finite God in a Pluralistic Universe," in Ruth Anna Putnam, ed. *The Cambridge Companion to William James* (New York: Cambridge University Press, 1997), 240.
7. Hunter Brown's book on James offers a compelling description of his expansive epistemology. See Hunter Brown, *William James on Radical Empiricism and Religion* (Toronto: University of Toronto Press, 2000).
8. These ideas are from James's piece "The Dilemma of Determinism," available online at http://www.rci.rutgers.edu/~stich/104_Master_File/104_Readings/James/James_DILEMMA_OF_DETERMINISM.pdf. For readers unfamiliar with the notion of determinism, it's the idea that all events are caused to happen just as they do, including human choices. Sometimes quantum indeterminacy is adduced as an exception, based on a particular interpretation of quantum mechanics, but, even if this interpretation holds, something at least close to determinism at the macro level seems likely on naturalism.
9. William James, *The Varieties of Religious Experience* (New York: Modern Library, 1994), 159. Germane to questions of moral transformation, James contrasted the emotional and practical difference between acceptance of the universe in the "drab way of stoic resignation to necessity, or with the passionate happiness of Christian saints": "If religion is to mean anything definite for us, it seems to me that we ought to take it as meaning this added dimension of emotion, this enthusiastic temper of espousal, in regions where morality strictly so called can at best but bow its head and acquiesce. It ought to mean nothing short of this new reach of freedom for us, with the struggle over, the keynote of the universe sounding in our ears, and everlasting possession spread before our eyes.... This sort of happiness in the absolute and everlasting is what we find nowhere but in religion." Ibid., 41–42.
10. Hunter Brown, *William James on Radical Empiricism*.
11. William James, "The Will to Believe," in *The Will to Believe and Other Essays in Popular Philosophy* (London: Collier Press, 1948), 109.
12. Aspects of the epistemology of James also have conspicuous parities with Plantinga's later Reformed epistemology. For this case see David Baggett, "Theistic Belief and Positive Epistemic Status: A Comparison of Alvin Plantinga and William James," *Asbury Theological Journal* 58, no. 1 (2003): 151–166, which describes about a dozen telling similarities.
13. Tim Madigan, "The Paradoxes of Arthur Balfour," *Philosophy Now*, 2010, https://philosophynow.org/issues/81/The_Paradoxes_of_Arthur_Balfour.
14. Ibid. Madigan continues, "What is most interesting is that early in their lives both men were torn between pursuing careers in politics or in academic philosophy. Russell chose the latter, but remained passionately committed to political activism (thrice running unsuccessfully for Parliament), whereas Balfour, with much heaviness of heart, chose to devote himself to political office. Originally elected to Parliament in 1874, he confided to his sister that if he was not re-elected he would 'leave politics

for philosophy'. But he was successfully returned to office, and thereafter remained in political service until the end of his life, while still finding time to be, among other things, Rector of St Andrews and Glasgow Universities, Chancellor of Cambridge and Edinburgh Universities, President of the British Association, Fellow of the Royal Society and of the British Academy, and both Gifford and Romanes Lecturer."

15. For readers interested in finding out more about the history and intent of the Gifford lectures, see Stanley Jaki, *Lord Gifford and His Lectures: A Centenary Retrospect* (Macon, GA: Mercer University Press, 1986).
16. Arthur James Balfour, *Theism and Humanism* (London: Hodder and Stoughton, 1915), 20.
17. Ibid., 21.
18. Ibid.
19. Ibid., 27. For an assessment of the religious philosophy of William James, see David Baggett, "On a Reductionist Analysis of William James's Philosophy of Religion," *Journal of Religious Ethics* 28, no. 3 (2000): 423–448.
20. Balfour wrote that he did not believe that any escape from these perplexities is possible, unless we are prepared to bring to the study of the world the presupposition that it was the work of a rational Being, who made it intelligible and at the same time made us, in however feeble a fashion, able to understand it. This conception does not solve all difficulties; far from it. But at least it is not on the face of it incoherent (as is the case with naturalism). "It does not attempt the impossible task of extracting reason from unreason; nor does it require us to accept among scientific conclusions any which effectually shatter the credibility of scientific premises." Arthur James Balfour, *The Mind of Arthur James Balfour: Selections from His Non-Political Writings, Speeches, and Addresses* (New York: George H. Doran, 1918), 347. It is fascinating that in both Balfour and Lewis we find variants of both the argument from reason and a moral argument. In chapters 3 and 5 of Lewis's *Miracles* is a most salient example of the two arguments dovetailing.
21. Balfour, *Theism and Humanism*, 51.
22. Ibid.
23. Ibid., 119.
24. Ibid.
25. Ibid., 126.
26. Ibid., 127.
27. Ibid., 128.
28. Ibid., 129.

Chapter 6

1. Charles Hamilton Sorley, "When You See Millions of the Mouthless Dead," https://www.poetryfoundation.org/poets/charles-hamilton-sorley.
2. J. H. Muirhead, "In Memoriam: William Ritchie Sorley," *Philosophy* 11, no. 41 (1936): 120.

3. William Sorley, *Moral Values and the Idea of God*, 3rd ed. (New York: MacMillan, 1930 [1918]), 189–190.
4. There's a parallel sort of reasoning here possible in the philosophy of mathematics. Intuitionists insist that the concepts and truths of mathematics depend on human minds, but to avoid a criticism that Gottlob Frege launched against such a view, they might opt for the additional idea that, though such truths depend on human minds, they don't depend on any *particular* human mind. This avoids the objection that, say, the number two in my mind is different from such a concept in yours. However, it still leaves open the challenge of accounting for why twice two was four prior to the emergence of any human minds. If such truths do in fact depend on the noetic functioning of a mind, and no finite mind will do, there are reasons for suggesting that an eternal Mind is needed to ground necessary mathematical truths. See Øystein Lennebo, *Philosophy of Mathematics* (Princeton, NJ: Princeton University Press, 2017), 76–79. In a similar fashion, Sorley argued that the only Person in whom the moral ideal can be fully realized is God himself. Much of this anticipates the theistic conceptualism of Plantinga's famous 1982 American Psychological Association presidential address in which he speculatively retained the invariance of necessary truths while rejecting their mind-independence, thus effecting a certain rapprochement of elements of constructivism and realism. Embedded here are the ingredients for a solution to both moral and modal variants of the Euthyphro dilemma. See Alvin Plantinga, "How to Be an Anti-Realist," *Proceedings and Addresses of the American Philosophical Association* 56, no. 1 (1982): 52.
5. William Lane Craig, *Reasonable Faith*, 3rd ed. (Wheaton, IL: Crossway, 2008), 104. Sorley's *Ethics of Naturalism* aimed to refute the historical, evolutionary approach to ethics, but this chapter will confine its attention to *Moral Values and the Idea of God*.
6. G. F. Stout, "W. R. Sorley (1855–1935)," *Mind* 45, no. 177 (1936): 124.
7. Sorley, *Moral Values*, 234–235.
8. Ibid., 239.
9. Horner, "Too Good Not to Be True."
10. David Bentley Hart, *The Experience of God: Being, Consciousness, Bliss* (New Haven, CT: Yale University Press, 2013), 251.
11. Sorley, *Moral Values*, 92.
12. Ibid., 105.
13. Ibid., 106.
14. Bertrand Russell, *Mysticism and Logic* (London: Longmans, Green, 1919), 30–31. Rik Peels, in his brilliant 2017 book *Responsible Belief*, distinguishes epistemic from nonepistemic reasons for believing that *p*. One may be motivated to believe something because it is an instance of wishful thinking that simply makes one happy. But this isn't epistemic, and why? Because epistemic reasons differ from other reasons in that they count in favor or against something—a belief, for example—in virtue of that belief's relation to our aim of having true rather than false beliefs. Then Peels writes, "Moral, prudential, and other non-epistemic reasons do *not* meet this criterion." Peels, *Responsible Belief* (Oxford: Oxford University Press, 2017), 111. We take his point regarding prudential reasons and other nonepistemic reasons, but mention

of moral reasons in this context gave us pause and tempted us to demur, because the suggestion, at face value, seems to be that moral and epistemic reasons are mutually exclusive. Moral reasons are included in the category of nonepistemic reasons, which suggests that moral reasons don't, and perhaps can't, function evidentially to enable us to get a better handle on the truth or to avoid error. The effort to infer from moral reasons to metaphysical conclusions, if so, would thus be misguided, unless we're misreading the suggestion, which would sink the moral argument before it set sail.

In response to this challenge, Peels (in personal correspondence) allayed our concerns and, in the process, revealed he was an advocate of (at least) two variants of the moral argument: "I think you're right I might have been insufficiently careful in phrasing things here. Just to be explicit: I accept and have defended various moral arguments for God's existence. What I wanted to say is that moral reasons don't count in favor of the truth of propositions in situations in which it would be morally good to believe a proposition (it would enhance cohesion, increase compassion, and so on). So, what I meant by 'moral reasons' is 'reasons that contribute to the moral goodness of believing the proposition but don't actually contribute to the likelihood of the proposition itself, don't give us any more reason to believe the proposition to be true.' If the proposition is itself a moral proposition and the moral reason is a reason to think that the proposition is true, then the moral reason is also an epistemic reason. I do believe that naturalism cannot explain the existence of moral facts and our ability to *know* moral facts, whereas theism has a plausible explanation of each."

15. A. E. Taylor, *Faith of a Moralist* (New York: Macmillan, 1930), 16.
16. See Jerry L. Walls, "Hume on Divine Amorality," *Religious Studies* 26 (1990): 257–266, for an argument that Hume ignored a crucial and telling part of the created order—namely, our moral intuitions. When these are taken into account, the argument for amorality is undercut and we are led to believe that God is either truly good or he is perverse.
17. Sorley, *Moral Values*, 332–333. "The moral consciousness carries with it a demand that reality shall be in accordance with it, and this demand requires us to postulate the freedom of man and his immortality and the existence of the one perfect being or God. We are therefore justified in affirming these as postulates of the moral life."
18. Ibid., 334.
19. Ibid., 335.
20. Ibid., 297.
21. Charles Taylor, *A Secular Age* (Cambridge, MA: Harvard University Press, 2007), 18.
22. Jean Moorcroft Wilson, *Charles Hamilton Sorley: A Biography* (London: Cecil Woolf, 1985), 12.

Chapter 7

1. Andrew Seth Pringle-Pattison, *The Idea of God in the Light of Recent Philosophy: The Gifford Lectures Delivered in the University of Aberdeen in the Years 1912 and 1913*,

2nd ed., rev. (New York: Oxford University Press, 1920 [1917]). Available online at https://books.google.com/books?id=lqEOAAAAIAAJ&printsec=frontcover&source=gbs_ge_summary_r&cad=0#v=onepage&q&f=false.
2. Ibid., 27.
3. We argued to this same effect in *God and Cosmos*.
4. Pringle-Pattison, *The Idea of God*, 30.
5. Rudolph Hermann Lotze was born in May 1817 into a physician's family living in Bautzen, Saxony, a city in what today is east Germany. Lotze was led to philosophy via poetry. He was made Professor Extraordinary at Leipzig in 1843 and called to Gottingen in 1844. The academic climate while he was there was described in terms of the fading Idealism of Johann Gottlieb Fichte and G. W. F. Hegel and the rising strength of empiricism. He set out later in life to write a three-volume work on metaphysics based on his lecture notes, which are published and translated as his outlines. Unfortunately, he was only able to complete the first two volumes before his death in 1881. As a result, we are left with something of an unfinished work. Still, there is much we can derive from what has been surmised as the ground for his third volume, his *Outlines of the Philosophy of Religion*. Thanks to Peter Van Kleeck.
6. Cited in Pringle-Pattison, *The Idea of God*, 42.
7. Ibid., 38.
8. Ibid., 40.
9. Ibid., 42.
10. Ibid., 41. From Arthur Balfour, *Foundations of Belief* (New York: Longmans, Green, and Company, 1895), 31. Although here PP quotes Balfour approvingly, elsewhere he lamented that Balfour on occasion fell into the unfortunate trap of anti-intellectualism, such as when Balfour subjectivized religious conviction, rendering it susceptible to invasions of superstition.
11. Ibid., 53. From Martineau's *A Study of Religion: Its Sources and Content*, vol. 1 (Oxford: Clarendon Press, 1888), 13.
12. Pringle-Pattison, *The Idea of God*, 132.
13. Ibid., 176.
14. Ibid., 246. "This idea, Descartes reminds us, is not just an idea which we happen to find as an individual item in the mind, like our ideas of particular objects. It is innate, he says, in his old-fashioned misleading terminology. He means that it is organic to the very structure of intelligence, knit up indissolubly with that consciousness of self which he treated as his foundation-certainty—so that our experience as self-conscious beings cannot be described without implying it."
15. Ibid., 248.
16. Ibid., 251. From William Wordsworth, *The Prelude* (Cambridge: Cambridge University Press, 1991 [1805]), book 6.
17. Ibid., 252.
18. Ibid.
19. Ibid.
20. Ibid., 411.

Chapter 8

1. Anthony C. Thiselton, *The Thiselton Companion to Christian Theology* (Grand Rapids, MI: Eerdmans, 2015), 602. For a fuller summary of Rashdall, see Thiselton's entry on the moral argument in the same volume.
2. Hastings Rashdall, *The Theory of Good and Evil: A Treatise on Moral Philosophy*, vol. 1 (Oxford: Clarendon Press, 1907).
3. P. E. Matheson, *The Life of Hastings Rashdall* (London: Oxford University Press, 1928).
4. Nicholas Mark Smith, *Basic Equality and Discrimination: Reconciling Theory and Law* (New York: Routledge, 2011), 37.
5. Jeremy Waldron, *One Another's Equals: The Basis of Human Equality* (Cambridge, MA: Belknap Press of Harvard University Press, 2017).
6. Elsewhere we have suggested that naturalists who live as if moral realism were true are better than their worldview, which is often the case. Some years ago in class I said this, and my student Brett Seybold perspicaciously added, "And we as Christians too often don't live up to our worldview."
7. Rashdall, *The Theory of Good and Evil*, 1:53–54.
8. Ibid., 61–62.
9. Ibid., 63.
10. Hare was perhaps more careful to distance himself from a eudaimonist construal than Rashdall could. Hare would say a providential God ensures the correspondence of happiness and holiness, while consistently insisting that these remain ontologically distinct, contra eudaimonism (even with that airtight connection).
11. This accounts, of course, for why ethics professors in class usually have to resort to something so specifically nuanced as "torturing children for the fun of it" to locate an example of something wrong that doesn't admit of exceptions. Even here, the example adduced is less one of an ethical first principle than an arguably exceptionless moral act-type.
12. Rashdall, *The Theory of Good and Evil*, 1:93.
13. Ibid., 97.
14. Generally Rashdall thought Kant confused the inclusion of an exception *in* a moral rule with the admission of an exception *to* a moral rule. Ibid., 116.
15. Ibid., 130.
16. Hastings Rashdall, *The Theory of Good and Evil: A Treatise on Moral Philosophy*, vol. 2 (Oxford: Clarendon Press, 1907), 189.
17. Ibid., 192–193.
18. Ibid., 193.
19. "In Ethics, as in many other branches of knowledge, the plain man who is content to know particular things without knowing the ultimate meaning and basis of knowledge itself, can get along without any Metaphysic at all; but when we are confronted by difficulties or objections based upon a bad Metaphysic, the only solution of them must be found in a better one." Ibid., 199.
20. Ibid., 200.

21. Ibid., 202–203.
22. Ibid., 203.
23. Ibid.
24. Ibid., 207.
25. Ibid., 209.
26. Ibid., 211.
27. Ibid., 212.
28. Ibid.
29. Ibid., 213.
30. Ibid. Note that Rashdall's moral argument on this score is more heavily content-theoretic than was Newman's. Another departure from Newman will arise momentarily.
31. Ibid., 214.
32. Whereas Kant thought eternal life was needed to approach a holy will only asymptotically, Rashdall's variant went like this: "If human life be a training-ground and discipline for souls where they are being fitted and prepared for a life better alike in a moral and a hedonistic sense than the present, then at last we do find an adequate explanation of the willing of such a world by a Being whose character the moral consciousness at its highest presents to us as Love." Ibid., 216.
33. "The real meaning of the belief that Virtue should be rewarded is that Virtue is not by itself the whole of human good; the real meaning of the theory that vice should be punished, not merely as a measure of social protection but as a demand of absolute Justice, is that happiness without goodness is not the true good. The good, we have seen, is neither goodness nor happiness, but both together," wrote Rashdall, echoing Kant once more. Ibid.
34. Ibid., 217.
35. Ibid., 258–259.
36. "And yet there is clearly no kind of personal affection or social emotion except the fear or love of God which can be trusted to range itself invariably on the side of the Moral Law. It is not easy to exaggerate the increase of emotional intensity which the Moral Law acquires when the reverence for it fuses inextricably with a feeling of reverence for a Person who is conceived of as essentially and perfectly good." Ibid., 259.
37. Ibid. One is reminded at this point of a quote from William James: "It makes a tremendous emotional and practical difference to one whether one accept the universe in the drab discolored way of stoic resignation to necessity, or with the passionate happiness of Christian saints. The difference is as great as that between passivity and activity, as that between the defensive and the aggressive mood." William James, *The Varieties of Religious Experience: A Study in Human Nature* (Cambridge, MA: Harvard University Press, 1985 [1902]), 41–42.
38. Earlier Rashdall's primary focus was on the phenomena in need of explanation, which implied theism; some of the present points approach it from the other side, that which is doing the explanation (captured by the explanans), which isn't necessarily apologetic. But their conjunction, Rashdall seemed to think with some justification, *is* apologetic, conducing to a fuller overall evidential case.

39. Rashdall, *The Theory of Good and Evil*, 2:267.
40. Ibid., 267–268.
41. Ibid., 268.

Chapter 9

1. Two-volume Memoirs written by Webb in the 1940s [ref. MPP/W 30/1,2], 44866 (e. 1157), Oriel College.
2. J. H. Muirhead, *Contemporary British Philosophy* (London: George Allen and Unwin, 1924). Ibid., 44867 (e. 1158).
3. Two-volume Memoirs written by Webb in the 1940s [ref. MPP/W 30/1,2], 44869 (e. 1159).
4. Ibid. So deeply experiential a faith might well have only exacerbated an already strained and complicated relationship to his cleric father, who remained characteristically critical of him. The younger Webb thought himself better able than his father supposed of critiquing the details of religious experiences without involving in his distaste for these the faith that inspired the experiences themselves.
5. Ibid.
6. "Rashdall as Philosopher and Theologian," in Matheson, *The Life of Hastings Rashdall*, 240–249. Their families even vacationed together on occasion.
7. A new edition of this 1883 classic edited by David O. Brink was published in 2004.
8. Needless to say, we're inclined to see his work on the moral argument as an example of apologetics rightly construed. Superficiality is not a necessary concomitant of apologetics, and it's in conflict with good apologetics. It's instructive, nevertheless, to remain aware of the negative connotations attached to apologetics in the minds of many and the reasons for them.
9. Clement C. J. Webb, *Studies in the History of Natural Theology* (Oxford: Clarendon Press, 2012), 113.
10. Ibid., 85.
11. The order of the heavens and the *consensus gentium*, the agreement of all races of men in the acknowledgment that there are gods.
12. Webb, *Studies*, 85–86.
13. Ibid., 113.
14. This corresponds to the axiological versus deontic categories in ethics.
15. Ibid.
16. "On the contrary it is the ground of his so-called 'moral argument for the existence of God,' of the postulation by the Practical Reason of a Summum Bonum and therefore of a Power capable of producing it. But his presentation of the thought suffers from the external and arbitrary air which he gives to it; and this again is due to the fact that he is ill at ease in treating that as a postulate of Morality the thought of which he yet held it could not but injure morality fatally to admit, if I may so express it, into the moral experience itself." Ibid., 128–129.
17. Ibid., 131.

18. Ibid.
19. Ibid., 132.
20. Ibid., 133. In addition to Webb, another thinker who cast Kant's philosophy of religion as an example of eliminative reductionism was Ernst Cassirer: "The substance of [Kant's] philosophy of religion comprises for him only a confirmation of and a corollary of the substance of his ethics. Religion 'within the limits of reason alone' ... has no essential content other than that of pure morality." Ernst Cassirer, *Kant's Life and Thought*, tr. J. Haden (New Haven, CT: Yale University Press, 1981), 381–382, 385. Webb echoed the sentiment in describing Kant's theory of religion as "an appendix to Ethics"; see Clement C. J. Webb, *Kant's Philosophy of Religion* (Oxford: Clarendon Press, 1926), 62. Or consider Rem Edwards's claim: "We have in Kant the complete reduction of religion to morality"; Edwards, *Reason and Religion* (Washington, DC: University Press of America, Inc., 1979), 46. For a counterpoint to such analyses, see Stephen Palmquist, "Does Kant Reduce Religion to Morality?" *Kant-Studien* (January 1992): 129–148.
21. H. P. Owen, *The Moral Argument for Christian Theism* (London: George Allen and Unwin, 1965), 49.
22. John Baille, Review of W. R. Matthews's *Studies in Christian Philosophy*, *Philosophical Review* 31, no. 181 (January 1922), 191. Alexander Campbell Fraser (1819–1914) was a Scottish philosopher, the eldest of twelve children, and the son of a parish minister, Rev. Hugh Fraser and his wife, Maria Helen Campbell. In 1856 he became professor of logic and metaphysics at Edinburgh University, and in 1859 he became dean of the Faculty of Arts at the university, a role he retained for thirty years. His autobiography, *Biographia Philosophia*, clearly showcased his theistic faith. In his career he spent a great deal of energy exploring the work of Berkeley, Reid, and Locke. His book *Philosophy of Theism* argued that theism (rather than panmaterialism, immaterialism, and pantheism) is the best answer to the "ultimate problem," the question about the deepest and truest interpretation of reality, a question to be answered by appeal to factual and evidential considerations. Most of the distinctively moral evidence to which Fraser pointed can be found in the penultimate chapter of the book, and can be quickly summarized here. There he directed attention to the "irresistible conviction of moral responsibility" for all deliberately intended acts, reflection on which demands self-origination. That *ought implies can* points to personal moral agency. It's "in the ethical conception of the universe we seem to have a deeper and truer hold of reality than when it is treated only as a scientifically interpretable system of sense signs. *Man at his highest*, acting freely under moral obligation, with its implied intellectual and moral postulates, is suggested as a more fitting key to the ultimate interpretation of things than man only as an animal organism, abstracted from the moral experience that is often unconscious in the human individual, but is realised fully in the Ideal Man, and can be disclaimed by imperfect men only by disclaiming human responsibility." Fraser added, "The religious instinct which interprets the final Power practically as perfect moral personality, not merely non-moral physical mechanism, must itself be taken into account as a verifying experience, for justifying the final interpretation of ourselves and things around us.

As developed in the religious experience which has found its highest expression in Hebrew and Christian Scripture, it gives therein the verification of facts to the theistic interpretation of the universe." In such ways Fraser argued that the spiritual conception of the universe is "more fully philosophical for man than the merely physical." See Alexander Campbell Fraser, *Philosophy of Theism* (Edinburgh: William Blackwood and Sons, 1895), 3–8, 269–274.
23. A powerful example of this can be found in Langdon Gilkey, *Shantung Compound: The Story of Men and Women under Pressure* (New York: Harper and Row, 1966).
24. For a paper on this topic, see David Baggett and Ronnie Campbell, "Omnibenevolence, Moral Apologetics, and Doubly Ramified Natural Theology," *Philosophia Christi* 15, no. 2 (2013): 337–354.
25. Another reductionist interpreter of Kant is Kwan Tze-wan in "Kant's 'Humanistic' Conception of Religion," *Tunghai Journal* 24 (June 1983): 95–118.
26. Clement C. J. Webb, *Divine Personality and Human Life* (Aberdeen: University of Aberdeen, 1920), 115–116.
27. Ibid., 118.
28. We are not affirming that Webb got Kant right here; he might well have not.
29. Webb, *Divine Personality*, 123.
30. James Martineau, *A Study of Religion*, vols. 1 and 2 (Oxford: Clarendon Press, 1888); *Types of Ethical Theory*, vols. 1 and 2 (New York: Cosimo, 2006).
31. Webb, *Divine Personality*, 124n14.
32. Martineau, *A Study of Religion*, 2:27.
33. See Webb, *Divine Personality*, 124.
34. Ibid., 125.
35. Ibid., 126.
36. Ibid., 124.
37. See Webb, *God and Personality*, 118–119.
38. Webb, *Divine Personality*, 129.
39. Webb, *Kant's Philosophy of Religion*, 192.
40. Ibid., 191.
41. Ibid., 192.
42. Ibid., 193. De Burgh would later be much less inclined to draw this conclusion.
43. Ibid., 202.
44. Ibid., 206.
45. Ibid., 135–136.
46. Ibid., 137.
47. Ibid.

Chapter 10

1. A. E. Taylor, "William George de Burgh, 1866–1943," *Proceedings of the British Academy* 29 (1943): 371–372.

2. Alan P. F. Sell, *Four Philosophical Anglicans: W. G. de Burgh, W. R. Matthews, O. C. Quick, H. A. Hodges* (Burlington, VT: Ashgate, 2010), 3–4.
3. Ibid., 1.
4. Taylor, "William George de Burgh," 386. De Burgh's view is not just that our understanding of reason needs to be broadened but that it needs to be supplemented by divine revelation. On its own reason can take us only so far. Natural revelation prepares the way for special divine revelation, de Burgh thought, echoing elements of Newman in this regard.
5. W. G. de Burgh, *From Morality to Religion: Being the Gifford Lectures, Delivered at the University of St. Andrews, 1938* (Port Washington, NY: Kennikat Press, 1938).
6. W. G. de Burgh, *The Legacy of the Ancient World*, 2 vols. (Harmondsworth, UK: Penguin, 1955), 356n2.
7. De Burgh, *From Morality to Religion*, 146.
8. Ibid., 146–147.
9. Ibid., 147.
10. Ibid., 151–152. De Burgh, incidentally, insisted on important distinctions between morality and religion; no purely ethical imperative could have prescribed to the poor widow the casting of all she had into the treasury, for example. De Burgh agreed with Søren Kierkegaard that the experience of *penitence* marks the point of transition from morality to religion.
11. Ibid., 154.
12. Ibid., 155.
13. Ibid., 157–158.
14. Ibid., 162.
15. Ibid.
16. Ibid., 167.
17. Ibid., 168–169.
18. Ibid., 171.
19. Ibid., 173–174.
20. Ibid., 171.
21. Ibid., 177–178.
22. Ibid., 182.
23. De Burgh, *Legacy of the Ancient World*, 564.
24. Sell, *Four Philosophical Anglicans*, 55. Sell writes, "De Burgh further tantalizingly suggests in his Gifford Lectures that religion resolves the following tensions in morality: (a) the fact that the moral law remains formal and defies embodiment in any empirical content; (b) the dilemma that 'if evil be illusory, the ethical struggle is a mockery; if it be real, how can good maintain its primacy?'; (c) the question, 'How can the freedom of choice, essential to moral responsibility, be reconciled with the freedom of inner necessitation, when the will responds with unhesitating spontaneity to the vision of the ideal good?' I say he 'tantalizingly suggests' this resolution because he immediately proceeds to hint that the solution in each case turns upon the truth of the doctrine of the incarnation, and then says that to elucidate this would

entail an apologetic for the Christian revelation which would be in defiance of Lord Gifford's trust."
25. Cited in Sell, ibid., 67.

Chapter 11

1. The Old Testament scholar Dennis Kinlaw, citing the Princeton Reformed philosopher Emile Caillier, wrote that "if you want to find the classical statement of the Reformed doctrine of holiness, you cannot look at Luther or Calvin. Rather, you must look to John Wesley, and when the Methodist movement calcified, to the Salvation Army and its doctrinal statement on entire sanctification. There is the classical statement of the Reformed doctrine of holiness." Dennis F. Kinlaw, *Lectures in Old Testament Theology* (Anderson, IN: Francis Asbury Press, 2010), 413.
2. The role of the school in Taylor's formative years is well acknowledged by him in his book *Socrates*, which was first published in England in 1933. Taylor dedicated the book "To the Boys and Masters of Kingswood School, Bath." See A. E. Taylor, *Socrates* (Boston: Beacon Press, 1951). Anthony Flew was among notable alumni, attending about sixty years after Taylor.
3. See A. J. D. Porteous, "A. E. Taylor (1869–1945)," *Mind* 55, no. 218 (April 1946): 187–191.
4. Ibid., 188.
5. Ibid.
6. Ibid.
7. His last work, *Does God Exist?* (1945), is also widely acclaimed in moral apologetics, unshackled from the constraints of the Gifford lectures. In that book, Taylor presented an essay of acute, cogent reasoning on a topical subject that has agitated the minds of philosophers and theologians ever since. His purpose for writing the book was "not to demonstrate 'the being of God,' but only to argue that some alleged and widely entertained 'scientific' objections to theistic belief are unsound, and that it is unbelief (not belief) which is the unreasonable attitude." A. E. Taylor, *Does God Exist?* (1945; repr., New York: Macmillan, 1947), v.
8. H. P. Owen, *The Moral Argument for Christian Theism* (London: George Allen and Unwin, 1965), 7.
9. H. P. Owen, *The Christian Knowledge of God* (London: Athlone Press, 1969), 95.
10. C. D. Broad, "The Faith of a Moralist, by A. E. Taylor," *Mind* 40, no. 159 (July 1931): 375. Obviously here we can't begin to do justice to all those fertile digressions.
11. Taylor also had Alfred North Whitehead in view, for example, whose *Process and Reality* was published just one year before *Faith of a Moralist*. Taylor wrote a review of Whitehead's book that echoed many of the same points made in *Faith of a Moralist*. See A. E. Taylor, "Some Thoughts on *Process and Reality*," *Theology* 31 (1930). In this milieu, Taylor needed to defend the notion that our ordinary temporal lives have moral significance.
12. A. E. Taylor, *Faith of a Moralist* (New York: Macmillan, 1930), i.12.

13. Ibid.
14. Ibid.
15. Ibid., 36.
16. Ibid., 60.
17. Ibid., 65.
18. Ibid., 66.
19. Ibid., 71.
20. Ibid., 74.
21. Ibid., 76.
22. Ibid., 81.
23. Ibid., 89.
24. Ibid., 90.
25. Ibid., 91–92.
26. Ibid., 92.
27. Ibid., 92–93.
28. Ibid., 98.
29. Ibid., 100.
30. Ibid., 101.
31. Ibid., 105. The resonance of Taylor's ideas with those of Rashdall and Sorley should be obvious, subtle distinctions notwithstanding. In light of the relevant parities between them, John Baxter attempted to forge a discursive argument on the basis of their shared themes. See "An Exposition and Critique of the Moral Argument for the Existence of God as Found in the Writings of Hastings Rashdall, W. R. Sorley, and A. E. Taylor," Baxter's 1982 MA thesis at Trinity Evangelical Divinity School.
32. Ibid., 163.
33. Ibid., 165.
34. Ibid., 174.
35. Ibid., 177.
36. Ibid.
37. Ibid., 187.
38. Ibid., 192.
39. Ibid., 193.
40. Ibid., 205.
41. Ibid., 207.
42. Ibid., 208.
43. Ibid., 209.
44. Ibid., 210.
45. Ibid., 94.
46. Ibid., 16.
47. See, for example, Sam Harris, *The Moral Landscape: How Science Can Determine Moral Values* (New York: Free Press, 2010). On the specific issue of moral obligation, Harris has next to nothing to say except to eschew its importance.
48. Charles W. Mason, *The Value-Philosophy of Alfred Edward Taylor: A Study in Theistic Implication* (Washington, DC: University Press of America, 1979), 33.

49. Steven D. Smith, *The Disenchantment of Secular Discourse* (Cambridge, MA: Harvard University Press, 2010), 25.
50. Interestingly enough, though, Taylor recognized that this can even happen within science itself. Contrary to a popular view, science is not always free of evaluations. Whether indications of intelligent design, for example, are taken to provide evidence for a Creator invariably depends on whether one accepts such a conclusion as rational or not, and rationality itself is evaluative. In foreseeing such a problem Taylor demonstrated remarkable prescience.
51. Taylor, *Faith of a Moralist*, 229.
52. Ibid., 230.
53. Ibid.
54. Ibid., 231.
55. The whole good can't be experienced at any one time, and we are left with disconnected experiences of a "good" that we know to be ultimately unified. Our experience of moral value implies an eternal and unified fulfillment—whole, simultaneous, and complete fruition of a life without bounds—which can only be accomplished by God, the ground of both value and being.

Chapter 12

1. Sell, *Four Philosophical Anglicans*, 69–142.
2. Recounted in his autobiography, W. R. Matthews, *Memories and Meanings* (London: Hodder and Stoughton, 1969), 18.
3. Ibid., 42–43.
4. W. R. Matthews, *Studies in Christian Philosophy* (London: Macmillan, 1921).
5. H. P. Owen, *W. R. Matthews: Philosopher and Theologian* (London: Athlone Press, 1976), 70.
6. Matthews, *Memories and Meanings*, 161–162. Sell adds, "It should be noted that Matthews was not alone in thinking that he would have done justice to the Gifford Lectureship. When he retired from St. Paul's in 1967, William Wand, noting that Matthews had held the Wilde Lectureship in the Philosophy of Religion from 1929 to 1932, continued, 'If only someone had had the sense to make him Gifford Lecturer after that, we might have had some more outstanding volumes in the philosophy of religion." *Four Philosophical Anglicans*, 77.
7. W. R. Matthews, *God in Christian Thought and Experience* (London: Nisbet, 1930).
8. Sell, *Four Philosophical Anglicans*, 78–92.
9. W. R. Matthews, *The Gospel and the Modern Mind* (London: Macmillan, 1930), 38.
10. Sell, *Four Philosophical Anglicans*, 91.
11. "If the universe is completely rational, judgments of value will be of determining importance in our interpretation of meaning." Matthews, *Studies in Christian Philosophy*, 118.
12. Ibid., 123.

13. Ibid., 125–126. In making his case, he took on reigning views of his day: absolute idealism and radical pluralism.
14. Ibid., 128.
15. Ibid., 142.
16. Ibid., 131.
17. Ibid., 132. Here Matthews and Taylor offer similar but subtly different analyses.
18. Ibid., 135.
19. Ibid., 136. Matthews proceeded to argue that theism most adequately makes sense of this picture, more so than absolute idealism (Baruch Spinoza and later F. H. Bradley), for which efforts to promote the good or abolish evil constitutes senseless impertinence, and more so, too, than either dynamic immanentism (Henri Bergson's vitalism) or radical pluralism.
20. Ibid., 146.
21. Ibid., 147.
22. Ibid., 153.
23. Ibid., 156–157.
24. Sell, *Four Philosophical Anglicans*, 102–103.

Chapter 13

1. Philip Zaleski and Carol Zaleski, *The Fellowship: The Literary Lives of the Inklings* (New York: Farrar, Straus and Giroux, 2015), 161–162.
2. C. S. Lewis, *Surprised by Joy* (New York: Harcourt, Brace & World, 1955), 228–229. Scholars have concluded that Lewis actually got the date of his conversion to theism wrong and that his conversion to theism happened in 1930, and his conversion to Christianity in 1931. See Alister McGrath, *C. S. Lewis: A Life* (Carol Stream, IL: Tyndale House, 2013), 135–146.
3. C. S. Lewis, *The Abolition of Man* (HarperSanFrancisco, 2001), 14–15.
4. Ibid., 18.
5. Ibid., 21.
6. Ibid., 22.
7. Ibid., 30.
8. Ibid., 40.
9. Ibid., 49–50.
10. Ibid., 73.
11. Cf. Lewis's line in his essay "The Poison of Subjectivism": "If we once grant that our practical reason really is reason and that its fundamental imperatives are as absolute and categorical as they claim to be, then unconditional allegiance to them is the duty of man." See C. S. Lewis, *Christian Reflections*, ed. Walter Hooper (Grand Rapids: Eerdmans, 1967), 79.
12. C. S. Lewis, *Mere Christianity* (San Francisco: HarperSanFrancisco, 2001), 8
13. Talk of "obedience" here is not meant to suggest that there's anything about such laws that goes beyond the merely descriptive.

14. Ibid., 5.
15. Ibid., 6.
16. Gilbert Meilaender suggests that Lewis was inconsistent on this score and that "self-evident" cannot mean the same as "obvious" for Lewis, and that "obvious" is a less satisfactory formulation of the argument. Part of Meilaender's reason is as follows: "Indeed, if Lewis really held that the precepts of the Tao were 'obvious,' the central theme of *The Abolition of Man* could make little sense; for it is a book about our need for moral education." "On Moral Knowledge," in *The Cambridge Companion to C. S. Lewis*, eds. Robert MacSwain and Michael Ward (Cambridge: Cambridge University Press, 2010), 124. This claim is doubtful, however, for the heart of moral education that Lewis is concerned with is training of the emotions, as well as our actions. Even if we correctly discern moral truth, we are not moral persons until the heart learns to follow the head. To be sure, correct emotional training also helps us to discern moral truth at a deeper level. But moral truth can be both self-evident as well as obvious in the sense that any normal person instinctively sees it, but emotional training does not automatically follow as a matter of course.
17. Lewis, *Mere Christianity*, 13.
18. Ibid., 20.
19. Ibid., 25–26.
20. Ibid., 30.
21. Ibid., 32.
22. "The Poison of Subjectivism," 80.
23. Ibid.
24. Lewis, *Mere Christianity*, 31.
25. Ibid., 52.
26. Lewis developed these themes in more detail in book 4 of *Mere Christianity*.
27. C. S. Lewis, *Miracles* (San Francisco: HarperSanFrancisco, 2001), 23.
28. Ibid., 34–35.
29. Lewis, "De Futilitate," in *Christian Reflections*, 65.
30. Ibid., 67. Lewis also gives a version of this argument in *Mere Christianity*, 38–39. He also developed the parallel between our logical judgments and our moral judgments in *Miracles*, 53–60.
31. Ibid., 69.
32. Ibid., 70.
33. Ibid.
34. For more on these issues, see Baggett and Walls, *God and Cosmos*, 79–111.
35. Friedrich Nietzsche, *Twilight of the Idols* and *The Anti-Christ*, trans. R. J. Hollingdale (London: Penguin Books, 1990), 81.
36. We have seen this question recur whenever pressed by those who have argued that theism is better than Platonism at accounting for the authority of the moral law (which includes nearly everyone this book covered). Still, some might defend Lewis by suggesting that if indeed his point is meant as exclusively epistemic rather than ontological, it underdetermines the metaphysical questions it raises.

37. For more on this see Baggett and Walls, *God and Cosmos*, 243–269.
38. Glenn Tinder, *The Fabric of Hope* (Grand Rapids, MI: Eerdmans, 2001), 34.
39. C. S. Lewis, "Man or Rabbit?" in *God in the Dock*, ed. Walter Hooper (Grand Rapids, MI: Eerdmans, 1970), 112.

Chapter 14

1. H. P. Owen, *The Moral Argument for Christian Theism* (London: George Allen and Unwin, 1965). H. P. Owen, "Morality and Christian Theism," *Religious Studies* 20, no. 1 (March 1984): 5–17.
2. Owen, *The Moral Argument for Christian Theism*, 7. Newman's influence is likely seen in Owen's emphasis on *intuition*.
3. Ibid.
4. Ibid., 12.
5. In a Platonic heaven, for example, or God.
6. Owen thought this view implies that all human beings have (potentially if not actually) a common moral nature.
7. "If goodness actually inheres as a 'non-natural' quality in objects it is apprehended by an intellectual act analogous to our perception of their physical qualities." Owen, *Moral Argument*, 12. In contrast, to call moral terms "subjective" is to locate their meaning in an activity of the subject-user. This is the classically expressivist understanding of moral discourse, according to which moral language conveys the speaker's approval, praise, commendation, or something in that vicinity. Expressivism is a noncognitivist account of moral language, and proponents of such a view in Owen's day included A. J. Ayer, Charles Stevenson, Patrick Nowell-Smith, and R. M. Hare. Sophisticated contemporary accounts of expressivism include Simon Blackburn's quasi-realism, Terry Horgan and Mark Timmons's nondescriptivist cognitivism, and Allan Gibbard's projectivism.
8. Russ Shafer-Landau and Terence Cuneo, eds., *Foundations of Ethics: An Anthology* (Oxford: Blackwell, 2013), 35–38. Since much of what Owen did in this section of his book was reply to what Shafer-Landau and Cuneo call "first-wave expressivism" (which has largely by now been eclipsed by more sophisticated analyses), much of what Owen did need not detain us for long. Among the criticisms lodged against the crudest and earliest versions of emotivism and prescriptivism was the so-called Frege-Geach problem: if moral discourse doesn't express propositions, how can sentences that express moral judgments form part of semantically complex sentences? Another standard criticism is how to account for genuine moral disagreements on expressivism.
9. Owen, *Moral Argument*, 23.
10. Note the similarity here with Martineau's way of taking Kant's insights that Webb endorsed.
11. Owen, *Moral Argument*, 27.
12. Ibid., 28.

13. Ibid., 29. Owen was following H. H. Farmer on this score: "It is the *form* of the demand as absolute and unconditional, and not so much the *content*, which is the significant thing." See Farmer's published Gifford lectures: H. H. Farmer, *Revelation and Religion* (London: Harper & Brothers, 1954), 141.
14. Owen thought that though this is tragic, it will be overcome in the final, reconciling act of God.
15. Owen, *Moral Argument*, 33.
16. Ibid., 34.
17. While the world depends wholly on God for its existence it also enjoys a relative independence insofar as its modes of operation can be partially understood without any reference to him.
18. Owen, *Moral Argument*, 35. In Webb we heard articulated that to recognize a Duty is to recognize God, which was echoed later by John Baille's claim that atheists who acknowledge moral duties possess "unconscious faith" in God, confessing God "in the bottom of their hearts" despite their denials at "the top of their minds." Maritain similarly asserted that the good pagan is a pseudo-theist who unconsciously knows without recognizing God. Owen didn't think this view is right because it confuses the orders of knowing and being.
19. Ibid., 37.
20. Ibid., 38.
21. T. W. Manson summed up the essence of Hebrew ethics like this: "The last ground of moral obligation is the command of God; and the supreme ideal is the imitation of a God who is at once king and father, who exhibits in the field of nature and history, and above all in his dealings with Israel, the qualities of holiness and righteousness, mercy and faithfulness, love and covenant-loyalty, which are to be the pattern for the behavior of his subjects and children." T. W. Manson, *Ethics and the Gospel* (London: SCM Press, 1966), 19.
22. Owen, *Moral Argument*, 43–44.
23. Ibid., 48.
24. W. D. Ross, *The Right and the Good* (Oxford: Oxford University Press, 1946), 20.
25. Owen, *Moral Argument*, 49–50.
26. As a case in point, see Illtyd Trethowan, *The Basis of Belief* (London: Hawthorn Books, 1960), 117.
27. Owen, *Moral Argument*, 53.
28. Speaking of Chesterton, we didn't accord him much space here. In personal correspondence, however, T. J. Gentry wrote to us, "There is a nexus of the rational, affective, and imaginative in Chesterton's apologetic writings, cultural critiques, and fiction by which he presses readers with the sense of both the intuitiveness and logic of belief in God based on morality and other considerations. Chesterton's use of imaginatively fired passional reason helps build a bridge between the good God and human perceptions of goodness, joy, and so on. While he does not offer a moral apologetic argument for God's existence, per se, Chesterton provides breadcrumbs—moral clues and segues—along the path. His is a rational-affective-imaginative triad of apologetic method that is at once cumulative and teleological, while at the

same time rooted in common sense and human experience. What may be true of Chesterton is that his moral apologetic intent is a culmination of his other implicit arguments for God's existence. All of these means, and possibly others found in Chesterton's works, reveal an undercurrent of morality and goodness that make Chesterton at least a support and cohort in moral apologetics, even if he is not a moral apologist particularly." January 1, 2019.

29. Owen, *Moral Argument*, 59. Owen recognized that this was a different moral argument—more a performative than an ontological one. This was one reason he didn't pursue this line further than he did. It's still significant, however, that he recognized that this was an important variant of moral apologetics.
30. Ibid., 66.
31. Ibid.
32. Ibid., 66–67.
33. Two observations: Owen is like Webb here in integrating insights from both Plato and Kant. Also, though, Owen, more so than Webb and many others, seemed especially keen to infer duties on the basis of goodness. This seems to do more than suggest that a theory of the right requires a theory of the good; it seems to suggest that goodness entails rightness, which, however, makes carving out space for supererogation require additional work.
34. Owen, *Moral Argument*, 79.
35. Ibid., 80.
36. Ibid., 85.
37. Ibid., 86.
38. Ibid., 84.
39. Ibid., 98. "The facts are that we are conscious both of serving claims and desiring happiness; that the two interact in many subtle ways; and that the interaction, so far from impoverishing, enriches both."
40. Ibid., 97–99.

Chapter 15

1. A. C. Ewing, *Value and Reality: The Philosophical Case for Theism* (New York: Humanities Press, 1971), 204–205.
2. David Elton Trueblood, *Philosophy of Religion* (New York: Harper & Brothers, 1957), 116–117.
3. Philip Curtis, *A Hawk among Sparrows: A Biography of Austin Farrer* (London: SPCK, 1985).
4. Michael Ward, "The Next C. S. Lewis? A Note on Austin Farrer," http://www.transpositions.co.uk/austinfarrer/.
5. Rowan Williams, "General Synod: Debate on the Gift of Authority," http://rowanwilliams.archbishopofcanterbury.org/articles.php/1836/general-synod-debate-on-the-gift-of-authority-archbishop-of-canterburys-remarks.
6. Cited in Curtis, *Hawk among Sparrows*, 230–231.

7. Austin Farrer, *Reflective Faith: Essays in Philosophical Theology* (Eugene, OR: Wipf & Stock, 2012).
8. George Mavrodes, "Religion and the Queerness of Morality," in *Ethical Theory Classical and Contemporary Readings*, 2nd ed., ed. Louis P. Pojman (New York: Wadsworth, 1995).
9. George Mavrodes, "There Was a Wind Blowing," in *God and the Philosophers*, ed. Thomas V. Morris (Oxford: Oxford, 1994), 212.
10. Basil Mitchell, *Morality, Religious and Secular* (Oxford: Oxford University Press, 1980).
11. That paper, which has recently served as the foundation for a book, outlined various arguments for God's existence, and the moral argument is a prominent example. See Jerry L. Walls and Trent Dougherty, eds., *Two Dozen (or So) Arguments for God: The Plantinga Project* (Oxford: Oxford University Press, 2018). Plantinga himself really came around on the moral argument; after ignoring it in *God and Other Minds*, more recently Plantinga suggested the moral argument might be the best piece of natural theology on offer.
12. Clement Dore, "A Moral Argument," in *Theism* (Boston: D. Reidel, 1984).
13. A person at least *to that extent*. Incidentally, Dore thought it's possible to show that this being may have a further characteristic that's traditionally been ascribed to God—namely, necessary existence. He argued we are justified in thinking that some moral obligation claims express necessary truths. This applies in every possible world, so significant wrongdoing needs to be able to be punished in every possible world; therefore, in every world there's a God-like person able to do so. Still, despite the attractions of parsimony, Dore admitted he hadn't shown that it's the same God-like punisher who exists in each possible world or, for that matter, that there is only *one* God-like punisher in any given possible world. Nor did he show, he said, that this person is perfectly good or that the person is omnipotent and omniscient. What he had shown, he claimed, is that the person is more powerful and knowledgeable than any wrongdoer could possibly be.
14. We know from observation that the morally innocent are just as apt to suffer in this world as are moral reprobates. And since this is a well-substantiated inductive generalization, it would be irrational to claim that all wrongdoers are worse off in this life than they would have been if they had remained relatively morally innocent. So, given the overriding nature of moral obligation, it follows that there is an afterlife in which those wrongdoers who flourish in this world are punished. But all of us are wrongdoers to some degree, and most of us sometimes do what is significantly wrong without suffering (here and now) for it. It follows that there is reason to believe that many of us survive our earthly death. An alternative argument would be that the overriding importance of morality entails not only that the wicked are worse off in the long run than the relatively righteous but also that the latter are better off in the long run than are the wicked, and that those among the relatively righteous who suffer greatly in this world will be compensated in the afterlife. But this would show at least some survive earthly death, which renders it more likely than it would be otherwise.

15. For space constraints, and no small amount of indolence, we refrained from elaborating on the American John Warwick Montgomery—born a few years before Adams, in 1931—who offered a variety of evidential arguments for God's existence. *The Law above the Law* and *Human Rights and Human Dignity* put forth a moral argument to the effect that classical theism provides the necessary explanation of human dignity and human rights.
16. The two main advantages Adams cites in favor of divine command ethics are (1) that it presents facts of moral rightness and wrongness as objective, non-natural facts, and (2) that it is relatively clear, certainly more so than, say, intuitionism or Platonism. He spends a fair bit of time defending divine command theory against objections, most especially arbitrariness concerns. Most relevantly in that regard, he predicates his divine command theory on a loving God.
17. Marilyn McCord Adams, *Horrendous Evils and the Goodness of God*, 156.
18. Linda Zagzebski, "Does Ethics Need God?" *Faith and Philosophy* 4, no. 3 (July 1987): 294–303.
19. J. P. Moreland, *The Recalcitrant Imago Dei: Human Persons and the Failure of Naturalism* (London: SCM Press, 2009), 3.
20. The way he shows how "natural" contrasts with "artificial" rather than "supernatural," in Aristotle's work, is just one small but potent example.
21. The Craig-Wielenberg debate will be published in 2020 as *God and Morality: What Is the Best Account of Objective Moral Values and Duties: A Debate between William Lane Craig and Erik Wielenberg*, ed. Adam Lloyd Johnson (with additional essays from David Baggett, Michaael Huemer, Adam Lloyd Johnson, Mark Linville, Stephen Maitzen, J. P. Moreland, and Wes Morriston) (Abingdon, UK: Routledge, forthcoming). It includes an essay I (Dave) wrote covering issues of supererogation and psychopathy that came up in the debate. Wielenberg and I also conducted a written debate on C. S. Lewis's moral argument in Gregory Bassham, ed., *C. S. Lewis's Christian Apologetics: Pro and Con* (Leiden: Brill, 2015).
22. Note that it focuses on the ontological matters of deontic and axiological morality. Incidentally, one might think that all that is needed to render the conclusion more likely true than false is that each premise be more likely true than false, but in fact what's needed is that the premise set taken collectively is more likely true than false. We owe the following example to Tim McGrew: Consider rolling a six-sided die. It's more likely true than not that the roll will yield a 1, 2, 3, or 4, and more likely true than not that it will yield 3, 4, 5, or 6. Deductively it follows that it will yield 3 or 4, but such a roll is less likely true than not (a one in three chance).
23. C. Stephen Layman, "A Moral Argument for the Existence of God," in Garcia and King's *Is Goodness without God Good Enough?*, 52. He's referring to more than merely *prima facie* duties.
24. Ibid., 54.
25. Ibid.
26. Ibid., 56.
27. Ibid., 58–59.

28. Jerry L. Walls, *Heaven: The Logic of Eternal Joy* (New York: Oxford University Press, 2002), 193. His trilogy also contains a book on hell and one on purgatory. Walls and I (Dave) have teamed up to write a few books on theistic ethics and moral apologetics. The first was *Good God: The Theistic Foundations of Morality* (New York: Oxford University Press, 2011), in which we defended theistic ethics against an assortment of Euthyphro-inspired objections; that book won the 2012 *Christianity Today* Book Award in Apologetics/Evangelism. Later, in *God and Cosmos: Moral Truth and Human Meaning*, we extended our abductive, cumulative, and teleological moral argument by critiquing the adequacy of various secular theories of morality and building our fourfold moral apologetic encompassing moral facts, knowledge, transformation, and rationality. With Gary Habermas, we have also edited a book called *C. S. Lewis as Philosopher*, an expanded version of which was published in 2017 (Lynchburg, VA: Liberty University Press). New topics broached issues like myth, epistemology, and remarkable analysis of the argument from desire (by the likes of Stew Goetz, Will Honeycutt, Bruce Reichenbach, and Sloan Lee). Recently we also collaborated with Jeremy Neill to edit *Venus and Virtue: Celebrating Sex and Seeking Sanctification* (Eugene, OR: Cascade Press, 2018). In 2018 I (Dave) collaborated on a more accessible book on moral apologetics with my wife, Marybeth, called *The Morals of the Story* (Downers Grove, IL: InterVarsity Academic, 2018), which won the 2019 *Christianity Today* Award of Merit in the Apologetics/Evangelism category. See our MoralApologetics.com website for a wide range of resources on the moral argument, covering pastoral, counseling, pedagogical, literary, historical, devotional, biblical, theological, and philosophical dimensions of the discussion.

29. His is an ambitious and sweeping account, canvasing the whole Western and ancient Near Eastern ethical traditions, starting with the Old Testament, moving to the New, traversing ancient Greece. Then it provides a rich examination of aspects of medieval thought and modernity, including the Renaissance and Enlightenment, their points of emphasis and innovations and a whole plethora of subsequent trends. This elaborate tracing of the history of ethical analysis proves tremendously useful in accounting for many of today's trends in ethical thought. Smith helps us get a better handle on them, understand their genesis, and subject them to scrutiny rather than simply assuming them as axiomatic or sacrosanct. See R. Scott Smith, *In Search of Moral Knowledge: Overcoming the Fact-Value Dichotomy* (Downers Grove, IL: InterVarsity Press, 2014).

30. That entry is available online here: https://appearedtoblogly.files.wordpress.com/2011/05/linville-mark-22the-moral-argument22.pdf. Linville's contribution to the forthcoming book on the Craig-Wielenberg debate will cover epistemological matters.

31. Linville has also written a helpful encyclopedia article on the history of the moral argument: "Moral Argument," in *The Blackwell Companion to Natural Theology*, eds. William Lane Craig and J. P. Moreland (Malden, MA: Blackwell, 2012); another recent piece is his "God Is Necessary for Morality" (which includes his rebuttal of the main essay by his debate partner, Louise Antony) in Michael Peterson and Ray

VanArragon, eds., *Contemporary Debates in Philosophy of Religion*, 2nd ed. (Malden, MA: Wiley-Blackwell, 2019).
32. See Paul Copan, *Is God a Moral Monster?* (Grand Rapids, MI: Baker, 2011). Copan and Matthew Flannagan teamed up to write another excellent book on this topic: *Did God Really Command Genocide? Coming to Terms with the Justice of God* (Grand Rapids, MI: Baker, 2014). Flannagan has also done top-tier work in the area of theistic ethics and the Euthyphro dilemma; he and his wife blog at http://www.mandm.org.nz/.
33. Philosophers call this a Gettier case. The "Gettier problem" in epistemology arises when cases are adduced in which a justified true belief obtains but presumably not knowledge, which seems to indicate that the right account of knowledge isn't "justified true belief." Menuge seems to be implicating weak EE in a "moral Gettier case."
34. Angus Menuge, "The Failure of Naturalism as a Foundation for Human Rights." *Moral Apologetics*. http://moralapologetics.com/the-failure-of-naturalism-as-a-foundation-for-human-rights/.
35. Angus Ritchie, *From Morality to Metaphysics* (Oxford: Oxford University Press, 2013). For a sustained case that Christian thought resonates with humanism rightly construed, see Angus Ritchie and Nick Spencer, "Humanism, and Humanists in Christianity," Theos, https://www.theosthinktank.co.uk/research/2014/12/05/the-case-for-christian-humanism.

Conclusion

1. See Marybeth Baggett's lovely blog about the documentary: "The Faithful Witness of Fred Rogers," Moral Apologetics, July 13, 2018, https://www.moralapologetics.com/wordpress/2018/7/13/the-faithful-witness-of-fred-rogers.
2. See Marybeth Baggett, "Kurt Vonnegut: Unlikely Apologist," Moral Apologetics, December 15, 2014, https://www.moralapologetics.com/wordpress/kurt-vonnegut-unlikely-apologist?rq=vonnegut.
3. This was in personal correspondence on September 26, 1900. See William James, *The Letters of William James*, vol. 2 (Boston: Atlantic Monthly Press, 2018 [1920]), 94.
4. C. S. Lewis, *The Four Loves* (Boston: Houghton Mifflin Harcourt, 1991), 71.
5. For an argument that moral apologetics may even be useful in distinguishing between rival Christian conceptions of God's character, see Baggett and Campbell, "Omnibenevolence, Moral Apologetics, and Doubly Ramified Natural Theology."
6. Paul Copan, "Reinforcing the Moral Argument: Appealing to the Historical Impact of the Christian Faith," paper presented at the Evangelical Theological Society, San Diego, CA, November 19–21, 2014.
7. David Bentley Hart, *Atheist Delusions: The Christian Revolution and Its Fashionable Enemies* (New Haven, CT: Yale University Press, 2009), 213–214.
8. For an essay on ways in which moral apologetics leads to Christianity, adducing such features of the latter as its being Christological, Trinitarian, transformative, soteriological, eschatological, and universal, see David Baggett, "Seven Reasons Why Moral

Apologetics Points to Christianity," Moral Apologetics, March 8, 2017, https://www.moralapologetics.com/wordpress/seven-reasons-why-moral-apologetics-points-to-christianity. On the issue of eschatology, an interesting issue that arises in the history of the moral argument is a case for a sanctification model of purgatory offered by several prominent moral apologists (Taylor, Owen, Lewis, and Walls, for example—all Protestants, by the way)—for distinctively moral reasons. For a defense of aspects of Walls's account of purgatory, see David Baggett and Jonathan Pruitt, "In the Twinkling of an Eye," in *Purgatory: Philosophical Dimensions*, eds. Kristof Vanhoutte and Benjamin W. McCraw (New York: Palgrave Macmillan, 2017).

Index

For the benefit of digital users, indexed terms that span two pages (e.g., 52–53) may, on occasion, appear on only one of those pages.

Page locators in **bold** denote a chapter.

The Abolition of Man (Lewis), 164–67, 169–70
absolutism, 63
action, abhorrent, 30
Adams, Marilyn McCord, 32, 202, 208–9
Adams, Robert, 9, 19–23, 201–2, 204, 208–9
Adickes, 127
affection, actualization of mutual, 63
afterlife
    beatitude and, 192
    existence of, 15
    happiness and, 192
    morality and the, 14, 15
    moral obligation and the, 248n14
    Rashdall on the, 109, 112–13
    Sidgwick's belief in, 50–51
    on television, 8
agape, 52
agnosticism, 63
Alexander the Great, 9–10
altruism, 100–1, 102–3
amorality, 177
Anscombe, Elizabeth, 174, 220n2
Anselm of Canterbury, 2, 14, 24–25, 103
anthropomorphism, 135–36
apologetics, 78–79, 82, 105–6
Apologia Pro Vita Sua (Newman), 35
apologist, 71, 77
Applebaum, David, 20
apprehension, assent and, 41
Aquinas, Thomas
    on desire, 221n11
    fourth way, 191
    God-man's relationship, 135–36
    mentioned, 2–3
    precursor to Kant, 10, 18
    Taylor's work and, 142
    way to God, 136
argument, moral, 156
argument from conscience, 44
argument from grace, 19, 22, 33
argument from providence, 19, 27, 33
argument from reason, 173–75
Aristotle, 9, 10, 18, 44, 98, 117
assent
    apprehension and, 41
    giving, 39–40
    inference vs., 41
    real vs. notional, 36, 41
atheism, 118–19, 123, 192
atonement, 46–47, 119, 120, 173
Augustine, 9, 10, 18, 24–25, 122–23, 220n8
Ave Maria (Gounod), 114

Bacon, Francis, 78
Baille, John, 121, 124
Balfour, Arthur James
    life and work, 67, 229n13
    Matthews and, 158
    prime minister, 67
    Rashdall and, 108
    run-down of the solar system, 93
    Russell relationship, 67
    Sidgwick and, 67
    synopsis, 71
Balfour, Arthur James, works
    Introduction to Mathematical Philosophy, 67
    Political Ideals, 67
    Theism and Humanism, 50, 68, 121
    Theism and Thought, 68
Balfour, Eleanor Mildred (later Sidgwick), 50, 51
The Balfour Lectures on Realism (Pringle-Pattison), 89
Barfield, Owen, 40
Baring, Thomas, 130
Barth, Karl, 131, 156
beatitude, 192, 195–96
beauty, goodness and, 93
Beck, Lewis White, 20
Beethoven, Ludwig van, 19
being, order of, 185–86
Bell, E. T., 14–15

254 INDEX

Bell, Kristen, 8
benevolence
    rational, 56–57, 58, 158
    self-evident, 160
    self-love and, 53, 55–57, 58
    sources to motivate and practice, 52–53
benevolence principle, 160
Benson, Edward White, 50
Benson, Mary Sidgwick, 50
Berkeley, George, 97, 221n15
Bernard, St., 136
Bertuzzi, Cameron, 34
Bjork, Daniel, 64
The Blackwell Companion to Natural Theology
    (Linville), 206
Bloom, Allan, 10
Boethius, 146–47
Bosanquet, Bernard, 89
Bradley, F. H., 89
Broad, C. D., 141–42
Broadcast Talks (Lewis), 212
Brown, Hunter, 221n9
Brownlow, William, 37
Butler, Joseph, 18, 97, 142, 159

Caldecott, Alfred, 155–56
Cassander, 9–10
Cassirer, Ernst, 237n20
certitude, 68, 226–27n29
Chesterton, G. K., 189, 246–47n28
The Christian Knowledge of God (Owen),
    141, 181
Christian Theism (Owen), 181
Christian Trinitarian theism, 172
Chronicles of Narnia (Lewis), 163
Churchill, Winston, 67
Cicero, 10
Clifford, W. K., 63
Closing of the American Mind (Bloom), 10
coincidence thesis, 17–18
Coleridge, Samuel Taylor, 164–65
common good, 128
Concepts of Deity (Owen), 181
conjunctive good, 224n19
conscience, 37, 41, 125, 127, 226n23
consciousness, moral, 106–7, 110, 111, 119,
    134–35, 151–52, 160, 191
consequence, abhorrent, 30
consequentialists, 104, 105
Contemporary British Philosophy
    (Muirhead), 114–15
contuition, 187
convictions, moral, 111

Copan, Paul, 206
cosmic futility, 175
Craig, William Lane, 9, 76–77, 80, 204, 206, 208–9
credibility vs. plausibility, 78
Creel, Richard, 32
The Critique of Judgment (Kant), 27–28
The Critique of Practical Reason (Kant),
    21, 27–28
The Critique of Pure Reason (Kant), 27–28
Crofts, Mary, 49
cumulative case-building, 133
Cuneo, Terence, 17
Curtis, Philip, 199

Danson, Ted, 8
Dante Alighieri, 92–93, 122–23
Davidman, Joy (later Lewis), 163–64
death, 50–51, 165–66, 248n14
de Burgh, Hannah Jane Monch Mason, 130
de Burgh, Hubert, 130
de Burgh, Maurice, 130
de Burgh, W. G.
    anticipated, 38
    the gregarious aristocrat, **130–38**
    Kant and, 133–34, 135
    life and work, 130–31, 138
    moral argument, 132
    synopsis, 138
de Burgh, W. G., works
    The Legacy of the Ancient World, 130
    The Life of Reason, 130, 137–38
    From Morality to Religion, 130–33
    Towards a Religious Philosophy, 130
de Burgh, William, 130
"De Descriptione Temporum" (Lewis), 3
"Dedicatory Letter to the Sorbonne"
    (Descartes), 13
deductivism, 133
"De Futilitate" (Lewis), 174, 180
demand, moral, 23–26, 29–30, 132–33
Dennett, Daniel, 205–6
Descartes, René
    "Dedicatory Letter to the Sorbonne," 13
    features salient to, 14
    Meditations, 13, 14
    precursor to Kant, 12, 18
    Third Meditation, 191
desire, 221n11
The Development from Kant to Hegel
    (Pringle-Pattison), 89
Dialogues Concerning Natural Religion (Hume),
    83, 90, 176–77
Dillahunty, Matt, 34

Divine Motivation Theory (Zagzebski), 202
"Divine Personality and the Human Life" (Webb), 121
doctrine of the postulates of practical reason, 85
Does God Exist? (Taylor), 240n7
Dore, Clement, 201
Douglass, Frederick, 98
"The Dream of Gerontius" (Newman), 35
"Dreams of a Visionary" (Kant), 20
dualism of good and evil, 173
dualism of practical reason, 54, 99–101, 102–3
duty
  authority of, 31, 128
  consequences of doing one's, 31
  grounds of, 123–24
  happiness and, 17, 50–51
  Kant on, 119
  life of, 132–33
  new testament teachings, 195–96
  objectivity of, 128, 184–85
  Owen on, 188
  pleasure and, 128
  Rashdall's attitude toward, 99–100
  Sidgwick's attitude toward, 99–100
  utilitarian, 58

Ebels-Duggan, Kyla, 29–30
egoism, 54
egotism, 100–1, 102, 103
Elgar, Edward, 35
Émile (Rousseau), 20
emotion, conscience and, 43
emotivism, 60
empiricism, 106–7
Epicureans, 27, 102
equal rights, 215
Essay in Aid of a Grammar of Assent (Newman), 22, 35–36, 40, 44, 45, 226n10
ethical theism, 121, 124
ethics
  the divine and, 71
  divine command, 249n16
  Hebrew, 246n21
  normative, 104
  theological view of, 193
Ethics (Aristotle), 117
Ethics of Naturalism (Sorley), 74
Euthyphro dilemma, 14, 171–72
Evans, C. Stephen, 9, 203, 208–9
evidentialism, 65
evil
  defeating, 32
  the problem of, 83, 90, 147

evil maxim, 24
evils of history, 32
evolution, ethics of, 74
Ewing, A. C., 137–38, 198, 208–9, 223n12
exclusive humanism, 86
existence, goodness vs., 186
The Existence of God (Swinburne), 2
explanandum, 109
expressivism, 245n7

fact and value, coherence of, 143
faith, moral, 22, 214
The Faith of a Moralist (Taylor), 139, 141, 150–52, 182
Farrer, Austin, 88, 199–203, 208–9
Finite and Infinite Goods (Adams), 201–2, 204
forgiveness, 23, 47, 214–15
The Four Loves (Lewis), 213
Four Philosophical Anglicans (Sell), 130, 131, 155, 239–40n24
frailty, moral, 24
Fraser, Campbell, 121
freedom, moral, 128
Frege, Gottlob, 231n4
friendship, 213
Froude, William, 36, 219n3

Gadamer, H. G., 38
Gentry, T. J., 246–47n28
Gettier case, 251n33
Ginsburg, Ruth Bader, 213
God
  conscience and, 46
  descriptors of, 48
  knowing about, 45–46
God and Evolution (Matthews), 156
God and Moral Obligation (Evans), 203
God and Other Minds (Plantinga), 2
God and Personality (Webb), 121
God and the Philosophers (Morris), 200
God in Christian Thought and Experience (Matthews), 156
God in the Dock (Lewis), 95
God's Command (Hare), 204
good
  defining, 79
  desirability of, 12
  God as the, 11
  goodness and, 9, 137
  idea of the, 157
  implications of the desire for, 132
  irrationality of indifference to, 15
  personal vs. general, seeking, 55–56

good (cont.)
  Plato, 9
  secular as defective, 152
  supremacy of the, 120
  ultimate, 54, 55
"The Good, Its Position among the Values"
  (Lewis), 162–63
good life, sacrifice in the, 120
good maxim, 24
goodness
  beauty and, 93
  divine, 32
  existence vs., 186
  of God, 10–12
  good and, 9, 137
  happiness and, 101, 103, 110
  main application of, 184
  making attractive, 210
  moral and nonmoral, 79
  new testament teachings, 195–96
  pleasure and, 183
  seminal evidential role of, 75
  source of, 137
  supreme value of, 104
The Good Place (television), 8, 18
good will, 79–80, 91
The Good Will (Paton), 192
Gounod, Charles-François, 114
grace, 51–52
grace, argument from, 19, 22, 33
Grammar of Assent (Newman), 182
The Great Divorce (Lewis), 163
Green, Thomas Hill, 97, 116–17
Greenwell, Andrew, 45
Grey, George, 130
Grey of Falloden, 130
Groundwork of the Metaphysics of Morals
  (Kant), 21, 117
guilt, 147, 189–90, 214

Habermas, Jürgen, 27, 215
Haldane, R. B., 88
Hamilton, Flora Augusta (later
  Lewis), 162
happiness
  afterlife and, 192
  altruism and, 101
  deserving, 103
  duty and, 17, 50–51
  duty vs., 193–94
  goodness and, 101, 103, 110, 192–93
  good will and, 91
  holiness and, 102, 103

  morality and, 22, 27, 29, 30
  personal, moral purpose vs., 84
  requirements for, 22
  sacrificing, 58
  self-sacrifice and worthiness, 101
  senses of, 193
  sympathy and, 57–58
  universal, 54–55, 58, 59
  virtue and, 102
Hare, John, 24–25, 29–30, 103, 203–4, 208–9
Hare, Richard M., 203–4
Harper, William Jackson, 8
Harris, Sam, 79
Hart, David Bentley, 215
Heaven: the Logic of Eternal Joy (Walls), 205
hedonism, 54, 99, 102
Hegel, G. W. F., 6, 64, 88–89
Hegelianism, 121
Hegelianism and Personality
  (Pringle-Pattison), 89
Hesiod, 118–19
Hicks, Dawes, 133
Hieronymi, Pamela, 8
A History of British Philosophy to 1900
  (Sorley), 73
holiness, 102, 103, 137
Homer, 118–19, 148
hope, 30–32, 33
Hopkins, G. M., 45
Horner, David, 78
humanism, exclusive, 51
human nature, law of, 169–70
human rights, 215
humans, purpose of, 10
Hume, David, 83–85, 90–91, 166, 176–77, 179
Huxley, Aldous, 163–64
Huxley, T. H., 63

ideal, the, 93–94
idealism, naturalism and, 92
ideals, 75–76, 93–94, 112–13, 231n4
The Idea of a University (Newman), 35
Idea of God (Pringle-Pattison), 121
The Idea of God in the Light of Recent Philosophy
  (Pringle-Pattison), 89
The Idea of Revelation (Matthews), 156
illative sense, 44–45
immanence, 135–36
immortality, 23, 109–10, 194
imperatives, categorical and hypothetical, 22
incarnation, 136
inference, assent vs., 41
innocence, 248n14

Introduction to Mathematical Philosophy (Russell), 67
intuitionism, 54, 56, 60, 103
intuitionists, 231n4
Irenaeus, 91

Jachmann, Eduard von, 21
James, Henry, 62
James, William
    Balfour compared, 68–69
    epistemology, 229n12
    friendships, 213
    influences on, 89
    Matthews' work and, 157
    mentioned, 156–57
    Newman compared and contrasted, 62–63, 64–65, 66
    synopsis, 71
    that adorable genius, 62
    The Varieties of Religious Experience, 64–65, 66, 229n9
Jesus, 173, 195
John (the biblical), 136
John of the Cross, 122–23
judgment, moral, 106–7
justice, 47, 215
justification, 23

Kant, Immanuel
    Adams' work and, 201–2
    argument from grace, 19, 22, 33
    argument from providence, 19, 27, 33
    Balfour compared, 69–70
    de Burgh's work and, 132
    "Dreams of a Visionary," 20
    on duty, 103
    duty, attitude toward, 99–100
    fact and value, severing, 144
    goodness-happiness relation, 103, 110
    Hume contrasted, 83–85, 90–91
    influence of, 119–20, 182
    life and ethical works, 20, 223n6
    mentioned, 3
    moral argument, 2, 60, 70, 121–24, 133–34, 135, 137, 138, 143–44
    Owen's critique of, 193
    philosophy of religion, 237n20
    precursors to, **8–18**
    Pringle-Pattison's work and, 88, 90–94, 96
    Rashdall's work and, 104–5, 109
    the sage of Königsberg, **19–33**
    senility, 19
    Sidgwick's work and, 50–51
    Sorley's work and, 74–75
    synopsis, 18
    Taylor on, 147
    Webb and, 91–92, 118, 119–20, 122, 123–24, 125–26
Kant, Immanuel, works
    The Critique of Judgment, 27–28, 74–75
    The Critique of Practical Reason, 21, 27–28, 143
    The Critique of Pure Reason, 27–28
    Groundwork for the Metaphysics of Morals, 21
    Groundwork of the Metaphysics of Morals, 117
    Lectures on Ethics, 21
    Metaphysic of Morals, 21
    Opus Postumum, 126
    Religion within the Bounds of Reason Alone, 21, 27–28
Kant's Philosophy of Religion (Webb), 126
Keats, John, 91
Keller, Tim, 208
Kennedy, John F., 163–64
Kierkegaard, Søren, 8, 203
King, Martin Luther Jr., 98
kingdom of ends, 25
Kinlaw, Dennis, 240n1
knowing, order of, 185–86
knowledge, 127, 184
Koukl, Greg, 208
Kuhn, Thomas, 37

Lady Grey, 130
Lamberth, David, 64
Lash, Nicholas, 38–39
law, moral
    authority of the, 125–26, 127–28, 159, 184
    as binding, 120
    binding of the, 22
    emotional intensity of the, 235n36
    God revealed in the, 126–27
    inspiration of the, 52–53
    Kant, Immanuel, 22
    Matthews, W. R., 159
    Newman, John Henry, 42
    obedience owed, 71, 106–7
    objectivity of the, 108, 159–60
    personified, 125
    reverence for the, 125–26
    transcendent, authority of, 84
law, natural, 11–12
law of nature, 169–70
law of right and wrong, 169, 170–71
Laws (Plato), 118
Layman, C. Stephen, 204–5, 208–9

"Lead, Kindly Light" (Newman), 35
Lectures on Ethics (Kant), 21
The Legacy of the Ancient World (de Burgh), 130
Leibniz, Gottfried Wilhelm, 201–2
Leo XIII, 35
Lessing, Gotthold, 91
Lewis, Albert James, 162
Lewis, Charles, 83
Lewis, C. S.
    anticipated, 38, 108
    defending morality without God, 164
    a dinosaur, **162–80**
    friendships, 199, 213
    influences on, 50, 68
    life and work, 162–64
    Matthews and, 158
    moral argument, 3–5, 162, 164, 212
    objective morality without God, 177
    objective moral truth implies God, 169
    Rashdall and, 108
    rationality, morality, and the problem of evil, 174
    synopsis, 180
    the Tao, 165, 166, 167–68, 169–70, 177
Lewis, C.S., works
    The Abolition of Man, 164–67, 169–70
    Broadcast Talks, 212
    Chronicles of Narnia, 163
    "De Descriptione Temporum," 3
    "De Futilitate," 174, 180
    The Four Loves, 213
    God in the Dock, 95
    "The Good, Its Position among the Values," 162–63
    The Great Divorce, 163
    "Meditation in a Toolshed," 95
    Mere Christianity, 2, 83, 162, 163, 164–67, 169, 170, 171, 172–73, 178–79, 180, 199, 200
    Miracles, 69, 163, 174, 175
    "The Poison of Subjectivism," 171–72, 180
    The Problem of Pain, 163
    "Right and Wrong: A Clue to the Meaning of the Universe," 164
    role of grace and forgiveness, 23
    The Screwtape Letters, 163
    Surprised by Joy, 163
Lewis, Flora Augusta Hamilton, 162
Lewis, Joy Davidman, 163–64
Li, Junlei, 210
life, meaningful, 212
The Life of Hastings Rashdall, D. D. (Matheson), 97, 116

The Life of Reason (de Burgh), 130, 137–38
limits, inference pattern of, 39–40
Linville, Mark, 206, 208–9
Locke, John, 16–17, 221n11
logic, 38–39
Lotze, Rudolph Hermann, 4, 92, 233n5
Lotze's dictum, 80, 214
love
    divine, 136–37
    ethic of, 215
    holiness and, 137
    Rogers on, 210
    universal, 53
Luther, Martin, 122–23

MacIntyre, Alasdair, 54, 60
Mackie, J. L., 200
Madigan, Tim, 66
mankind, voice of, 46–47
Manson, T. W., 246n21
Man's Place in the Cosmos (Pringle-Pattison), 89
Martineau, James, 93, 121, 124–26, 127, 129
Mascall, E. L., 187
Masefield, John, 72
Mason, Charles, 152
Mason, Hannah Jane Monch (later de Burgh), 130
materialism, 53
mathematicians, 12–13, 14–15
mathematics, philosophy of, 231n4
Matheson, P. E., 97, 116
Matthews, Edgar, 155
Matthews, Hubert, 155
Matthews, Olive, 155
Matthews, W. R. (Walter Robert)
    background, 155
    dean of St. Paul's, **155–61**
    ethical method, 160
    historical method, 158
    James and, 157
    moral argument, 156
    on naturalism, 158
    psychological method, 159
    synopsis, 161
    task of apologetics to, 212–13
Matthews, W. R. (Walter Robert), works
    God and Evolution, 156
    God in Christian Thought and Experience, 156
    The Idea of Revelation, 156
    The Psychological Approach to Religion, 156
    Studies in Christian Philosophy, 155–56
Mavrodes, George, 9, 200, 208–9

May, Todd, 8
Mead, George Herbert, 89
"Meditation in a Toolshed" (Lewis), 95
Meditations (Descartes), 13, 14, 191
Men of Mathematics (Bell), 14–15
Menuge, Angus, 207, 208–9
Mere Christianity (Lewis), 2, 83, 162, 163, 164–67, 169, 170, 171, 172–73, 178–79, 180, 199, 200
Metaphysic of Morals (Kant), 21
metaphysics
  Lotze's dictum, 80
  morality and, 21–22, 80, 106, 111–12, 151–53
Methodism, 139
The Method of Ethics (Sidgwick), 49, 51, 54, 55–56
Mill, John Stuart, 36, 55–56, 116–17
Milton, John, 123
Miracles (Lewis), 69, 163, 174, 175
Mister Rogers' Neighborhood (television), 210–11
Mitchell, Basil, 199, 200–1
monism, 76–77
Moore, G. E., 51, 97, 147
moral agents, 24, 30–31, 120
The Moral Argument for Christian Theism (Owen), 181, 182, 245n7
moral dilemma, 31
moral experience, 125
moral gap, 24
The Moral Gap (Hare), 203–4
morality
  afterlife and, 14, 15
  atheism vs., 123
  authority of, 101–2
  autonomy of, 16, 17–18, 120, 186
  core of, 109
  criterion of, 104
  defending without God, 164
  happiness and, 22, 27, 29, 30
  incentive for, 13
  language in understanding, 183
  meaning of, 195
  metaphysics and, 21–22, 80, 106, 111–12, 152–53
  motivations for, 16–17, 112
  objective without God, 177
  Owen on, 183–85
  punishments, rewards and, 16
  rational authority of, 29, 57
  rational stability of, 102
  reductionist analysis of, 151–52
  religion and, 111, 185
  religion vs., 133, 134
  self-sacrifice in, 120
Morality, Religious and Secular (Mitchell), 200–1
"Morality and Christian Theism" (Owen), 181
From Morality to Metaphysics (Ritchie), 207
From Morality to Religion (de Burgh), 130–33
The Moral Life and Moral Worth (Sorley), 73
moral order, reality of a, 134
moral order of mutual benefit, 51
moral terms, 183–86
moral truth, objective, 164, 166, 167–68
Moral Values and the Idea of God (Sorley), 73, 74, 121
Moreland, J. P., 15, 203, 205–6, 208–9
Morris, Tom, 200
motivation, moral, 29, 30, 33
Muirhead, J. H., 73, 114–15

naturalism
  Balfour, Arthur, 65–66, 69–70, 71
  de Burgh, W. G., 134
  idealism and, 92
  Lewis, C. S., 174
  Matthews, W. R., 158
  Sorley, William, 74
  Taylor, A. E., 151, 153
Natural Signs and Knowledge of God (Evans), 203
nature, law of, 169–70
neo-Stoicism, 52
Newman, John Henry
  Balfour compared, 68–69
  conscience, existence of, 110
  conscience, phenomenology of, 41
  conscience and imaginative apprehension of God, 41
  a contentious, contemplative cardinal, **34–48**
  empiricism, 226n10
  epistemology, 35
  friendships, 213
  goodness-happiness relation, 110
  James compared and contrasted, 62–63, 64–65, 66
  life and work, 35, 38
  Matthews' work and, 157
  mentioned, 82, 93–94, 189–90, 196–97, 211
  on moral guilt, 214–15
  synopsis, 48
  Taylor compared, 150–51

Newman, John Henry, works
   Apologia Pro Vita Sua, 35
   "The Dream of Gerontius," 35
   Essay in Aid of a Grammar of Assent, 22, 35–37, 40, 44, 45, 182, 226n10
   The Idea of a University, 35
   "Lead, Kindly Light," 35
   "Praise to the Holiest in the Height," 35
   role of grace and forgiveness, 23
   Tracts for the Times, 35
Nietzsche, Friedrich, 4, 6, 142, 177–78
norms, moral, 185

obedience, 16, 188–89, 190, 243n13
objective value, doctrine of, 164–66
objectivity, 42, 183–85
obligation
   afterlife and, 248n14
   consciousness of, 125–26, 127–28, 133, 134
   to hope, 32
   last ground of, 246n21
   mentioned, 132–33
   Owen, H. P., 184
   political, 127–28
   source of, 125, 134
   unconditionality of, 134
Opus Postumum (Kant), 126
Otto, Rudolf, 48
oughtness, 75, 123–24
Owen, H. P. (Huw Parri)
   beatitude, 192, 196
   Christian revelation, 195
   de Burgh's work and, 137–38
   duty, 188, 196
   a few preliminaries, 182
   goodness, 195–96
   life and work, 181–85
   Matthews' work and, 156
   morality, nature of, 183
   morality and religion, 185
   on moral law, 199
   a reverend don, **181–97**
   synopsis, 196–97
   Webb and, 121
Owen, H. P. (Huw Parri), works
   The Christian Knowledge of God, 141, 181
   Christian Theism, 181
   Concepts of Deity, 181
   The Moral Argument for Christian Theism, 181, 182, 245n7
   "Morality and Christian Theism," 181
   Revelation and Existence, 181
Owen, Wilfred, 72, 73
Oxford Movement, 35

Pascal, Blaise, 12, 14–15, 18, 122–23
Pascal's wager, 15
Passmore, Edmund, 140
Passmore, Lydia Justum (later Taylor), 140
Paton, H. J., 192
Paul, St., 45, 47, 85, 122–23, 132–33, 185
Peirce, Charles Sanders, 63
Pensées (Pascal), 14–15
perfection, 11–12, 23, 26, 94
personality, autonomous, 120
Personal Knowledge (Polanyi), 38
phenomenology, 122
Phillips, Gordon, 199–203
philosopher, a moral, 78
Philosophy of Religion (Trueblood), 198–99
philosophy on television, 8
phronesis, 44
Piano Sonata in A major (Schubert), 45
Plantinga, Alvin, 2, 38, 158, 201, 222n23, 229n12
Plato
   account of the 'Forms,' 220n4
   atheism, 118–19
   canon of theology, 118–19
   good and, 9, 120, 137, 191
   influence of, 10
   Matthews and, 157
   precursor to Kant, 9, 18
   principle of goodness, 137
   on sacrifice, 120–21
   Sorley and, 78
   Taylor and, 82, 132, 142, 147, 153–54
   television and, 8
   Webb and, 118–19, 122, 129
Plato, works
   Laws, 118
   Republic, 80, 109, 117, 118–19, 140
Platonism, 132, 134–35, 220n4
Plato: The Man and His Work (Taylor), 141
pleasure
   duty and, 128
   goodness and, 183
   personal vs. general, 100–1
pluralism, 76–77
poetry, 72, 145
"The Poison of Subjectivism" (Lewis), 171–72, 180
Political Ideals (Balfour), 67
Porteous, A. J. D., 140
possibilism, universal, 13
pragmaticism, 63
pragmatism, 63
"Praise to the Holiest in the Height" (Newman), 35

Principia Ethica (Moore), 147
Pringle-Pattison, Andrew Seth
  answering Hume's challenge, 93
  an Edinburgher, **88–96**
  idea of good and the problem of evil, 90
  influence of, 89
  life and work, 88
  naturalism and idealism, 92
  synopsis, 96
Pringle-Pattison, Andrew Seth, works
  The Balfour Lectures on Realism, 89
  The Development from Kant to Hegel, 89
  Hegelianism and Personality, 89
  Idea of God, 121
  The Idea of God in the Light of Recent Philosophy, 89
  Man's Place in the Cosmos, 89
  Studies in the Philosophy of Religion, 89
Pringle-Pattison, Eva Stropp, 88
Pringle-Pattison, James, 88
Pritchard, Duncan, 225n8
The Problem of Pain (Lewis), 163
Process and Reality (Whitehead), 240n11
progress, rational, 158–59
Prolegomena to Ethics (Green), 116–17
"The Proof of Utilitarianism" (Sidgwick), 56
propitiation, 119, 120
providence, argument from, 19, 27, 33
prudence, 44, 56–57
Pruitt, Jonathan, 34
The Psychological Approach to Religion (Matthews), 156
Ptolemy, 9–10
purpose, personal happiness vs., 84

racism, 98
Rashdall, Hastings
  biography of, 97, 116
  friendships, 97
  intuitionism and the categorical imperative, 103
  Kant and, 182
  life and work, 97–99
  metaphysics and morality, 106
  rationalistic utilitarianism, 99
  religion and morality, 111
  Sorley and, 76
  synopsis, 113
  Taylor and, 151–52
  the theo-philosopher of Carlisle, **97–113**
  The Theory of Good and Evil, 97
rationality, 38, 102
reality
  insight into, 122
  knowing, 93–94
  moral, 73
  morality of, 176–77
  nature of, 65, 94, 120
  rational, 110
reason
  argument from, 173–75
  disengaged, 52–53
  limitations of, 131–34
The Reasonableness of Christianity (Locke), 16–17
reasoning, moral, 184
The Recalcitrant Imago Dei (Moreland), 203
Recent Tendencies in Ethics (Sorley), 73
Reflective Faith (Farrer), 200
Reformed doctrine of Holiness, 240n1
regret, moral, 65, 71
Reid, Thomas, 16, 17–18
relationality, 62–65
religion
  morality and, 111, 185
  morality vs., 133, 134
  natural, 45–48
  true, 47
"Religion and the Queerness of Morality" (Mavrodes), 200
Religion within the Bounds of Reason Alone (Kant), 21, 27–28
religious experience, authentic, 95
repentance, 120–21
Reppert, Victor, 158, 222n23
Republic (Plato), 80, 117, 118–19, 140
responsibility, 189
revelation, 195
Revelation and Existence (Owen), 181
reverence, 132–33, 189
rewards and punishments, 192
Richter, John Paul, 114
right and wrong, law of, 169, 170–71
"Right and Wrong: A Clue to the Meaning of the Universe" (Lewis), 164
rightness, moral, 184
Rist, John, 220n4
Ritchie, Angus, 207, 208–9
Ritchie, D. G., 88
Robinson, N. H. G., 137–38
Rogers, Fred, 210–11
Rorty, Richard, 215
Rosenberg, Isaac, 72
Ross, W. D., 185, 188
Rousseau, 20
Royce, Josiah, 63, 213
Russell, Bertrand, 51, 67, 81, 89, 144, 229n13

sacrifice, 120–21, 165–66
sanctification, 23
Santayana, George, 89
Scalia, Antonin, 213
Schubert, Franz, 45
Scotus, John Duns, 24–25, 103
The Screwtape Letters (Lewis), 163
Scruton, Roger, 5
In Search of Moral Knowledge (Smith), 205–6
secularism, 51–52
self-determination, 128
self-interest
  altruism and, 102–3
  morality and, 101–2
self-love, benevolence and, 53, 55–57, 58
self-sacrifice, 120
Sell, Alan P. F., 130, 131, 155, 156, 239–40n24
Sermons on the Canticles (Bernard, St.), 136
Seth, Andrew. *see* Pringle-Pattison, Andrew Seth
Shaw, Kegan, 225n8
Shur, Michael, 8
Sidgwick, Eleanor Mildred Balfour, 50, 51
Sidgwick, Henry
  an agnostic moralist, **49–61**
  Balfour and, 67
  benevolence, self-love and universal, 56
  dualism of practical reason, 54, 99–101, 102–3
  exclusive humanism, 51
  hedonism, 102
  life and work, 49–51
  mentioned, 72–73, 97
  moral argument, 58–60
  moral order of mutual benefit, 51
  principle of benevolence, 160
  Rashdall and, 99
  synopsis, 61
Sidgwick, Henry, works
  The Method of Ethics, 49, 51, 54, 55–56
  "The Proof of Utilitarianism," 56
Sidgwick, Mary (later Benson), 50
Sidgwick, William, 49
The Sidgwick Group, 50
sin, 47, 120–21, 147
Slaughterhouse-Five (Vonnegut), 1, 212
Smith, Janetta (later Sorley), 73
Smith, Nicholas Mark, 98
Smith, R. Scott, 205–6, 208–9
Smith, Steven D., 152–53
social virtue, 57–58
Society for Psychical Research, 50, 67
Socrates, 9, 47
Socrates (Taylor), 240n2

Sorley, Charles Hamilton, 73, 81, 86, 212
Sorley, Janetta Smith, 73
Sorley, William
  de Burgh's work and, 132, 134–35
  evil in the world, 91
  an imaginative apologetic, 82
  influences on, 92
  an integrative mind, 85
  a Knightbridge professor, **72–87**
  life and work, 72–74, 83
  Lotze's dictum, 73–74, 80
  mentioned, 88, 93–94, 196–97
  moral argument, 4, 73, 74, 212
  on moral guilt, 214–15
  moral philosopher, 77
  Owen's work and, 184
  problem of evil, 83
  Rashdall and, 76, 107
  synopsis, 86–87
  Taylor compared, 150–51
  what is good? 79
Sorley, William, works
  Ethics of Naturalism, 74
  A History of British Philosophy to 1900, 73
  The Moral Life and Moral Worth, 73
  Moral Values and the Idea of God, 73, 74, 121
  Recent Tendencies in Ethics, 73
soul, the, 15, 50–51
Spencer, Herbert, 116–17
Spener's problem, 224n15
Spinoza, Baruch, 64
"Spring and Fall" (Hopkins), 45
stability, rational, 29
Stevens, Wallace, 3–4
Stoics, 27, 102
Stout, G. F., 77
Stropp, Albrecht, 88
Stropp, Eva (later Pringle-Pattison), 88
Structure of Scientific Revolutions (Kuhn), 37
Studies in Christian Philosophy (Matthews), 155–56
Studies in the Philosophy of Religion (Pringle-Pattison), 89
A Study of Religion (Martineau), 124–25
suffering, 32
Summa Theologica (Aquinas), 221n9
Surprised by Joy (Lewis), 163
Swinburne, Richard, 2
sympathy, 52–53, 57–58

Tao, the, 165, 166, 167–68, 169–70, 177
Taylor, A. E.
  biography, 139

coherence of actuality (facts) and (moral) value, 143
critiquing naturalism, 151
de Burgh's work and, 131–33, 134–35, 137–38
an eminent and erudite Platonist, **139–54**
epistemology, 150–51
friendships, 130
human sinfulness, 147
influences on, 92
interdisciplinary approach, 82
mentioned, 24–25, 90, 93–94, 189–90, 196–97, 199
methodology, 149
on moral guilt, 213–15
moral philosopher, 77
moral transformation, 153
personal guilt, 147
power of theistic explanation, 153
the problem of evil, 147
Rashdall compared, 107
role of grace and forgiveness, 23
synopsis, 154
work and context, 141
Taylor, A. E., works
  Does God Exist? 240n7
  The Faith of a Moralist, 139, 141, 150–52, 182
  Plato: The Man and His Work, 141
  Socrates, 240n2
Taylor, Alfred, 139
Taylor, Charles, 51–53, 86
Taylor, Lydia Justum Passmore, 140
teachers, moral, 173
Theism and Humanism (Balfour), 50, 68, 121
Theism and Thought (Balfour), 68
The Theory of Good and Evil (Rashdall), 97
Third Meditation (Descartes), 191
Thirty-Nine Articles of Religion of the Church of England, 49–50, 156
Thiselton, Anthony, 97
Thus Spake Zarathustra (Nietzsche), 142
tikkun olam, 210
Tinder, Glenn, 179
Tolkien, J. R. R., 163
Towards a Religious Philosophy (de Burgh), 130
Tracts for the Times (Newman), 35
transcendence, 135–36, 215
transformation, moral, 26, 145–46, 153, 173, 220n8, 229n9
trinitarian theism, 171–72
The Trinity (Augustine), 11
Trueblood, David Elton, 198–202, 208–9
truth
  contingency of, 13
  finding, 65
  objective moral truth implies God, 164, 166, 167–68, 169
  self-evident vs. obvious, 169–70
  sinks slowly, 36, 38
Truth and Method (Gadamer), 38
"Two Dozen (or So) Arguments for God" (Plantinga), 201
Types of Ethical Theory (Martineau), 124–25

universalism, egalitarian, 27
universe, phenomena of the moral, 156
utilitarianism, 54, 55–56, 57–58, 104, 105
  rationalistic, 99

value
  moral, 70, 75–76, 79–80
  statements of, 164–65
Value and Reality (Ewing), 198, 223n12
The Varieties of Religious Experience (James), 64–65, 66
virtue
  genuine, requirements for, 17
  happiness and, 27–28, 102
  intrinsic goodness of, 16–17
  a life of, 10
  practical, 44
  rewarded, 235n33
  well-being and, 17
Vonnegut, Kurt, 6–7, 212

Waldron, Jeremy, 98
Webb, Clement
  consciousness of obligation, political implications, 127
  on duty, 188
  friendships, 97
  influences on, 119
  Kant and, 91–92, 119–20, 122, 123–24, 125–26, 182
  memoir, 114
  mentioned, 82, 93–94
  moral argument, 118
  Owen and, 121
  an Oxford Nolloth professor, **114–29**
  short biography, 114
  studies in the history of natural theology, 117
  synopsis, 129
  Taylor compared, 150–51
Webb, Clement, works
  "Divine Personality and the Human Life," 121
  God and Personality, 121
  Kant's Philosophy of Religion, 126

Webb, Clement (*cont.*)
   The Life of Hastings Rashdall, D. D.,
      contributor, 116
well-being, virtue and, 17
Wesley, John, 23, 122–23
Whitbread, Samuel, 130
Whitehead, Alfred North, 9, 62, 240n11
Wielenberg, Erik, 79

Wilberforce, William, 98
Willey, Basil, 189
wisdom, practical, 44
Wordsworth, William, 221n16
The World Is Not Enough (film), 139

Zacharias, Ravi, 208
Zagzebski, Linda, 202–3, 208–9